RUINS IN A
LANDSCAPE

Lizars sc.

SIR ROBERT SIBBALD BART. M.D.

1721. Ætatis. 80.

STUART PIGGOTT

RUINS

IN A

LAND

SCAPE

ESSAYS IN
ANTIQUARIANISM

at the
University Press
EDINBURGH

FOREWORD

A reprinted collection of essays written at various times over a quarter of a century requires justification if not apology, but at least two reasons seem to me valid. In the first place, they do in fact follow a consistent theme and though not originally written strictly in the sequence now presented, cover consecutively aspects of the history of antiquarian thought in Britain from the sixteenth to the nineteenth century; from William Camden to the Cambridge Camden Society. Camden forms the common ground where my beginnings overlap with the end of Sir Thomas Kendrick's brilliant survey of the transition from medieval to Renaissance antiquarianism in this country,[1] and a general study of the ensuing centuries up to the modern thinking of the nineteenth century has yet to be made. I hope to attempt this task myself, but in the meantime offer some observations on a few of the aspects of this rewarding subject. A second, and if minor perhaps not negligible factor, is that half a dozen of the essays are in their original form scattered through as many publications; two appear here for the first time.

As a background to their writing a brief autobiographical note may be thought useful rather than egotistical. As a young archaeologist beginning his career in the early 1930s I was excited and captivated by Kenneth Clark's *The Gothic Revival* of 1928, and this, together with Christopher Hussey's *The Picturesque* of the previous year, made me look at my own subject from a new, and to me interesting, viewpoint. A few years later I published an immature essay on prehistory and the Romantic Movement, but in it I saw the lines along which my further thinking would go, when I wrote that I believed we might see 'that the accurate and precise science which some of us would consider modern archaeology to be, began merely as an episode in the history of taste'[2] — a phrase taken from the sub-title of *The Gothic Revival*. This was in 1937; later acquaintance with the work of A. O. Lovejoy and his school in the history of ideas, and of Margaret Hogden in the history of anthropology, has confirmed me in this approach.[3]

To an archaeologist in Wessex, working with O. G. S. Crawford and Alexander Keiller, the early antiquaries such as John Aubrey and William Stukeley, William Cunnington and Sir Richard Colt Hoare, were familiar and respected figures in the landscape. At Avebury, Alexander Keiller directed my particular attention to Stukeley and the rich manuscript sources in his own library, and after the war I was able to complete a full-length study of this eighteenth century antiquary in 1950: subsequent field-work at Stonehenge prompted a cool hard look at the Druids in 1968.[4] As a consequence these two subjects, both fascinatingly interwoven with the ideas of Noble Savages and Golden Ages, are only touched on in the studies in this volume.

Six of the papers reprinted here were given as public lectures on various occasions, and repetitions and overlapping inevitably occurred. So far as possible, this has been mitigated or eliminated in the form in which they now appear; all have been edited to a greater or less degree, and additional references have been supplied throughout. No. VII has been substantially re-written and enlarged, No. VIII has had a new section added, thereby altering its original title, No. V was written *de novo* but had its origin in a short note published in 1945, and No. VI appears here for the first time. For further details, see page 196.

NOTES
1 T. D. Kendrick, *British Antiquity*, London 1950.
2 S. Piggott, *Antiq.* XI, 1937, 31.
3 A. O. Lovejoy, *The Great Chain of Being*, Harvard 1936; *Essays in the History of Ideas*, Johns Hopkins 1948; M. T. Hogden, *Early Anthropology in the sixteenth and seventeenth centuries*, Philadelphia 1964.
4 S. Piggott, *William Stukeley: an eighteenth century antiquary*, Oxford 1950; *The Druids*, London 1968.

CONTENTS

O ils sunt as peles alees
G rem denant et de trauers
B ien ont enpointe a bn pote
E t bien retrait a bn enole
N e par force a la meiom
E e purrent fair peindre un tou

D riathe uons dit cherlin en dns
I l a par force ne fopez plus
O e roirez engine a semon
A euls qe roient de corpsualle
M mc alait analit es bestuot
E ntour qardast le leue uint
I nu fide qe fift qrostim
L e ban fil fift qurisimq
D mue ad les zhrevmt s alpetez

I.

ANTIQUARIAN THOUGHT IN
THE SIXTEENTH AND
SEVENTEENTH
CENTURIES

In studying the origins and development of historical disciplines, we are in effect engaged in the investigation of the history of ideas; ideas about the past held by those who are now the objects of our own historical investigation, and the techniques they devised, deliberately or accidentally, to obtain and interpret the basic material from which history can be written. The sixteenth and seventeenth centuries constitute a formative period in the development of such ideas in Britain, and we can see at that time the construction of disciplines to organise and investigate more than one type of historical source-material.

The enquiry into the whole human past which constitutes history in its widest sense utilises two main groups of sources. On the one hand we have written records of all descriptions — documents on clay, metal, parchment, paper; monumental inscriptions on tombs or temples or in public places; coins and medallions. And on the other, there are the sources which consist of what one may call the unconscious evidence provided by the tangible remains of man's day-to-day activities, which may range from Canterbury Cathedral or Stonehenge to a flint axe-blade or the ridge-and-furrow pattern of pre-Inclosure fields. Although documentary sources may be and very often are used to elicit from them information not intended by their original writers, they are nevertheless in origin conscious expressions of an intention to place something on more or less permanent record — something less transient than the spoken word, but nevertheless with an implicit or explicit content of motive and

1. *Merlin building Stonehenge. MS of mid-14th C.*

thought. The alternative sources, those involving material remains, are not the result of any such intent, except in so far as a temple or a tomb may have been conceived as a monument for posterity—and in the absence of dedicatory inscription or epitaph the message it was intended to convey may be ambiguous enough.

To utilise any sources for knowledge of the past, techniques of enquiry must be devised if any but the most superficial and erroneous deductions are to be made. The potential sources will only yield the evidence they contain (and often conceal) if the proper questions are asked. As Collingwood insisted, 'historical procedure, or method, consists essentially of interpreting evidence', and as regards our non-documentary sources he goes on to say: 'Prehistoric flints or Roman pottery acquire the posthumous character of historical evidence, not because the men who made them thought of them as historical evidence, but because *we* think of them as historical evidence.'[1] This capacity to visualise the potentialities of latent evidence is fundamental to all historical study: by the seventeenth century we see it being affected by the transference to the field of history of the Baconian and Cartesian approaches to natural phenomena. But in fact, once the critical process had been applied to documentary sources, especially archive material involving the techniques of palaeography and diplomatic, it was potentially available for the study of the material remains which constitute the unwritten sources. Once 'students were beginning to use their eyes as well as their heads', as Professor Galbraith said of Thomas of Elmham in the early fifteenth century,[2] the conditions for the study which we now call archaeology existed *in posse* at least.

To define our terms, I would suggest that we recognise certain distinctions. If we use the phrase 'historical research' to denote the discipline of obtaining knowledge of the human past from written records, we can recognise in 'archaeology' a complementary group of techniques which utilises material remains for the same ends. For extinct communities which were non-literate, archaeological evidence is the sole means of recognising their very existence, and the interpretation and assessment of this evidence should lead to the writing of prehistory. But archaeological techniques can be applied to any period of the human past, supplementing and complementary to the historical documents in degrees varying with the quality and quantity of the latter. Furthermore, the relationship between the two disciplines may vary in accordance with the kind of history which is being written, the sort of enquiry into the past which is involved. For instance, for the history of technology, or of art and architecture, or even in economic studies, evidence derived from material remains, archaeological evidence, would inevitably bulk larger than in legal or constitutional history.

As we have seen, the nature of archaeological techniques applied to material remains of the past is comprised in the recognition of the unconscious historical content of the source employed rather than their obvious and overt qualities. The use of palaeographical and linguistic techniques to assign a Middle English document to its time and place of origin is within the same frame of reference as the archaeological methods of assigning the *disjecta membra* of a prehistoric midden to their chronological and cultural position; the reconstruction of Domesday woodland from the figures of pannage for swine is an inferential process of the same order as the use of pollen-analysis to demonstrate the advent of agriculturalists in a prehistoric landscape. In fine, once a critical approach to documentary sources could be formulated, side by side with the development of the techniques of investigation in the natural sciences, the archaeological approach to the past was theoretically possible. Our enquiry will be to see how far these potentialities were realised in this country in the sixteenth and seventeenth centuries. Of course we cannot, and should not, expect to find any conscious distinction made between historical, topographical and archaeological research in the period under review; indeed such distinctions were hardly envisaged before the end of the nineteenth century. We are concerned with that engaging figure, the Antiquary, a figure distinctive enough to be satirised by Earle in the 1620s and to be accorded an entry in *A New Dictionary of the Canting Crew* of 1690.

Although antiquarian thought in the period under review was not in a position to make the distinction, the problem as we can see it today has two aspects—the use of archaeological techniques for the prehistoric past which is dependent entirely upon such techniques for its recognition and definition, and the application of the same principles to the historical period. But it is here that we must remember that almost until the nineteenth century the concept of any literally prehistoric past for mankind

3

did not and could not exist, since the essentials of early human history since the Creation had been authoritatively recorded in a document of unimpeachable authority. True, the Bible narrative was confined in detail to a restricted region of western Asia, but the repeopling of the entire world after the Flood formed a divinely constituted and inescapable frame of reference within which all remote antiquity had to be contained. For classical antiquity, there were the ancient historians of Greece and Rome, whose narratives, it was widely held in the Renaissance and later, could be commented upon, but had an undisputed authority.[3] And throughout the Middle Ages and for some time to come, the British History of Geoffrey of Monmouth provided a narrative source of particular application to pre-Roman Britain. For Britain this, and the classical writers for immediately pre-Roman times, gave an historical background to all archaeological remains. When prehistoric finds occasionally obtruded themselves on the mind of the medieval scholar, they could either be disposed of as natural wonders, or interpreted by the Bible or another written authority.[4]

At the beginning of the fourteenth century, a *Tractatus de mirabilibus Britanniae* includes Stonehenge, the Rollright Stones, and the Uffington White Horse among the marvels of this island. Of the lintelled stones of the first monument the writer expresses amazement and incomprehension—'one cannot imagine by what art they were erected, nor by what kind of people it was built' he says, and at Rollright, though recognising the circle there as man-made, he has to admit that 'at what time this was done, or by what people, or for what memorial or significance, is unknown'.[5] On the other hand, Geoffrey of Monmouth had placed Stonehenge in a firm historical context unknown to or ignored by the writer of the *Tractatus*, and a fourteenth-century chronicler had therefore inserted what is the earliest known drawing of the monument *sub anno* AD 483, with a note derived from Geoffrey stating that it was brought in that year from Ireland by Merlin, *non vi sed arte*, to its present position.[6] Such writers as these looked at these structures with the unquestioning eyes of those to whom incomprehensible wonders were of the accepted order of things, or even if miraculous, could be placed in a secure chronological position by reference to an historical source as reputable as Geoffrey then appeared to be.

Early in the thirteenth century Ralph of Coggeshall, always

4

interested in local folklore and oddities, records what must have been the find of a mammoth's bones on the Essex coast: enormous ribs and a couple of teeth so huge that 200 human teeth could have been cut from them. These, he said, were no doubt the bones of a giant, and indeed the head of a giant had been found on the shore in Yorkshire.[7] So too the chronicler who records the finding of huge bones at Bardney near Lincoln in 1344 has no doubt of the former existence of giants in England.[8] In antediluvian times they had scriptural warrant, after all; Geoffrey had put it on record that this island of Albion was originally inhabited by giants, and later, John Rous wrote a treatise on them. Such finds were to be marvelled at, but not to be understood: in Ralph's *Chronicon* the section *De giganteis dentibus* is appropriately sandwiched between the story of the Green Children of Woolpit and that of a poltergeist named Malekin.

The excavations in the Roman city of Verulamium by the Abbots Ealdred and Eadmar in the eleventh century were frankly conducted in search of building material. The former had 'brought together a great quantity not only of stones and tiles, but also of timber-materials for the building of his church' from this source before his sudden death. Eadmar made a sensational find of Roman documents, one of which of course was a life of St Alban; whether or not this story, handed down by Matthew Paris, had any foundation in fact is another matter, but the description of the 'ancient stone floors with tiles and columns . . . the foundations of ancient buildings and underground hollows, jugs and amphorae of well-made pottery turned on the wheel, and glass vases containing the dust of the dead' is circumstantial enough.[9] St Albans carried on the excavation tradition into the next century, when the monks of the abbey, in response to a miraculous dream, excavated a barrow at Redbourn in 1178, finding in it a skeleton with iron weapons (likely enough Saxon) which was triumphantly claimed as that of St Amphibalus.[10] But perhaps the most direct interest shown in field archaeology in the Middle Ages was the unashamed search for treasure, instigated at the highest level, as is shown by King John's unrewarding excavation at Corbridge in 1201[11] and by the repeated royal commands to dig barrows for this end. Records of such barrow-digging go back at least to 1237, and continue into the seventeenth century.[12]

In the later Middle Ages there was a certain amount of conscious antiquarianism, whereby some attempt was made on occasion by painters or sculptors to dress historical figures in costume or armour which was at least old fashioned, if not more precisely defined. Instances of this antiquarian feeling have been noted by Sir James Mann:[13] two outstanding figures of the fifteenth century concerned in such matters, William Worcester and John Rous, have been further discussed by Sir Thomas Kendrick.[14] In the former we see a topographer-antiquary much of the type of Leland a century later. Rous, in his two Warwick Rolls, depicted the ancestors of the earls of Warwick in consciously archaic dress; the representations of the armour in particular 'are so good', in Mann's words, 'that one wonders whether the early armours of the Earls were still preserved in the castle at his time', and so available for direct copying.

But this medieval antiquarianism is no more than sporadic and exceptional. With the sixteenth century we come into a new world of learning in which antiquarian studies as such take a place from the start. They took this place, not as a disinterested intellectual activity, but as part of the contemporary search for precedent and authority in all branches of life and thought, and above all in the quest for respectable antecedents. Scholars, churchmen, and statesmen in Tudor England were concerned with establishing their new world on newly defined foundations, but these foundations had themselves to be recognisably a part of the ancient world of classical or Biblical antiquity. I have noted elsewhere that the papers contributed to the Elizabethan College of Antiquaries 'were written with an eye to determining and confirming by historical or archaeological precedent the institutions of the contemporary England of the writers,'[15] though, as Dr Joan Evans has commented, '"Antiquity" figures in most of the discourses, but never visible antiquity'.[16] On the whole, archaeological evidence was not amenable to such interpretation, though by the eighteenth century Stukeley was using his Stonehenge and Avebury field-work to 'combat the Deists from an unexpected quarter' and to demonstrate that not only were the Druids 'of Abraham's religion entirely' but had 'a knowledge of the plurality of persons in the Deity' and so were acceptable founders of patriarchal Christianity in England. It was left for the nineteenth century to use the ecclesiastical architecture of the Middle Ages as in itself an argument for the revision of liturgy and ceremonial in the Church of England, and to discover the moral qualities of the Pointed or Christian Style.

Nevertheless, Renaissance thought was deeply concerned with antiquities, and in England there were plenty of antiquities which had to be accounted for. Those of the Roman period did not present great difficulties, and we shall see how Camden used them to make just that link between the England of his day and the respectable antecedents of classical antiquity that I have mentioned. Prehistory, however, was another matter; we have seen how the concept of non-historical antiquity was almost impossible to grasp, and with the demolition of the myth of the British history from Polydore Vergil onwards, an unfortunate gap was left. It was necessary to construct a new documentation for the remote past, which would again link British antiquities to the historically documented past of either the Bible, or the world of classical mythology and history. The bolder spirits managed to combine the two, and so make the best of two ancient worlds, sacred and pagan. Bale, for instance, produced in 1548 a splendid scheme by inventing a character called Samothes, son of Japhet, as the first post-diluvian King of Britain in the third millennium B C, with a collateral descendant, Albion, who was the son of Neptune and great-grandson of Ham, and who later came to the British throne. Twyne, in 1590, little knowing what damage he was doing, introduced the Phoenicians, eager for Cornish tin, for the first time: these grave Tyrian traders have, alas, haunted British antiquarian studies to their detriment ever since. In the seventeenth century the Phoenicians and the sons of Japhet held their own as the respectable ancestors of British prehistoric man, supported by what seemed to be a mass of convincing evidence from philology.[17]

It is worth while considering for a moment the relation between antiquarian and philological studies in the sixteenth to eighteenth centuries, and to recognise that the chaotic state of the latter did much to inhibit the development of even a rudimentary sort of prehistory. There was of course the necessary premiss that as the world had been repeopled after the Deluge and the episode of the Tower of Babel, there must have been an original language for all mankind, and this, by more or less general consent, was inevitably thought to have been Hebrew. From this point, of course, there were no rules of linguistics or philology to guide the wary or hamper the bold, and Welsh,

7

Hebrew, and Greek could be equated with all the conviction needed to support the new foundation-myth which had been concocted to replace that of Geoffrey of Monmouth. Only rarely does one see philological problems being approached from a reasonable standpoint, as when Scaliger (and following him, Camden) noted the genuine similarities within the Indo-European language group in the vocabularies of Persian, Germanic, and Crimean Gothic, or still more, the acute grasp of the problems of the Celtic languages shown, as we shall see, by Edward Lhwyd late in the seventeenth century.

It was in this climate of thought, then, that any consideration of ancient British antiquities in the sixteenth or seventeenth centuries would take place, with the added evidence of the classical writers for the condition of Britain at the time of the Roman Conquest, and the new view of primitive mankind made possible by the discovery of America and its aboriginal inhabitants. The Ancient Britons were not only discussed but their appearance reconstructed in a series of related drawings from about 1575 to 1611, the importance of which has been demonstrated by Kendrick. It is instructive to analyse the sources of these drawings, and those of the current concepts of prehistoric Britain as presented in verbal form.[18]

The essential questions, as they would have presented themselves to any scholar from Camden onwards, were asked and answered by John Aubrey in the middle of the seventeenth century in a passage which serves as an admirable opening to the enquiry we are about to make. It forms part of the Introduction to his *Essay Towards the Description of the North Division of Wiltshire*, composed in 1659 as part of a larger work for the whole county, modelled on Dugdale's *Warwickshire*.

Let us imagine then [writes Aubrey] what kind of countrie this was in the time of the ancient Britons. By the nature of the soil, which is a sour woodsere land, very natural for the production of oakes especially, one may conclude that this North Division was a shady dismal wood: and the inhabitants almost as savage as the beasts whose skins were their only rayment. The language British, which for the honour of it was in those dayes spoken from the Orcades to Italie and Spain. The boats on the Avon (which signifies River) were basketts of twigges covered with an oxe skin: which the poore people in Wales use to this day. They call them *curricles*. Within this shire I believe that there were several *Reguli* which often made war upon another: and the great ditches which run on the plaines and elsewhere so many miles (not unlikely) their boundaries: and withall served for defence against the incursions of their enemies, as the Pict's wall, Offa's Ditch: and that in China, to compare things small to great. Their religion is at large described by Caesar. Their priests were Druids. Some of their temples I pretend to have restored, as Avebury, Stonehenge, &c., as also British sepulchres. Their waie of fighting is lively sett down by Caesar. Their camps with their way of meeting their antagonists I have sett down in another place. They knew the use of iron. They were 2 or 3 degrees, I suppose, less savage than the Americans.[19]

You will have noticed several interesting points in this charming vignette. Aubrey supplies coracles from the classical sources, and from his knowledge of the survival of these craft in Wales (where indeed they may still be seen); from Caesar the Druids and chariot-warfare, and the use of iron. His own field-work in Wiltshire provides stone circles, hill-forts, linear earthworks, and barrows. And finally, he introduces a touch of comparative ethnography as the Britons are set against the still novel Indians of the New World. It is possible that the inter-tribal warfare Aubrey suggests for prehistoric Wiltshire may not be unconnected with Samuel Daniel's comparison in 1612 of the Indian tribes with the conditions likely to have obtained in prehistoric Britain.

This revelation of primitive man in the Americas was then of the greatest importance in moulding antiquarian thought in the sixteenth and seventeenth centuries, particularly so far as visual concepts of Ancient Britons were concerned. In the representations we are about to discuss the relationship of John White's drawings of Virginian Indians to his of Britons is clear. But the story seems to start ten years before White's drawings of *c.* 1585, with de Heere's couple of naked and melancholy Britons, tattooed (or woad-painted), mustachio'd and carrying spear, sword, and shields, one of which is a long oval in shape. Now these details derive from references to Celts in the classical writers, partly in Caesar but mainly in other writers such as Dio Cassius and Diodorus Siculus (who specifies long shields). John Speed's descriptions of Ancient Britons in his *Histcrie*, for instance, are built up from references in such Greek and Latin authors and form the verbal counterpart to these drawings. Representations of Red Indians were becoming available in England from the 1560s at least: they climb among the strapwork on Edmund Harman's monument of 1569 in Burford church in Oxfordshire,[20] derived here from unknown sources, and de Bry's *America* (with some of White's drawings) was published in 1590. White's drawing of a 'Pict' is clearly related not only to his Red Indian drawings, but to the de Heere drawing as well, with which it shares the oval shield and curious sword, but White has also added a severed human head to be brandished by his Pict, presumably inspired by the references in Diodorus to Celtic head-hunting. Here and in his *Native of Britain* drawing, he has developed de Heere's sword into a sort of fantastic semi-Oriental scimitar, and this weapon continues to adorn ancient Britons up to Speed's illustrations of 1611: Mann has noted the medieval predilection for fantastic accoutrements such as scimitars in representations of mythological and even Roman personages. But John White's Briton has an addition, not in de Heere, in the form of a globular butt to his spear, a feature taken up and exaggerated by de Bry and Speed, which must derive from Dio Cassius' description, as contained in Xiphilinus, of spear-butts of this form among the Scottish tribes (also attested, incidentally, by archaeological evidence).[21] The tattooing of the Picts, mentioned by more than one classical writer, may have come into Renaissance antiquarian thought from the New Learning, but may be a heritage of the early Middle Ages, since it is described by that great encyclopaedist Isidore of Seville. On the whole, literary sources alone had been used in reconstructing these ancient Britons, but we are on the threshold of a new approach when we turn to Leland, and to that greatest of Elizabethan antiquaries, William Camden.

These reconstructions of Ancient Britons seem to stand alone, and apart from drawings of medieval buildings of varying degrees of inaccuracy, illustrations of antiquities seem hardly to have survived before those of the later seventeenth century. The likelihood that more may have been made than is generally thought, however, is suggested by such occasional records as the charming drawing, with notes and measurements, of the skull and antlers of an extinct Irish Giant Deer found in 1588 and preserved by Adam Loftus, Lord Chancellor of Ireland, in

2. *Extinct Irish Giant Deer. Drawing c. 1588.*

Rathfarnham Castle near Dublin.[22]

Leland, much of whose unpublished material was used by Camden, was a topographer-antiquary whose allegiance was more to the medieval tradition than to the new learning, despite his Paris training in the Renaissance modes of thought, yet he and his work symbolise the beginning of the topographical study of Britain which was to culminate in the great county histories in the later eighteenth century. Like William Worcester, he had an omnivorous curiosity for ancient and contemporary alike, and, while primarily concerned with the task set him by Henry VIII's commission 'to peruse and diligently to serche al the libraries of monasteries and colleges of this yowre noble realme', made in his famous travels that mass of miscellaneous notes which was to be the quarry in which succeeding generations of antiquaries dug. His approach was in the main from the documents to the things he saw, but he inevitably noted pre-Conquest antiquities when they caught his attention—the Roman Wall and the Vallum, Offa's Dyke, The Devil's Arrows, but curiously enough not Stonehenge nor Silbury Hill. He got as far as guessing that hill-forts could sometimes be pre-Roman, and his interest in Roman antiquities was doubtless partly stimulated by his association in Paris with Guillaume Budé, the eminent numismatist. But throughout his work antiquities took their place side by side with other topographical features, natural or artificial, and his studies seem at no time to have been planned with any definite idea of how he might utilise the source material he so industriously gathered.

Camden, however, had specific ideas about studying antiquities for their own sake while still a schoolboy, and deliberately set about training himself as an antiquary while still a young man. There were no precedents — 'it was a sort of Learning, that was then but just appearing in the world' — but he recognised the need of a knowledge of Anglo-Saxon and Welsh if he was to attempt to understand place-names, and a knowledge of antiquities at first hand if he was to consider these in their historical framework. And he set about the composition of the *Britannia* with a clearly conceived plan in his mind. As I have said in another place,

> I do not think we can escape from the conclusion that the *Britannia* was originally planned to elucidate the topography of Roman Britain, and to present a picture of the Province, with reference to its development through Saxon and medieval times, which would enable Britain to take her rightful place at once within the world of antiquity and that of international Renaissance scholarship. Language and title alike declared its purpose : it was to have a European appeal, and, with the destruction of the myth of Trojan Brutus, was to establish Britain as a member of the fellowship of nations who drew their strength from roots struck deep in the Roman Empire.[23]

It is well known how he travelled in Wales and England, and made his famous visits to Hadrian's Wall. In the second of these he was accompanied by Sir Robert Bruce Cotton, who had been his pupil at Westminster and who collected not only manuscripts but coins. His influence on numismatic studies in the first decade of the seventeenth century was considerable — 'the few years 1609–11, witnessed, in each case under the influence of Cotton, the creation of a royal coin cabinet, and also Camden's immensely successful first English edition, and Speed's no less epoch-making book — both full of coins'.[24] Perhaps Camden's most notable contribution to numismatics and to British pre-history was his recognition of a native coinage at the time of the Roman Conquest, the identification of coins struck by Cunobelin and Commius, and the mints of Verulamium and Camulo-dunum. But he hardly goes beyond the classical writers for a brief description of the ancient Britons, turning with enthusiasm rather to the coming of the Saxons — 'this warlike, victorious, stiffe, stout, and vigorous nation'.

The Anglo-Saxons do not, however, really enter into British archaeology until a century and a half after Camden's day. Though the cremation-cemetery which gave rise to *Hydrio-taphia* was in fact that of a pagan Saxon community, Sir Thomas Browne considered the sad sepulchral pitchers to be Roman, and no identification of archaeological finds as Anglo-Saxon seems to have been made before Bryan Faussett recognised the Kentish cemeteries he excavated for what they were in the 1750s.[25] Of course coins of the later Saxon period had long been identified, together with the inscribed monuments or such objects as the great silver brooch found at Sutton, Isle of Ely at the end of the seventeenth century and published by Hickes,[26] or the Alfred Jewel itself, found in 1693. This was described by William Musgrave, author of *Antiquitates Britanno-Belgicae* (1719): 'the Work very fine', he comments, 'so as to make some Men question its true Age: But in all probability it did belong to that great King'.[27]

The antiquarian spirit of the age, so well exemplified in Cam-den, touched not only scholars but country gentlemen as well. In the Isle of Wight Sir John Oglander not only made historical and antiquarian notes on his own and adjacent parishes at the beginning of the seventeenth century, but also excavated.

At my fyrst cominge to inhabit in this Island Anno 1607 [he records] I went to Quarr, and inquyred of divors owld men where ye greate church stood. Theyre wase but one, Father Pennie, a verye owld man, coold give me anye satisfaction; he told me he had bene often in ye church whene itt wase standinge, and told me what a goodly church itt wase; and furthor sayd that itt stoode to ye sowthward of all ye ruins, corn then growinge where it stoode. I hired soome to digge to see whethor I myght finde ye fowndation butt cowld not.[28]

His interests were not only medieval, but extended to barrow-digging.

You may see divors buries on ye topp of owre Island hills
[Oglander noted] whose name in ye Danische tounge signi-
fieth theyr nature, as being places onlie weare men were
buryed . . . I have digged for my experience in soome of ye
moore awntientest, and haue found manie bones of men
formerlye consumed by fyor, accordinge to ye Romane
custome . . . Wheresoever you see a burie in any eminent
place, moste commonlye on ye toppe of hilles, you may presume that there hathe been soome buryed; according to ye
etimoligie of ye woord,—digge, and you shall find theyre
bones.[29]

Fortunately for future archaeologists, there seem to have been
relatively few antiquaries at this time who, like Sir John, digged
for their experience in barrows. The general opinion was that
tumuli covered mass burials of those slain in ancient anonymous battles. Dugdale corresponded with Dr Langbaine and
Mr Bysshe on these matters, and it is in a way characteristic that
he and his friends still approached the problem entirely from
the literary end—'Upon the most diligent search into the
Roman Storye I am yet able to make, I meet not with anything
that comes any way home to yr. demand concerning the burying
of Soldiers in the field', writes Bysshe to Dugdale in 1650.[30] The
more empirical approach of digging into the mound and seeing
whether it covered one or many burials, inhumations, or crema-
tions, did not suggest itself, but a new spirit of enquiry was
already in the air by the middle of the century, as we shall see.

In the meantime, the early seventeenth century, largely due
no doubt to the effect on the educated public of Camden's
Britannia in its successive Latin and English editions, was seeing
a growing spirit of antiquarianism. In 1636, for instance, the
rector of Rodmarton of Gloucestershire recorded in his parish
register the find of a Roman pavement and coins in the vicinity.[31]
A more curious record of parochial antiquities and curiosities is
afforded by the stone sundial with carved and inscribed panels,
dated 1639 and now in the church of Trelleck in Monmouth-
shire. This depicts on one face the nearby Norman motte
(*Magna mole*), on another the three prehistoric standing stones
which give their name to the parish (*Maior saxis*), with their
heights indicated, and finally a local well (*Maxima fonte*).

In the early decades of the seventeenth century too, the performance of such plays as Beaumont and Fletcher's *Bonduca* in

1618, or the pastoral *Stonehenge* by John Speed, performed at St John's College, Oxford, in 1635, show the public interest in such matters and indicate how by their performance they would tend to encourage it. But on the whole we have to wait until after the Civil War before we really see the beginning of antiquarianism of the kind which was then to persist well into the nineteenth century. In the 1640s the meetings which were to give rise to the foundation of the Royal Society began to take place, and even if in these early years antiquities did not form a topic for discussion, within a couple of decades we find that the new spirit of empirical enquiry which the Society was to set afoot had taken antiquarian studies within its ambit. Aubrey dated the change in viewpoint to just before the middle of the century. Before about 1649, he wrote, when Baconian science was first discussed in Oxford, any 'Innovation in Learning' was frowned upon. We are reminded of Camden mastering the New Learning rather less than a century before, and Aubrey saw his kinship in scholarship with his great predecessor — 'I could not rest quiet 'till I had obeyed this secret call. Mr. Camden, Dr. Plott and Mr. Wood confess the same'.[32] With the second half of the seventeenth century we are confronted not only with the mighty team of historians, but with those who are partly or wholly concerned with antiquities — Aubrey and Plot, Lhwyd and Sibbald, Ashmole, and Dugdale.

Before turning to these figures, we must consider for a moment the possible influences from continental antiquarian scholarship on the English scene. There was for instance the literature of Druidism,[33] with such works as the *De Dis Germanis* of Elias Schedius published in 1648, but so far as field archaeology was concerned, with the odd exceptions such as a sixteenth century French painting showing Ste-Geneviève in a prehistoric stone circle (probably a destroyed site at Nanterre),[34] the first publication of drawings of megalithic chambered tombs were by such writers as Picardt in Holland (1660)[35] and by Ole Worm in Denmark (1643, 1651)[36] and had an importance in demonstrating to British antiquaries that monuments similar to those of this country could also be found on the European continent. Direct comment on this fact seems first to have been made by Georg Keysler in the early eighteenth century,[37] but there is little doubt that some of these illustrated foreign publications, especially Worm's first book, did serve to increase the interest shown in megalithic monuments by our own antiquarian scholars.

Of these the most remarkable and significant is that engaging character John Aubrey.[38] This is not the place to deal with Aubrey's many-sided antiquarian activities except from the standpoint of the study of material remains, but here alone there is much that is new and individual. His major contribution to such studies still unfortunately remains in manuscript, the famous *Monumenta Britannica* mainly written in the 1670s.[39] Its sub-title is 'a Miscellanie of British Antiquities', and is essentially planned as a descriptive work dealing with field monuments and antiquities from prehistoric times to the Middle Ages. It opens with what has always been the best known part of the work, the *Templa Druidum*, containing the first description of Avebury and the first satisfactory account of Stonehenge, together with notes on other stone circles and allied monuments. The literary sources for Druidism are then set out, with an 'Apparatus of Bards', and part of a correspondence with Dr Garden of Aberdeen on Scottish stone circles.[40] Dugdale and others had urged that whatever might be the state of the rest of the *Monumenta*, the *Templa Druidum* at least should be printed, but this was never achieved, and a summary of Aubrey's account of Avebury, and of his general ideas on stone circles and Druids, printed in Gibson's edition of Camden in 1695, was all that saw the light of print.

The *Monumenta* goes on to deal with field monuments, mainly those of Wessex known to Aubrey at first hand. Part II deals with pre-Roman and Roman camps and forts, and Roman civil settlements; Part III goes on to barrows, pottery, burials in general, linear earthworks, roads and trackways, Roman pavements (rather out of place), and coins. What makes this collection of material so important is that it is assembled and set out for its own sake, and not to illustrate a fictitious or quasi-historical narrative. Aubrey is at pains to bring together a corpus of archaeological evidence which seems to him to relate to pre-historic and Roman times, and to present it as source material with the minimum of comment or theory. He is in fact applying to this material the same classificatory method and presentation as his colleagues in the Royal Society were using in the natural sciences; the methods of Ray in botany or Lhwyd in palaeontology. And what is more remarkable, he continues this approach

16

into the field of medieval architecture.

Part IV of the *Monumenta* was never finished, and is even more disjointed than the earlier sections of the work: it was well entitled by its author *ΣΤΡΩΜΑΤΑ sive Miscellanea*. But it was planned to include investigations into the chronological sequence of architectural styles, handwriting, heraldic shields, and clothing. The first of these, the *Chronologia Architectonica*, is especially interesting, including as it does over fifty drawings of details of doors and windows taken largely from buildings which could be dated from documentary evidence, and used as a reference series to build up a sequence of styles. 'The windows ye most remarqueable', he notes, 'hence one may give a guess about what Time ye Building was'. This was a pioneer work in medieval archaeology if ever there was one, and Aubrey's sound but unpublished principles had to await rediscovery in the nineteenth century.[41]

Another work of Aubrey's shows clearly how he came within the Royal Society atmosphere. The *Natural History of Wiltshire* was begun in 1656, and continued under the encouragement of Robert Plot, Evelyn, Ray, Tanner and Thomas Gale. Its plan, ranging from Air and Springs Medicinall, through Formed Stones, Architecture, Agriculture and Antiquities, to Things Praeternatural in 36 chapters, is clearly related to the parochial enquiries or questionnaires which were being sent out from the 1670s onwards by such as Ogilby, Machell, Plot and Lhwyd.[42] These schemes set out to arrange in more or less standardised form the objective phenomena, whether natural or artificial, which could be observed and described in a county or other area, with a view to presenting a systematic picture. The inclusion of antiquities within these surveys, projected or carried out, makes it clear that they were regarded as coming more within the purview of the natural scientists than of the historians.

At the level of archaeological investigation possible at the Restoration, or for a couple of centuries more, this approach to antiquities was in fact the only one in which the study could progress and develop. It meant, so far as prehistoric antiquities were concerned, an emancipation from legend and from the fantastic substitutes for history concocted by those who reverenced written authority rather than the evidence of their own empirical investigations. There were die-hards, of course. Aylett Sammes, for instance, published a folio in 1676 entitled *Brit-*

annia Antiqua Illustrata, in which he wrote a complete and con-secutive history of Britain from the Deluge to King Ine by com-bining Geoffrey of Monmouth, Bale's Samothes and his kin, and Twyne's Phoenicians (as resurrected by Bochart) into one extraordinary fantasy: his isolation from contemporary anti-quarian activity is shown by the fact that archaeological, as opposed to literary, evidence is nowhere used in the book.

But throughout the correspondence and informal writing of most of the antiquaries in the second half of the century, rather more perhaps than in their published work, we see this objective interest in field archaeology. The heralds were by no means only concerned with the business of the College of Arms; the Camden tradition seems to have taken firm root there. Dugdale, who as we saw corresponded about tumuli with his learned friends, had visited the Roman wall, and was still interesting himself in the problems presented by Wall and Vallum in 1685.[43] This visit was presumably made in 1664–65, when he was engaged on the Visitation of Westmorland and Cumberland, and his manu-script volume of this tour includes, after the strictly heraldic and genealogical material, notes and drawings of shields and effigies in churches in that area, and of the cross-shafts and hog-back stones in the churchyard at Penrith, and an account, with sketch-plans, of the two 'Henge Monuments' of Mayborough and King Arthur's Round Table at Eamont Bridge.[44] Elias Ash-mole, writing to Dugdale in 1657, gives a long factual account of a stretch of Watling Street from Weedon to Mancetter: he not only notes the character of the road, and the visible remains at such sites as High Cross (*Venonae*) and Mancetter (*Man-duessedum*) but at New Inn (now Cave's Inn, the site of *Tripon-tium*) he did some original field-work: 'spying some smale tren-ches lately made to draine the adjacent meadow, I went to them, and found many pieces of Romane brick and tyle cast up'.[45]

John Anstis, Garter King of Arms early in the eighteenth century, was a Cornishman much interested in the field monu-ments of his own county, and of England and Wales in general. He compiled a large series of notes and drawings of antiquities,[46] including stone circles and chambered tombs, and some extrem-ely interesting plans of hill-forts, which, once thought to be by Edward Lhwyd, are now identified as by a young assistant of his, William Jones.[47] Anstis was a friend of Aubrey, and of that great figure Edward Lhwyd of the Ashmolean, who made

18

pioneer studies in palaeontology and other branches of natural history, as well as being the most notable Celtic scholar before the development of philological disciplines upon their present foundation in the last century.[48]

Lhwyd's notes on field monuments are now mainly known to us through transcripts made by Anstis and others, including William Stukeley in the early eighteenth century, as the originals largely perished in various vicissitudes, including fire, in the last couple of centuries. From these, and from surviving letters, we can see that the acumen Lhwyd brought to bear on the problems of linguistics or the natural sciences was also turned to antiquities. He describes the great chambered tomb of New Grange in Ireland for the first time (Anstis has a drawing of it, perhaps by Lhwyd or an assistant), and makes sensible use of the American Indians once again when commenting on flint arrow-heads. 'I doubt not but you have often seen of those Arrow-heads they ascribe to elfs or fairies', he writes from Scotland in 1699, 'they are just the same chip'd flints the natives of New England head their arrows with at this day: and there are also several stone hatchets found in this kingdom, not unlike those of the Americans'.[49] Dugdale, in fact, had earlier commented on stone axe-heads in similar terms — they were 'weapons used by the Britons before the art of making arms of brass or iron was known',[50] and Plot had said the same. The first recognition of a Palaeolithic flint implement was also at the end of the seventeenth century, when a hand-axe was found near Gray's Inn Lane with the skeleton of what was claimed as one of the elephants brought over by Claudius — pretty certainly a mammoth. The flint tool, published at the beginning of the next century, was recognised as an artifact, and the product of an Ancient Briton, but it was left to John Frere in 1797 to make the first classic pronouncement on Palaeolithic implements, assigning them 'to a very remote period indeed; even beyond that of the present world'.[51]

One of Lhwyd's friends and correspondents was Sir Robert Sibbald, first Professor of Medicine in the University of Edinburgh, who combined the study of antiquities with that of botany and natural history. He drew attention to the recumbent stone circles of north-east Scotland,[52] and published drawings of an important Late Bronze Age hoard from Fife as well as of other northern antiquities,[53] and he contributed to the 1695 edition of Camden's *Britannia* additions relating to Scotland, as well as a separate *Discourse Concerning the Thule of the Ancients*.

The re-editing of the *Britannia* by a team of historians and antiquaries under young Edmund Gibson at the end of the seventeenth century marks the culmination of the phase of antiquarian study we have been considering.[54] The work was a real achievement, and the revised edition, still owing much to the soundness of Camden's original plan, was almost a new work, embodying the results of three-quarters of a century's work by a notable succession of scholars in several fields.

The appearance of the first (and only published) part of Lhwyd's *Archaeologia Britannica*, dealing with Celtic philology, at the beginning of the eighteenth century should have been the turning point in the study of Celtic antiquities in general in the British Isles. But Lhwyd was a pioneer ahead of his time, with the prescient recognition of 'an hypothesis of C Britons and P Britons',[55] fundamental to the classification of the Celtic languages, and his sound linguistic approach in general did little to stem the flood of nonsense of the type popularised by Aylett Sammes, which was to continue well into the nineteenth century.

By the end of the seventeenth century the conditions for the scholarly study of antiquities had in fact been created, largely as a result of the application of the nascent scientific disciplines, and the empirical approach of Bacon and Descartes which lay behind them, which one associates essentially with the Royal Society; among its Fellows were to be found several of the leading antiquaries of the time. We have seen how this viewpoint made possible the liberation of archaeological studies from a dependence on literary sources, so many of dubious validity, and from any entanglement in the quest for antecedents or the hunt for respectable ancestors. This for the prehistoric material; Aubrey had even perceived how historical sources could be used in conjunction with the evidence of material culture (in this instance the development of medieval architecture) to build up a new frame of reference based on the architectural styles themselves. Scholars like Aubrey, Anstis and Lhwyd appreciated that so far as field antiquities were concerned, the need was for the record and collation, preferably in visual form, of the sites and monuments themselves, as an essential preliminary to any interpretation. Lhwyd in particular, in his classification of fossils, had in fact set out a possible typological approach to archaeological material which was basically that employed at the end of the nineteenth century by Sir John Evans.

We may note, in parenthesis, that these developments were not taking place within the framework of university disciplines, but were the achievement of individual scholars whose connection with the universities was either non-existent or, as with Lhwyd, the accidental result of holding a museum post. Nor, after the extinction of the Elizabethan College of Antiquaries, does there appear to have been any attempt to create a specifically antiquarian society until the early years of the eighteenth century, when the present Society of Antiquaries of London was brought into being. It was founded, as it happened, just as the studies it stood for were starting on their notable decline and, it must be confessed, it did little to arrest the process.

But promising though conditions may have seemed, the development of archaeological studies hardly, in fact, moved beyond the stage reached by the middle of the century. William Stukeley, brought up in the Restoration tradition, did, it is true, carry on the tradition of sound field archaeology into the 1720s, but his own lamentable lapse from scholarship after that time is but a single instance of the general collapse of standards in historical and antiquarian research after about 1730. The necessity of an empirical approach was forgotten, the British foundations-myths were rewritten, philological speculation took on even more fantastic forms, and antiquarian studies became, understandably enough, discredited by serious scholars in other fields. By the end of the eighteenth century a revived interest in antiquities appeared under the dubious aegis of the Romantic Movement which, however much it may have quickened a general apprehension of ancient monuments, hardly served to tighten the disciplines by which they were studied. It was not until the end of the nineteenth century that the reintroduction of the scientific approach to archaeology enabled it to build a secure foundation upon which the fabric of prehistory and protohistory could be constructed and, establishing its own techniques and authority, enabled it to take its place side by side with the older discipline of history itself.

NOTES

1 R. G. Collingwood, *The Idea of History*, Oxford, 1946, 12.
2 V. H. Galbraith, *Hist. Research in Medieval England*, London 1951, 42.
3 Cf. A. Momigliano, *Journ. Warburg and Courtauld Inst.* XIII, 1950, 291 ff.; *Studies in Historiography*, London 1966, 1.
4 Cf. M. Hunter in P. Clemoes (ed.), *Anglo-Saxon England* III, 1974, 29.
5 Corpus Christi Coll. Cambridge, MS. 59, f. 140^v; T. H. Ravenhill, *The Rollright Stones*, Rollright, 1926, frontispiece.
6 C.C.C.C. MS. 194, f. 57^r; *Stonehenge* H.M.S.O., 1955, pl. opp. p. 12. I am indebted to Professor C. R. Cheney for help in tracing these manuscripts in default of references in the two publications cited. Merlin is depicted building Stonehenge in a mid-XIV century manuscript; British Library MS. Egerton 3028, f. 30.
7 *Chronicon Anglicanum* (Rolls Series, 1875), 120.
8 *Chronicon Petriburgense* (ed. Giles, 1845), 168.
9 *Vitae Abbatum*, quoted in full translation by R. E. M. Wheeler, *Verulamium*, Oxford 1936, 35-37. Cf. J. C. Higgitt, *Journ. Brit. Arch. Ass.* 3rd S. XXXVI, 1973, 1, for the medieval attitude to Roman Britain.
10 Roger of Wendover, *Flores Hist.* (Rolls Series, 1886), i, 109.
11 Roger of Hoveden, *Chronica* (Rolls Series, 1871), 157.
12 G. F. Hill, *Treasure Trove*, London 1936, 251-5; cf. *Trans. Devon Assoc.* xviii, 1886, 106; *Proc. Isle of Wight Nat. Hist. Soc.* iii, 1941, 185-6; *Folklore* LXXVIII, 1967, 1.
13 *Arch. Journ.* LXXXIX, 1932, 254.
14 T. D. Kendrick, *British Antiquity*, London 1950; J. H. Harvey, *William Worcestre: Itineraries*, Oxford 1969.
15 *William Stukeley*, Oxford 1950, 4.
16 *History of the Society of Antiquaries*, Oxford 1956, 11.
17 For Bale and Twyne, cf. Kendrick, *British Antiquity, passim*. Cf. No. IV below.
18 Kendrick, *Brit. Ant.* 121 ff.; for John White's drawings of Indians and Ancient Britons, P. Hulton and D. B. Quinn, *The American drawings of John White . . .*, London 1964.
19 Conveniently available in *Brief Lives and other selected writings of John Aubrey*, ed. A. Powell, London 1949, 1-2.
20 S. Piggott, *Antiq.* XXXVIII, (1964), 134. Cf. No. II below.
21 V. G. Childe, *Prehistory of Scotland*, London 1935, 228.
22 G. F. Mitchell and H. M. Parkes, *Proc. R. Irish Acad.* LII, B, 1949, 294; Pl. XVII, where the drawing is assigned to the sixteenth century and the skull recorded as having been sent to Hatfield House in 1597. But the note on the drawing giving the Rathfarnham provenance also describes Loftus as Lord Chancellor, an office he did not assume until 1619, so that the inscription must be between this date and 1622, when he was created first Viscount Loftus of Ely. For a later record with drawing of a similar skull from Dardistown, Co. Meath, cf. T. Molyneux in *A Natural History of Ireland by Several Hands*,

Dublin 1726, 137, from *Phil. Trans.* XIX, 1697, 489.

23 *Proc. Brit. Acad.* XXXVII, 1951, 207; No. III below.

24 M. Grant, *Proc. Royal Numis. Soc.*, 1954, viii. For Cotton, H. Mirrlees, *A fly in amber . . . an extravagant biography of the romantic antiquary Sir Robert Bruce Cotton*, London 1962, is, as the title suggests, hardly an adequate treatment.

25 Cf. R. Jessup, *Anglo-Saxon Jewellery*, London 1950, 70 ff.

26 Cf. R. L. Bruce Mitford in *Dark-Age Britain*, London 1956, 193 ff.; *Aspects of Anglo-Saxon Archaeology*, London 1974, 330. The brooch was subsequently lost sight of, reappearing in 1950, when it was noted that the Hickes drawing was 'of an extremely high degree of accuracy'.

27 Jessup, op. cit., 87.

28 *Oglander Memoirs*, ed. W. H. Long, London 1888, 199.

29 Ibid., 117-18.

30 W. Hamper, *Life . . . Diary and Correspondence of Sir William Dugdale*, London 1827, 232.

31 S. Rudder, *History of Gloucestershire*, Cirencester 1779, 631.

32 Britton, *Memoir of John Aubrey*, London 1845, 93.

33 Cf. Kendrick, *The Druids*, London 1927, 21 ff.: S. Piggott, *The Druids*, London 1968.

34 S. Piggott, *Antiq.* XLVII, 1973, 292; J. Peek, ibid., XLVIII, 1974, 134.

35 *Korte beschryvinge van eenige Vergetene en Verborgene Antiquitaten. . . .* Amsterdam 1660.

36 *Danicorum Monumentorum Libri Sex*, Copenhagen 1643; *Danica Literatura Antiquissima*, Copenhagen 1651.

37 *Antiquitates Selectae Septentrionales et Celticae*, Hanover 1720.

38 M. Hunter, *John Aubrey and the realm of learning*, London 1975.

39 Bodleian MSS. Top. gen. c. 24-25. I am much indebted to Mr R. J. C. Atkinson for making his photostats of the manuscript available to me in advance of his critical edition of the *Monumenta*.

40 Edited by C. A. Gordon, *Miscellany*, *Third Spalding Club* III, 1960, 1.

41 H. M. Colvin, in J. Summerson (ed.), *Concerning Architecture*, London 1968, 1.

42 For these questionnaires, cf. Piggott, *William Stukeley*, 11 ff.; R. T. Gunther, *Life and Letters of Edward Lhwyd*, Oxford 1945. For Machell, J. M. Ewbank, *Antiquary on horseback*, Kendal 1963.

43 Hamper, op. cit., 462.

44 College of Arms, MS. C. 39. The drawings were copied by Aubrey into his *Monumenta* MS.; cf. G. Bersu, *Trans. Cumb. & West. Arch. Soc.* NS XL, 1940, 199.

45 Hamper, 323-7; C. H. Josten, *Elias Ashmole* I, Oxford 1966, 117.

46 Notably in British Library MSS. Sloane 1023, 1024.

47 F. Emery, *Edward Lhuyd*, Cardiff 1971, 65.

48 For Lhwyd, Gunther, op. cit.; G. Daniel in *Proc. Brit. Acad.* XL, 1954, 145 ff.; F. Emery, op. cit.; *Antiq.* XXXII, 1958, 179;

M. Herity, *Studia Hibernica* VII, 1967, 127.

49 Gunther, 425. Cf. No. VII below.

50 *Antiquities of Warwickshire*, London 1656, 788. These observations, and the deductions drawn from them, seem to have been independent of the similar comparison made by Mercati, Curator of the Vatican Botanical Garden, in the late sixteenth century, but in fact not published until 1717. Cf. No. VI below.

51 G. Daniel, *Hundred Years of Archaeology*, London 1950, 26-7.

52 *History Ancient and Modern of the Sheriffdoms of Fife and Kinross*, Edinburgh 1710, 25.

53 *Miscellanea quaedam eruditae Antiquitatis* . . ., Edinburgh 1710, 12 ff. No. VII below.

54 Cf. *Proc. Brit. Acad.* XXVII, 1951, 209 ff. No. III below.

55 Gunther, 491. Cf. No. IV below.

II

BRAZILIAN INDIANS ON
AN ELIZABETHAN MONUMENT

To the student of antiquarian thought in Britain, Red Indians have a peculiar interest on account of the influence of their discovery by the western world on concepts of primitive man, and hence Ancient Britons, from the later sixteenth century onwards.[1] Representations of New World Indians, and even of Eskimos,[2] were to become increasingly plentiful in drawings and engravings by European artists from the second half of the sixteenth century onwards, but Brazilian Indians at least had been depicted in England from early in the century, as for instance in a woodcut of apparently German origin in the English book (though printed in the Netherlands) *Of the Newe Landes* of 1511 or 1523. Of English artists, the earliest and most famous to depict American Indians, in this case Virginian, was John White, whose well-known drawings in the British Museum belong to the Roanoke voyages of Raleigh and others and cannot be earlier than 1584.[3]

It is therefore of some interest to find an English representation of New World Indians antedating John White's drawings by some fifteen years, and in the form of sculpture. Against the north wall of the parish church of Burford, Oxon, is a remarkable monument erected, according to the Latin inscription it bears, in 1569, during the lifetime of one Edmund Harman, and as a memorial to God's goodness to him. The monument contains Harman's arms within a triangular pediment, and the lower part carries a pair of relief panels with kneeling figures of his children between pilasters. The main panel of the monu-

Overleaf. 3. Monument to Edmund Harman, 1569.

ment, however, set back below the pediment, which is carried on slender detached columns, has an elaborate allegorical composition in high relief, consisting of a central rectangular panel on which is painted the inscription and date, surrounded by strap-work within which, in place of the usual *putti* or *amorini*, four naked figures, recognisably those of American Indians with feather head-dresses, are symmetrically contrived, together with baskets of what may well be heads of maize, and unambiguous tropical fruit including gourds (*cucurbitae*). The sculpture is of a high quality and, in addition to the distinctive feather head-dresses, there has been a deliberate attempt to give the features a non-European appearance, even if they have in fact been rendered more Negroid than Amerindian in the process.[4]

The early date of 1569 makes it inherently likely that the Indians depicted were Brazilian, and in the opinion of Professor D. B. Quinn of Liverpool University, and Professor Virginia Rau of Lisbon University, they must in fact be considered as Brazilian, probably of the Tupinamba tribe. We are then confronted with two problems : why do Brazilian Indians appear on Edmund Harman's monument, and what sources could the sculptor have used ?

Harman is a well-documented figure. Born *c.* 1509, a member of an Ipswich family, he became Barber Surgeon to Henry VIII, being admitted to the freedom of the Barber Surgeons' Company in 1530, and serving as Master in 1540; his portrait is included in the well-known painting by Holbein depicting the granting of the charter to the Company. In 1544 he was granted the Hospital of St John the Evangelist at Burford, and two years later the Manor of Taynton a couple of miles away; in the same year he was one of the witnesses to the will of Henry VIII, in which he was bequeathed £40. He married as his second wife a Burford woman, Agnes Sylvester, but at no time lived in that town, his country residence being in Taynton, where on his death in 1577, he expressed in his will his desire to be buried. He was in fact buried at Taynton but without a surviving monument.[5]

But at no point in the documentary sources relating to Edmund Harman are there any references to associations with the New World which might explain the allegorical panel on the monument of 1569, nor any hint as to why it was erected in that year. Mr W. R. Le Fanu, Librarian of the Royal College of Sur-

28

4. *Brazilian Indian, Harman monument.*

geons, points out that a tenuous connection with foreign trade might be inferred from the fact that Harman was King's Packer (i.e. Revenue Officer) for exports at the Port of London from 1536 to *c.* 1540, while Dr Alwyn Ruddock of Birkbeck College draws attention to the fact that his first wife was a Dame Dorothy Gwydott, widow of a member of an Italianate family settled in Southampton, and herself a daughter of a prominent Southampton merchant, Henry Huttoft. Neither of these facts, however, substantiates any real connection with the Americas, nor does an interesting suggestion by Mr A. H. Hall, Librarian of the Guildhall Library, that Harman might have participated in some unrecorded City venture to Brazil, similar to that of 1567, when certain gentlemen, forming themselves into a 'Society or Company, did furnish a fleet of six ships for a voyage to Guinea and other foreign regions'.[6]

There remain only the famous voyages of William Hawkins of Plymouth, the first known English contacts with Brazil, and the bringing back of a Brazilian chieftain to London in 1532. This 'Brazilian king' 'was brought up to London and presented to K. Henry the 8, lying as then at White-hall: at the sight of whom the King and all the nobilitie did not a little marvelle, and not without cause: for in his cheekes were holes made according to their savage manner, and therein small bones were planted. . . . He had also another hole in his nether lip, wherein was set a precious stone about the bignes of a pease. All his apparel, behaviour, and gesture, were very strange to the beholders'.[7] The chieftain remained in England for a year but died on the return voyage to his native country.

Harman must certainly have seen this 'king' and doubtless, like the rest, 'did not a little marvelle' at him, but no more direct connection can be traced. He might conceivably, as Professor Quinn suggests, have been entrusted with his care, or become interested in Brazil as a result of his visit, but confirmatory evidence is completely lacking. We must reluctantly admit that we cannot trace any convincing reason for Harman having commissioned the allegorical panel on his monument in the remarkable form in which it exists, and turn to the second puzzle, the source or sources from which the anonymous but accomplished sculptor derived his design.

The first, but perhaps the least likely would be that the sculptor had seen and sketched actual Brazilians in the 1560s.

We know of no others in England except the 'king', but the large-scale French contacts with Brazil resulted in many being brought back to France, especially to the Normandy ports: a whole village of Indians were transported there in 1550 and there may have been others brought to, for instance, Flanders. It is even conceivable that the artist had visited Brazil with the William Hawkins expedition. But for all these suppositions there is no evidence, and in view of the anonymity of the sculptor, such a source would be virtually impossible to substantiate. We do not know, after all, whether he was even an Englishman.

We are left then with drawings or engravings by other artists as the more likely origin for the figures and their appropriate fruit. The non-European cast of countenance suggests that the prototype drawing was at first hand or a close copy of a first-hand sketch; if an engraving, it must similarly have been fairly close to nature and not a more symbolic version with an approximately European face adorned with the necessary feather head-dress and other exotic trappings. The Brazilians in Hans Burg-kmair's engraving in *The Triumphs of Maximilian*, *c*. 1512, for instance, are of this class, and can hardly have formed the prototypes for the Burford sculpture, though feather head-dresses, maize and baskets of fruit are all represented.[8] John White's and Le Moyne's later drawings of the Virginian Indians are supreme examples of direct portrayal, even if Le Moyne made his actual paintings on his return to Europe. No original drawings of Brazilian Indians of the earlier sixteenth century survive but the engravings, especially those decorating contemporary maps, presuppose their existence. Professor Rau draws attention to the two Brazilians who occupy most of the centre of South America in a map by Petrus Plancius of 1592–4,[9] which have generic but not precise resemblances to the earlier Burford figures, and might suggest a common Flemish origin. She is in favour of a map source, but neither she nor Professor Quinn can discover, on any maps before 1570, a convincing prototype. We are left, as with our enquiries as to Edmund Harman's part in this strange affair, with an unsolved problem. We cannot explain the circumstances whereby an impressive and accomplished piece of stone sculpture depicting Brazilian Indians should have been set up by a Barber-Surgeon in 1569 in an Oxfordshire church, nor can we detect the sources from which the artist derived his convincing details. It is only hoped that publication may lead to further information on one or other aspect of the problem coming to light.

NOTES

1 Cf. T. D. Kendrick, *British Antiquity*, London 1950. No. 1 above.
2 K. Birket-Smith, *Folk* I, 1959, 5.
3 The John White drawings are well known (*B. M. Cat. Drawings Brit. Artists* IV (1907), 326); nine were reproduced in the Walpole Society's vol. XIII (1924-5), pls. XXIV-XXIX, and some engraved in de Bry's *America* (1590), together with others by Jacques Le Moyne. The full publication is P. Hulton and D. B. Quinn, *The American drawings of John White* . . ., London 1964.
4 The monument has several times been referred to, and the 'Red Indians' mentioned without further comment: R. H. Gretton thought it 'dull and uninspired', *The Burford Records*, Oxford 1920, 115. I am indebted to Mr Patrick Wise of Burford for the photographs of the monument reproduced here.
5 For Harman, cf. S. Young, *Annals of the Barber-Surgeons of London*, London 1890, *passim*; Sir d'Arcy Power in *Proc. Royal Soc. Medicine* IX, 1915-6, 67; Gretton, *The Burford Records*, *passim*. Harman's will (P.C.C. 43 Daughtry) makes no mention of possible New World interests, and his burial is recorded on 10 April 1577 in the Taynton Parish Register (transcript in Bodleian Library MS. Top. Oxon. c. 525: I owe this reference to Mr Howard Colvin).
6 Mr Le Fanu and Mr Hall *in litt.*, Dr Ruddock through Professor Quinn.
7 *Principal Navigations* XI, London 1904, 24. Three Indians 'found by merchaunts from Bristoll' were exhibited to Henry VII in 1502; for other European incidents of this kind, M. T. Hodgen, *Early Anthropology in the Sixteenth and Seventeenth Centuries*, Philadelphia 1964, 111 ff.
8 W. Oakshott, *Some Woodcuts by Hans Burgkmair*, London, Roxburge Club, 1960.
9 A. Cortesão and T. Da Mota, *Portugaliae Monumenta Cartographia* III, Lisbon 1960, No. 381.

III.

WILLIAM CAMDEN AND
THE *BRITANNIA*

The choice of the year 1951 for the inauguration of a series of archaeological lectures is a singularly happy one. The story of antiquarian studies in Britain may fairly be said to begin with the New Learning, in Tudor and Elizabethan times, and of the scholars of that period the acknowledged leader in such researches, in his own day and for a couple of centuries later, was William Camden, born just 400 years ago, in 1551. It is therefore fitting that the first of the Reckitt Lectures should in part take the form of a *laudatio* of Camden, appropriate to his quatercentenary, and that an estimation of the place of his work in seventeenth- and eighteenth-century antiquarian scholarship should be made. His *Britannia* is his monument, and the dates of its original publication in 1586, followed by those of the two great revisions and enlargements by Gibson in 1695 and Gough in 1789, form significant milestones in the history of British antiquarian thought from the Renaissance to the Regency.

The intellectual background of the Elizabethan antiquaries has been discussed by Sir Thomas Kendrick with characteristic scholarship and wit.[1] He has shown how the myth of the British History invented by Geoffrey of Monmouth in the twelfth century, in which the Trojan Brutus founded a pre-Roman dynasty in these islands no less respectable than that of Aeneas, was still dominating men's ideas about the early history of Britain in the beginning of the sixteenth century, and indeed the accession of the Tudors gave to the legend an added propaganda value. But the Italian, Polydore Virgil, and the Scotsman, John Major, had launched an attack on the British History early in the six-teenth century that had soon gathered momentum, and by the 1550s the new objective and critical approach to the materials of British history and archaeology had all but established itself, and certainly represented the prevailing intellectual temper among the antiquaries. In the first half of the century, too, John Leland was making his tours, recording at first hand the lib-raries, the topography, and the antiquities of town after town in England and Wales, gathering material for a great work that he seems to have visualised sometimes as a map, sometimes as an elaborate annotated gazetteer. But he died, his notes still in manuscript, a year after Camden was born, and it was he who realised a part of Leland's dream, in some measure with Leland's own materials.

William Camden was a Londoner, born in 1551 the son of a father described as *pictor*, and his markedly visual approach to antiqutities may have owed something to a painter likely to have been engaged at least in heraldic draughtsmanship, if not in portraiture. He attended St Paul's School, and went up to Oxford in 1566 where, apparently partly as a result of his partici-pation in religious controversy, he was refused a B.A., and came down in 1571. He was already interested in English topography and antiquities, and spent three years travelling about the country and evidently making notes which were later to be used in the *Britannia*. In 1575, at the age of twenty-four, he was appointed Second Master in Westminster School, a position he was to hold, as it happened, for the next twenty-three years of his life. Here was a position congenial enough for a young man of antiquarian tastes, and vacations afforded an opportunity for further travel—we know, for instance, that he made tours in Norfolk and Suffolk in 1578, when the plan for the *Britannia* was taking definite shape in his mind.[2]

He had determined on a study of antiquities as a schoolboy, when 'he could neither hear nor see any thing of an *antique* appearance, without more than ordinary attention and notice'. This enthusiasm had continued at the university, and although he seems to have made attempts, perhaps rather half-hearted, to give up these activities when a schoolmaster, yet 'whenever a Vacation gave him liberty to look abroad, his thirst returned, and . . . it was not in his power to restrain himself from making Excursions into one quarter or another, in quest of Antiquities'.

Sir Philip Sidney and other men of taste and influence had encouraged this enthusiasm while he was at Oxford, and it is clear that while he was at Westminster his reputation as an antiquarian scholar had been spread abroad by his friends, so that when in 1577 the great European geographer Abraham Ortelius came to England, it was with Camden that he mainly discussed British topography and antiquities. He saw the notes that had already been collected and recognised in them and in their compiler a potential addition to European scholarship of no mean order, and after much persuasion induced the diffident Camden to complete the task he had set himself, and reduce his materials to a book. Nine years later the *Britannia* was published.

In the compilation of the material for this book, Camden seems from the first to have planned a course of studies for himself which would enable him to make the best use of his sources. 'He enter'd upon it', his biographer remarks, 'with all the difficulties, that could attend an Undertaking. It was a sort of Learning, that was then but just *appearing* in the world, when that heat and vehemence of *Philosophy* and *School-Divinity* (which had possess'd all hearts and hands for so many hundred years) began to cool'. Apart from the observations made on his travels, Camden was, of course, in possession of the necessary knowledge of Latin required for reading the medieval texts (mainly chronicles) on which he was to base his historical conclusions, but since, as we shall see, he was particularly concerned with the elucidation of contemporary English place-names, in relation to those recorded from the Roman Province, he recognised the necessity of acquiring a knowledge of a Celtic tongue, as well as of Old English.

To obtain a knowledge of Welsh was not difficult in Tudor England — 'he had the comfort to think, that it was a *living* language, and that he wanted not Friends, who were Criticks in it' : Aubrey tells us he kept a Welsh servant for conversation in that language.[3] But Anglo-Saxon was another matter — 'a Language, then, which had lain dead for above four Hundred Years, was to be reviv'd; the Books, wherin it was bury'd, to be (as it were) rak'd out of the ashes; and (which was still worse) those Fragments, such as they were, exceeding hard to be met with'.

The beginnings of Saxon studies in Elizabethan England and the recovery of the language, have been described to the Academy by the late Dr Flower in a notable study of Laurence

Nowell, for whom we can claim the distinction of the founder of Old English studies in this country.[4] It was to Nowell and his circle—Archbishop Parker, Sir Robert Cotton, William Lambarde[5]—that Camden would most naturally turn. He was in fact a close friend of Sir Robert Cotton, with whom he made tours in the north of England, and Lambarde, who had worked in close collaboration with Nowell and inherited his library, was on sufficiently intimate terms with Camden for the *Britannia* to be sent to him in manuscript for his comments in 1595. An even closer link can in fact be established. In his book of *Remaines* Camden quotes an Old English version of the Lord's Prayer from 'an antient *Saxon* glossed *Evangelists*, in the hands of my good friend Master Robert Bowyer'. Now this must be the collection of glossaries in what is now Cotton MS. Cleopatra A. iii which Dr Flower showed was used by Laurence Nowell, and later given by Bowyer to Sir Robert Cotton. Camden could not have learnt his Anglo-Saxon under more auspicious circumstances.

I should like, if you will permit me, to reserve, for a moment, discussion of the scope and content of the *Britannia* as originally planned and written, and in the meantime to review, very briefly, the remainder of Camden's life, and to consider what we know of the man himself, his tastes, and his approach to antiquarian studies. He continued to make antiquarian tours after the publication of the book in 1586, collecting additional material which was to be inserted in the successive editions that appeared in 1587, 1590, 1594, 1600, 1607, and 1610. Between 1589 and 1596 he travelled in Wales, Devonshire, Wiltshire, and Somerset, and in 1599 he visited Cumberland and the Roman Wall with Sir Robert Cotton, though he had been to the Wall before the first edition of the *Britannia* appeared.[6] But meanwhile, in 1597, by which time he had become Headmaster at Westminster, he was offered and accepted the vacant post of Clarenceux King of Arms in the College of Heralds, which came as near to being an Institute of Antiquarian Research as could have been conceived of in Elizabethan England. So far as one can judge, Camden's interests were not in fact primarily genealogical, and indeed there seems to have been criticism from those concerned with family history that the *Britannia* did not contain enough pedigrees—'There are some', he wrote in his revised preface, 'there are some peradventure who apprehend it disdainfully and offensively that I have not remembered this or that family, when it was not my purpose to mention any but such as were more notable, nor all them truly (for their names would fill whole volumes) but such as happened in my way according to the methode I proposed to myselfe'.[7] But a herald was at least an avowed and recognised antiquary, and once established as such, Camden could pursue his studies in any direction that interested him. The early and abortive attempts to found a Society of Antiquaries naturally concerned Camden, and it was no fault of his or his colleagues that the schemes were unsuccessful.

Sir Thomas Kendrick has reviewed the heraldic controversies in which Camden was involved almost immediately upon taking up his new duties, and they need not detain us here. In his later years he published two books containing materials gathered during the preparation of the *Britannia*, a collection of chronicles and the little commonplace book of *Remaines concerning Brittaine* which, to judge by the succession of editions after its first publication in 1607, met with a receptive and appreciative public.

The *Remaines* do give us, I think, glimpses of Camden's own tastes, and some idea of his attitude to antiquities. In discussing the history of costume, for instance, he draws attention to the use of medieval effigies as evidence for contemporary dress and armour — 'what the habits both civil and military were in the time of King *John*, *Henry* the third, and succeeding ages, may better appear by their monuments, old glasse-windowes and antient Arras, than be found in Writers of those times'. He gives an essay on British coins, which clearly fascinated him, and another on Anglo-Saxon, with examples; a very full list of proverbs current in his day, and two selections of medieval Latin verse, divided into *Poems*, in classical metres, and *Rhymes* in rhyming stanzas: in the *Poems*, too, he includes a long passage from Chaucer's *Nun's Priest's Tale*.

He obviously enjoyed the rhyming Latin verses, but in an age when the classical mode was the undisputed canon of taste among scholars, he finds it necessary to apologise — 'I could present you with many of them, but few shall suffice, when as there are but few now which delight in them', he writes. He gives us a remarkable selection of medieval secular Latin peotry, perhaps the most notable items being the extracts from Joseph

of Exeter's *Antiocheis*, which, in default of surviving manuscripts, are our sole authority for the poem. In addition, we may
notice the passages from John de Hanville's *Architrenius*, and,
among the rhyming verse, the *Quisquis cordis et oculi* of Philip
de Grève and the Goliardic *Prisciani regula penitus cassatur*.
Best of all in this section are two passages from the masterly
Confessio of the twelfth-century Archpoet.[8] He attributed many
of the rhyming verses to Walter Map, as did subsequent editors
up to the last century, and it is likely that he obtained many, and
perhaps most, of the fragments of medieval Latin verse he
quotes from those enormous compilations of texts made by
Bale, Flacius Illyricus, and others for the purpose of anti-
Catholic propaganda in the Reformation. But what is important
about Camden's choice is that he is unconcerned with this attitude of the Protestant apologists, and prints the verses because
they entertained and intrigued him. His anthology, then, must
rank as the first printed collection of the secular verse of the
Middle Ages presented to the reader for its own sake.

I have just used the phrase 'the Middle Ages', employing it,
as we all do, as an essential part of our historical vocaulary. But
it was Camden who, so far as it is known, was the first Englishman to make use of this term, and the concept it implied, in a
printed work.[9] In introducing his collections of *Poems* he refers
to contemporary Renaissance Latin verses, 'But' he goes on
'whereas these latter are in every man's hand . . . I will onely
give you a taste of some of middle age, which was so overcast
with darke clouds or rather thicke foggs of ignorance, that every
little sparke of liberall learning seemed wonderful; so that if
somtime you happen of an uncouth word, let the time treat
pardon for it'. As an Elizabethan, he cannot feel that the 'middle
age' was anything but barbarous, but he does realise its existence, and recognises that it has qualities of its own which cannot
be ignored.

Camden's work on British coins, contained in the *Remaines*
and in the *Britannia*, is of pioneer importance. Leland had
denied the existence of a native coinage at the time of the Roman
Conquest, but Camden not only recognised the non-Roman
coin types for what they were, but correctly appreciated the
significance of the abbreviated titles and mints in the inscriptions of CVNOB . . ., COM . . ., VER . . ., and CAMV. . . . His investigations were carried out with the assistance of Sir Robert

5. British coins, from Camden, Britannia, *1600.*

F3

Cotton, who 'with curious and chargeable search', formed the collection from which the engravings in the 1600 edition of the *Britannia* were made.

The chapter on *Inhabitants* is noteworthy for its complete omission of the Trojan myth, and for its enthusiasm for the Saxons. Here one can see the influence of Nowell and his circle, and Camden, relegating the Britons, now bereft of the glamorous Brutus, to a minor prefatory position, begins the theme of the greatness of England, and of the English language, with the *adventus Saxonum*.

> This warlike, victorious, stiffe, stout, and vigorous nation [he writes] after it had as it were taken roote here about one hundred and sixtie yeares, and spread its branches farre and wide, being mellowed and mollified by the mildnesse of the soyle and sweete ayre, was prepared in fulnesse of time

for the acceptance of Christianity. From this it is an easy step to discuss the origins of the English language—'extracted (as the Nation) from the *Germans*, the most glorious of all now extant in Europe, for their moral and martial vertues', and to commend the thoroughness of the Saxon conquest—'To the honor of our progenitors, the *English-Saxons*, bee it spoken, their conquest was more absolute here over the *Britains*' than anywhere in Europe where the Romance languages survived.[10]

Camden wisely refuses to accept any wild ideas on the remote origins of the English language, but does draw attention to Scaliger's observations of words similar to Germanic forms in Persian, and to the remarkable little vocabulary of surviving Gothic which Busbecq, the Dutch Ambassador at Constantinople, had fortunately recorded in his letters from conversation with men from the Crimea. All these, of course, are genuine parallel forms within the Indo-European language group, the significance of which were not to be appreciated until the end of the eighteenth century, but already the Renaissance scholars were approaching the subject from the right point of view.

To the chapter on the English language is added a delightful little eulogy on *The Excellence of the English Tongue*, by Richard Carew, with a list of all the great contemporary writers ending—'will you have all in all for prose and verse ? take the Miracle of our Age, Sir *Philip Sidney*'. And Camden ends his chapter with a passage which would, I feel, please Sir Ernest Gowers:

> I may be charged by the minion refiners of *English*, neither

to write State-English, Court-English, nor Secretarie-English, and verily I acknowledge it. Sufficient it is for me, if I have waded hitherunto in the fourth kind, which is plaine English.

It is in the grand Elizabethan manner that the book should end with *Epitaphs*, introduced in solemn prose that not only echoes Camden's contemporary, Sir Walter Raleigh, but curiously foreshadows the cadences of *Hydriotaphia*:

> And that we may not particulate, the Romans so far exceeded in funerall honours and ceremonies, with Oyntments, Images, Bonfires of most pretious wood, Sacrifices and banquets, burning their dead bodies until the time of Theodosius, that Lawes were enacted to restrain the excesse. Neither have any neglected buriall but some savage Nations, as Bactrians, which cast their dead to the dogs; some varlet Phylosophers, as *Diogenes*, which desired to bee devoured of Fishes; some dissolute Courtiers, as Mecaenas. . . .

> Notorious it is to all, how the same *Lucian* bringeth in *Diogenes* laughing and out-laughing King *Mausolus*, for that hee was so pitifully pressed and crushed with an huge heape of stones under his stately monument *Mausoleum*, for the magnificence accounted among worlds wonders: But monuments answerable to mens worth, states, and places, have alwaies been allowed, yet stately sepulchres for base fellowes have alwayes lyen open to bitter jests.

In the last years of his life Camden decided to endow a Chair of History in the University of Oxford, an idea which seems to have been in his mind since the compilation of the *Britannia*, and in 1622, the year before his death, the foundation of the Camden Chair was announced in Convocation. It involved reading lectures 'on Florus or other antient historians, twice a week, Mondays and Saturdays',[11] and was held in the first instance by Degory Wheare, nominated by Camden. During the ensuing couple of centuries the only Camden Professor of distinction was Thomas Warton, that learned and eccentric eighteenth-century historian of English poetry: after Warton's death, in 1790, one notes, with eyebrows mildly raised, that the Chair was held until 1861 by three successive Principals of St Alban Hall: this Society, now defunct and perhaps never over-endowed, doubtless saw in the Camden foundation an admirable sinecure for the Head of a House, But in the later nineteenth century, the Chair recovered its intended dignity with George Rawlinson and H. F. Pelham, and in Haverfield we have seen a Camden Professor who perhaps most of all would have delighted the founder.

It is now time to turn from Camden to his *Britannia*, and to consider first of all exactly what was the intended scope and content of this work. And here we must clear our minds of the picture of the *Britannia* which we usually carry, and see not the great three-decker Gough in calf-bound folios, nor those of Gibson in two volumes or one; and not the rather smaller Philemon Holland translation, but the dumpy little quarto in Latin, with no maps and a woodcut of a medieval inscription as its only illustration, published in 1586.

Camden's first biographer, Dr Thomas Smith, who published a Latin life in 1691, revised and translated in Gibson's edition of the *Britannia* a few years later, had no doubt of the purpose of the book.

> *Italy* was the place [Smith wrote] where these *Topographical Surveys* were first attempted, for the more easie and delightful Reading of the *Roman* Histories; and there the difficulty was very inconsiderable. The express remains of the old names, preserved in the new ones, was a sufficient direction in many cases. . . . *France*, *Spain*, and *Germany* had not this advantage in so high a degree; but as they were subdued by the Roman Arms, so had they the good fortune to fall under the notice of the Roman Historians. . . . But Britain was *another world* to them; and accordingly . . . their Accounts were unavoidably confused and imperfect. In the case before us, the best direction seems to be the *Itinerary* of Antoninus.

You will notice the insistence on two things, the Roman Empire and place-names, and we find them again when we turn to Camden's own words in his Preface, in the 1610 English version:

> Truly it was my project and purpose to seeke, rake out, and free from darknesse such places as *Caesar*, *Tacitus*, *Ptolemee*, *Antonine* the Emperor, *Notitia Provinciarum* and other antique writers have specified and *TIME* hath overcast with mist and darknesse by extinguishing, altering, and corrupting their old true names.

Camden goes on to say that the place-names of Roman Britain, 'as easie and elegant as they sounded, were generally barbarous, and of a pure *British* extraction'; this led him to acquire a knowledge of Welsh, and then, to follow the place-name development into the Middle Ages, Old English. He was particularly insistent on collating all the available documents on Roman Britain, and obtained details of the Peutinger Map (discovered in 1507), before its publication. Smith sums up the sequence of Camden's work:

> The old *Itinerary* being settled, the *British* and *Saxon* tongues in a good measure conquer'd, our ancient Historians perused, and several parts of England survey'd, he now began to think of reducing his Collections to method and order.

I do not think we can escape from the conclusion that the *Britannia* was originally planned to elucidate the topography of Roman Britain, and to present a picture of the Province, with reference to its development through Saxon and medieval times, which would enable Britain to take her rightful place at once within the world of antiquity and that of international Renaissance scholarship. Language and title alike declared its purpose: it was to have a European appeal, and, with the destruction of the myth of Trojan Brutus, was to establish Britain as a member of the fellowship of nations who drew their strength from roots struck deep in the Roman Empire.

It is for this reason, I suggest, that the framework of the *Britannia*, persisting through every edition, is that of the Celtic tribal areas of Britain as recorded in the classical geographers, with the English shires grouped within their accommodatingly vague boundaries. In such a scheme, too, the descriptions of British and Roman coins, and the recording of Roman inscriptions in growing numbers in each edition, so that by 1607 nearly eighty are included, would have significance, and not least of all, Camden's famous first-hand account of the Roman Wall, the most considerable monument in the Province, would form an appropriate climax, between the tribal area of the Brigantes and that of the Ottadini, the last tribe named before he reaches the remote regions of Scotia, and the outer Ocean.

If we accept this view of the original intention of the *Britannia*, we can also recognise that the scheme, in the simplicity outlined above, was not pedantically followed. To the Roman skeleton Camden added English flesh and blood. If some of his material was lifted, at times verbatim, from Leland's notes, it was none the less treated with so systematic a thoroughness, and subordinated to such a clearly conceived and individual pattern, that it takes on the character of original work.

Of the six editions of the *Britannia* which appeared in Camden's lifetime all were in Latin except the last, that of 1610, which was translated by Philemon Holland, the 'translator-general', and a second edition of this version appeared in 1637, after the author's death. By the 1607 Latin edition, the *Britannia* had already reached the status of a folio, and contained the well-known Saxton and Norden maps of the English counties, as well as the illustrations of British and Roman coins, and of Stonehenge, which had first been included in the edition of 1600, dedicated to Queen Elizabeth. The Stonehenge view is a version of a Dutch drawing of 1574, through the intermediary of an engraving dated a year later,[12] and Camden inclines to a cautious acceptance of the legend of Aurelius Ambrosius and Hengist which is engraved beneath the 1575 print.

The appearance of the English versions of the *Britannia* show in themselves a changing antiquarian public in this country. The original Latin work was addressed to the world of European scholarship, as the interchange of letters between Camden and his contemporary colleagues on the Continent show. But by Jacobean times a new class of reader had grown up in England, anxious to read antiquarian literature written in English: a taste which the *Britannia* itself had gone far to create. We have moved out of that Latin-speaking fraternity of learning which, up to the time of Elizabeth, had carried on the tradition of the scholars' *lingua franca*, and are in the new, self-confident, national state in which, with the increase of literacy, an interest in local history was no longer confined to the learned professions, but was as likely to be found in the merchant or the country squire.

It is one of the greatest ributes that can be paid to Camden's sound planning and construction, that when, at the end of the seventeenth century, it was realised that a drastic re-editing of the *Britannia* would have to be made in order to bring it into line with contemporary antiquarian thought, it was possible to carry out this enlargement within the original framework rather than to embark on a separate work *de novo*. This revised version appeared in 1695, and we fortunately know the story of its progress and achievement in some detail.

The 1695 *Britannia* is perhaps the best known of the editions, either in its original one-volume form, or in the subsequent two volumes of 1722, and as a work of that great figure of the Restoration church, Edmund Gibson, Bishop successively of Lincoln and London, we probably most of us have taken it without further thought, as the product of the ripe scholarship of a dignified and mature churchman, his honours thick (and perhaps a trifle heavy) upon him. But it is nothing of the kind. Gibson's scheme for re-editing the *Britannia* originated while he was still an undergraduate, and the whole admirable achievement was the work of a young man who was twenty-six years old when the book was published.[13]

The story begins, it is interesting to note, among a group of scholars concerned with Old English studies who were, in the late seventeenth century, taking up the tradition of Nowell, Lambarde, and Camden. They were centred on Queen's College, Oxford, which became famous for its 'proluvium of Saxonists', led by Nicolson and Thwaites. Gibson came up to Queen's in 1689, and at twenty-three published an edition of the *Anglo-Saxon Chronicle*: in the same college he found, as a slightly junior fellow undergraduate, Thomas Tanner, later to be 'one of the most erudite members of a learned Church',[14] and the two became fast and lifelong friends. Gibson went down before Tanner, and it is from the letters written by him in London to his friends in Oxford that we hear much of the progress of the great task of re-editing the *Britannia* which he had taken upon himself.[15]

From the first, Gibson saw that the revision of the *Britannia* must be the work of a team of scholars under his general direction and editorship, as the task was far beyond the unaided efforts of a single individual. The initial problem presenting itself was that of translation, for it was generally agreed that Philemon Holland's version was in many ways unsatisfactory, and furthermore he had himself made unauthorised additions to the text. There appears to have been some discussion as to whether the new work should be in Latin or English, but the latter was decided upon, and it is interesting to note that Samuel Pepys, who was actively interested in the project, strongly recommended the use of English: here we presumably have the influence of the Royal Society's campaign for the use of the 'plaine English' which Camden had himself advocated, as we saw, as early as 1607. Gibson had met Pepys, on the introduction of Dr Arthur Charlett, Master of University College, Oxford, and would dine with him to discuss the work on the *Britannia* from time to time. New translations of the Latin text were therefore sponsored by Gibson, county by county, and he revised and collated the whole.

But more important was the question of additional material, similarly divided on a county basis. Here lay Gibson's main task as editor, and eventually he assembled some thirty contributors from among the antiquaries and historians of the day. They ranged in age from young Mr Tanner, not yet twenty-five, to old Mr Aubrey, who was nearly seventy, and included such famous names as John Evelyn, Samuel Pepys (who was responsible for the sections concerned with naval history), White Kennet, Ralph Thoresby, Robert Plot, Edward Lhwyd, and William Nicolson the Saxon scholar. It was a notable team, and it is a tribute to Gibson's charm and competence that he so successfully brought them together in the common enterprise. It is also significant of the growth of antiquarian interest since Camden's day that such a body of persons could be found.

The task of the editor was not however a uniformly easy one: contributors had to be handled with tact and firmness, or a rapid substitution made when an unsatisfactory choice had inadvertently been made. One of Gibson's triumphs was to secure from John Aubrey the use of material from his famous unpublished *Monumenta Britannica*, despite Aubrey's fear, voiced in a letter to Tanner in 1693, that the inclusion of extracts from the *Templa Druidum* section might prejudice its eventual publication as a complete work. But Tanner persuaded Aubrey to lend him the manuscript for transmission to Gibson in London, and his delay in sending it occasioned an amusing protest from the editor, with a lively sketch of the idle undergraduate's morning in Oxford—

> If you were to trot every day along *Cat-street*, and after a turn or two in the Schools quadrangle, to adjourn to Tom Swift's, I could excuse you for not sending your papers sooner. But when a man's cloysterd up in an old Monkish Lodge and the very Phys of his chamber is nothing but antiquitie itself; for such a one to make delays, is a little intolerable. If you knew how I am persecuted, you would not keep them a mom[t] longer; old John Aubrey is dayly upon me, and the blame is as dayly layd upon poor Mr. Tanner.[16]

The papers arrived safely enough, but Gibson's reaction was one which will be appreciated by anyone who has tried to use Aubrey's still unpublished manuscript today:

The accounts of things are so broken and short, the parts so much disorder'd, and the whole such a mere Rhapsody, that I cannot but wonder how that poor man could entertain thoughts of a present Impression.[17]

More serious trouble (but also, it must be confessed, some entertainment) was caused to Gibson by his unwary choice of that extraordinary character, John Toland, as the consultant on Ireland. Toland, whose books were to be burned by the public hangman and who was to be denounced with scandalised horror from every pulpit as the avowed champion of free thought, but whose enquiries into comparative religion show a mind of real anthropological acuteness, was at this time about Gibson's age, and already the centre of more than one scandal. There had been wild affairs with the students in Glasgow, and in Edinburgh (of which university he was a graduate) he had created a panic by declaring himself a Rosicrucian and setting off chemical flares which passed for the products of Black Magic; in London he had publicly burnt a prayer-book in a coffee-house. Gibson was intrigued and fascinated, and every piece of gossip was reported back to Tanner and Charlett in Oxford, where Toland was now living, but before any Irish memoranda were forthcoming they quarrelled—Gibson could not stand Toland's 'insolent conceited way of talking'—and this odd minor incident in the editing of the *Britannia* was closed.[18]

The work continued briskly in London and Oxford, with Gibson and Tanner in constant light-hearted consultation. The fact that the newly edited *Britannia* should be a paying proposition was not ignored:

Hang't man, to lay too much stress upon *filthy lucre* is below the dispensation of Learning and a scholar; not but a great many good uses may be made of 40 l. too. . . . After all, neighbour, it's a good honest way of getting money[19]

wrote Gibson in connection with another literary project, and the editorial business was conveniently discussed over beer at Mother Shepherd's in Oxford, or wine at the Dog Tavern or Black Susan in London. Dr Gale was helpful, Dr Bentley was interested, Ray was to do botanical notes—'what between herbs, camps, high-ways, families, etc. we shall have meat for all palats'.[20]

After some discussion over the dedication, the new edition was published early in 1695. It had been kept to one volume, despite the urgent desire of the country gentry that the inclusion of all their pedigrees and details of their estates should swell the work to several vast genealogical tomes. Camden's newly translated text was followed by the additions, placed at the end of each county. In Gibson's second edition, published in 1722 when he was Bishop of London, the extra material was incorporated into the text, though distinguished by enclosing it in square brackets, and the work had grown to two folio volumes. As well as an introduction and a bibliography, Gibson printed a translation of Thomas Smith's *Life* of Camden, originally published in Latin together with Camden's letters in 1691, and the main body of the work was prefaced by a transcript of the Antonine Itinerary based on William Burton's edition. In addition to re-engraved plates of British and Roman coins, a new section on Saxon coins was given, compiled by Walker and Thoresby. The county maps were by Robert Morden, and the Stonehenge plate was re-engraved by Kip.

The new translation has precision, and a comfortable dignity, though one regrets at times the enthusiastic, if wayward, style of Holland. We lose, for instance, the charming phrase which describes Camden's visit to Hadrian's Wall—'Verily I have seene the tract of it over the high pitches and steepe descents of hilles, wonderfully rising and falling', which is accurately, but how flatly, rendered 'I have observ'd the track of it running up the mountains and down again, in a most surprising manner'. But it is to Gibson that we owe the exquisite rendering of the Elizabethan sentiment expressed by Camden in his Introduction, in which Britain:

is the master-piece of Nature, perform'd when she was in her best and gayest humour; which she placed as a little world by it self, by the side of the greater, for the diversion of mankind.

Here then was the *Britannia* adapted to the needs of the new school of antiquaries of the early eighteenth century, the circle of William Stukeley and the Gales, of Francis Wise, Ralph Thoresby and Sir John Clerk. Essentially, it was still Camden's work, with its Romano-British plan emphasised by the addition of the Itinerary and of Smith's new surveys of Hadrian's Wall given in the 1722 edition. But by this time the Act of Union of England and Scotland of 1707 necessitated an introductory essay describing this event, and after the word SCOTLAND in the title of the ensuing section are put in square brackets the significant words [OR NORTH-BRITAIN], and considerable additions based on Sir Robert Sibbald's work are given. There is also an account of the Antonine Wall, with half a dozen inscriptions and a plan of part of the Wall near Bo'ness by Timothy Pont, and a separate *Discourse Concerning the Thule of the Ancients* by Sibbald. *Britannia* now extended to the farthest bounds of the Roman Province.[21] Prehistory, too, had benefited, particularly by Gibson's summary of the seventeenth-century controversy on the date and origin of Stonehenge, and by the inclusion of a short description of Avebury from the *Monumenta Britannica*.

For nearly seventy years the 1722 edition of the *Britannia* was to hold the field, the third, and last, major revision being published in 1789 and reprinted in 1806. In the 1720s the great tradition of the Restoration historians was still alive, and works of outstanding scholarship in English medieval studies were being published; William Stukeley was carrying out his finest piece of field-work at Avebury, which would have set a new standard in the observation and record of a major prehistoric monument, had he published it then in its original form and not, twenty years later, as a religious tract involved in the fantasies of his Druidic Christianity.

But already by the middle of the century, and increasingly in its second half, the standard of historical and archaeological studies was sadly on the decline. Let me quote Professor David Douglas:

Medieval scholarship in England [he writes] underwent during the eighteenth century not a development but a reaction. These studies between 1730 and 1800 made no advance comparable to that which had been achieved in the previous seventy years. The stultifying of so promising a growth, the slackening of an endeavour which had been marked by such devoted labour was a phenomenon in the development of English culture which was very remarkable.[22]

So much for medieval research, the low state of which in the later eighteenth century Professor Douglas has shown in melancholy detail in the work from which I have quoted. In antiquarian or archaeological studies the story was much the same. Stukeley's own intellectual decline and fall after about 1725–30 is now familiar, and among its unedifying events stands out his acceptance of the forged Itinerary of Roman Britain by the bogus Richard of Cirencester, which bedevilled the study of Roman Britain for generations.[23] But Stukeley was not alone in acclaiming Richard as an authority equal to, or rather better than, the Antonine Itinerary, and the state of contemporary archaeological scholarship and textual criticism is only too well shown by the enthusiastic election of Charles Bertram, the undergraduate who had invented Richard and written his Itinerary for him, as an Honorary Fellow of the Society of Antiquities of London in 1750.

It is, I think, in the second half of the eighteenth century that we really see the emergence of the antiquary as Sir Walter Scott saw him; Jonathan Oldbucks who eagerly identified Roman camps from hearsay rather than field-work, collectors of curios and old armour, uncritical and credulous, and ignorant of the essential disciplines of their scholarship in a way which would have horrified Gibson or Tanner or the young Stukeley. It was in this atmosphere of ponderous but ineffective dilettantism that the final editing of the *Britannia* took place.

Richard Gough, who undertook this work, was a country gentleman who, after going up to Corpus Christi College, Cambridge, had devoted his time to antiquarian travels in England. We today have reason to remember Gough with gratitude for his vast collection of topographical material—maps, drawings, plans, notes—which forms, in the Bodleian Library, a source of invaluable information still waiting for a detailed catalogue,[24] but we cannot come to his edition of the *Britannia* with the enthusiasm which Gibson's work unconsciously inspires in us. He began the task, he says, in 1773, when he was thirty-eight, and had already published his *Anecdotes of British Topography*, but it was sixteen years before the three folio volumes were published in 1789.

It is clear from Gough's preface that he regarded the task as one of antiquarian piety rather than the provision of a work of contemporary scholarship newly fashioned from the old stock. 'Without entering into the details of a county historian', he writes, 'or adopting the mode of a modern writer of a description of England I have endeavoured to do that for Mr. Camden, which Mr. Camden in the same circumstances, would have done for himself'. What we are to understand by 'in the same circumstances' is obscure, but the general tenor is plain. The approach is that of one who reveres the antique for its own sake, with the *Britannia* padded out with miscellaneous topographical notes, the annotating of a curious old book with affectionate antiquarian memoranda.

In this work Gough enlisted the help of his fellow antiquaries, but with very few exceptions the list he gives is one of nonentities. Pennant's help for Wales and Scotland must however be noted, and for the latter country Gough also received an important contribution from General Robert Melville, whose field-work first revealed the existence of Roman military works north of the Tay, and who encouraged and assisted Roy in the preparation of his great *Military Antiquities of the Romans in North Britain*, eventually published in 1793.[25]

The new edition continued to preserve the general form of the *Britannia* as contained in Gibson's recension, with the addition of a great deal of miscellaneous topographical information in the text, and the provision of a considerably enlarged number of illustrations. Maps of Roman and Saxon Britain are provided, the former unfortunately owing much to Richard of Cirencester, and prehistoric, Roman and Saxon antiquities bulk large in the engraved plates: in addition to those recorded in the text, there are over 220 Roman inscriptions and sculptures illustrated in the counties of Cumberland and Northumberland. The standard of the illustrations varies considerably—there is an excellent plan of Maiden Castle, Dorset, for instance, probably taken from that by Watson and Roy of 1756,[26] but the plans of Wiltshire hill-forts such as Yarnbury or Chiselbury are woeful. Yet there is a very great deal of material recorded in these plates, ranging from the Cerne Giant (unfortunately emasculated) to a plan of Silchester, from Kentish Saxon jewellery to Welsh Early Christian monuments and plans and details of major ecclesiastical buildings of the Middle Ages. Scotland is dealt with in greater detail than before, and Melville's notable additions to the knowledge of Roman antiquities in that region have been mentioned, while the Irish section contains illustrations of a very large series of Bronze Age antiquities, including the famous Irish Royal Crown (which is really a gold bowl of the Late Bronze Age illustrated upside-down).

But despite these important records, it is impossible to avoid the conclusion that Gough's edition of the *Britannia* is really a failure. It was undertaken too late, when the usefulness of Camden's great pioneer work was diminishing with the appearance of detailed county or regional histories, and it was undertaken at a time when historical and archaeological studies were at a noticeably low ebb. By the opening years of the nineteenth century, when such studies were reviving, antiquarian topography was to be better served by such works as the Lysons' *Magna Britannia* series, by individual county histories, or such archaeological monographs as Sir Richard Colt Hoare's *Ancient Wiltshire*.[27] From the time of its first publication in 1586, Camden's *Britannia* had remained a source of inspiration to British antiquarian studies until their own decline in the first third of the eighteenth century, and Gibson's second edition of 1722 really marks the end of an epoch. The age of the great pioneers was at an end, after a century and a half of inspired and devoted labour which culminated, with the Restoration historians, in an achievement of scholarship and industry that we can still regard with respectful and astonished admiration. Then was to come the anti-climax, even though local history was less affected than the wider field of investigation of the English medieval past, and we must not forget that Edward Gibbon, having completed his Olympian study of the dying fall of the classical world, recommended in 1793 the systematic publication of English medieval records that was later to become a national undertaking. But this was at the end of the century, and Horace Walpole, to whom the Middle Ages was a bric-à-brac shop from which he could pick out material for an elegant (and inaccurate) historical essay, or Gothic rococo ornament that had 'the true rust of the Barons' Wars', is a more representative figure of the age. Richard Gough admired Camden, but did not appreciate that the time had come to begin afresh, as Camden himself had done as he stood with his back to the Middle Ages and set down the historical links that bound the topography of his England to the medieval world, the Saxon past, and to Rome herself.

NOTES

1 T. D. Kendrick, *British Antiquity*, London 1950.

2 The main facts of Camden's life are contained in the Latin *Vita* prefaced by Dr Thomas Smith to his edition of the *Epistolae* in 1691. My quotations are from Gibson's translation of this printed in the 1695 and 1722 editions of the *Britannia*. For Camden as historian, H. Trevor-Roper, *Queen Elizabeth's First Historian* (Neale lecture in English history), London 1971.

3 Cf. Bromwich, *Bull. Board Celtic Studies* XXIII, 1968, 14; ibid., '*Trioedd ynys Prydain' in Welsh literature and scholarship*, Cardiff 1969. No. IV below.

4 *Proc. Brit. Acad.* XXI, 1935, 47.

5 Cf. R. M. Warnicke, *William Lambarde*, London 1973.

6 Cf. Haverfield in *Trans. Cumb. & West. Arch. Soc.* NS XI, 1911, 343 for Camden and the Wall.

7 Preface to 1610 edition.

8 Raby, *Secular Latin Poetry*, Oxford 1934, II, 100, 132, 299, 225. The stanzas of the *Confessio Archipoetae* are arranged in two groups numbering 12, 13, 16, 17, 18, 19, and 5, 4, 8 of Manitius's edition (*Gedichte des Archipoeta*, 1929, No. III).

9 Cf. G. S. Gordon, *Medium Aevum and the Middle Age* (S.P.E. Tracts, XIX, 1925).

10 Cf. No. IV delow.

11 Gough's *Life* of Camden, prefaced to the 1789 *Britannia*.

12 E. H. Stone, *The Stones of Stonehenge*, London 1924, 147.

13 For a Bibliographical Note on the 1695 *Britannia*, Gwyn Walters in facsimile ed., Newton Abbot 1971, 14.

14 David Douglas, *English Scholars*, London 1939, 200 and *passim* for Gibson's work.

15 The letters to Tanner are in Bodleian MS. Tanner XXV, and those to Dr Charlett in Ballard V; some were published by Ellis, *Letters of Eminent Literary Men* (Camden Soc. XXIII), London 1843.

16 Gibson to Tanner, 21 March 1693-4; Bodleian MS. Tanner XXV, f. 100.

17 Gibson to Tanner, 12 April 1694; MS. Tanner XXV, f. 134.

18 For the Toland gossip, see Ellis, op. cit., 226-9; Gibson to Charlett, 21 June 1694 (Bodleian MS. Ballard V, f. 48); Piggott, *William Stukeley*, Oxford 1950, 99.

19 Gibson to Tanner, 18 May [1694]; MS. Tanner XXV, f. 152.

20 Gibson to Charlett, 19 March 1693; MS. Ballard V, f. 14.

21 Cf. No. VII below.

22 David Douglas, op. cit., 355.

23 Piggott, op. cit., 154.

24 For summary list see now M. W. Barley, *Guide to British Topographical collections*, London (C.B.A.) 1974, 95.

25 G. Macdonald in *Arch.* LXVIII, 1917, 161-228.

26 R. E. M. Wheeler, *Maiden Castle, Dorset*, Oxford 1943, 6.

27 Cf. No. VI below.

IV.

CELTS, SAXONS, AND THE
EARLY ANTIQUARIES

The terms of the O'Donnell foundation are to provide for lectures on some aspect of the relations between what were conceived of at the time of the endowment as the Celtic and the Saxon peoples of Britain from the earliest times. I have taken as my theme part of the history of the concept of Celts and Saxons as antithetical entities, and will explore with you the circumstances in which such ideas originated among antiquaries, historians and linguists between roughly the sixteenth and the eighteenth centuries. I hope I may have something original to offer, but I must acknowledge my indebtedness to others who have harvested in these delectable fields, notably Sir Thomas Kendrick and Dr A. L. Owen.[1] If as a prehistorian I may be thought to have put my sickle to the perilous grain while standing amid the alien corn, I hope I may escape the fateful Lityerses.

I find myself, before a Scottish audience, in a position of phonetic ambiguity. Do I say Kelt and Keltic, or Selt and Seltic? As an Englishman, I use the former pronunciation from habit, though aware that Scottish usage favours the soft 'c', as does the *O.E.D.*, giving 'Keltic' only as a secondary alternative. I have not pursued this phonetic hare further than to note that in 1872 a distinguished English archaeologist, Sir John Evans, referred to 'those who have thought fit to adopt the modern fashion of calling the Celts "Kelts"':[2] the *O.E.D.* began publication only a decade later. The point is not without historical interest, as I suspect that the change may be the result of the impact of German philological studies of the Irish language

6. *Stukeley at Avebury. Drawing by Stukeley, c. 1723.*

about this time: 'Keltic' seems standard Anglo-Irish today. So I will unrepentantly use the hard 'c', and if 'Kelt' sounds fishy to a Scot, at least 'Keltic' avoids confusion with a football team.

Before turning to Celts in linguistic or personal form, we had better dispose of a word 'celt', belonging to older archaeological diction but still sometimes in use, with the sense of an axe-head of stone or bronze. This has no connection with either people or language, but derives from a rare Latin word *celtis*, allegedly cognate with *caelum*, a graver, occurring in an epistle by St Jerome and in his Vulgate version of the Book of Job—*vel celte sculpantur in silice*—and thence re-appearing in medieval Latin from the late eleventh century onwards. Its first recorded use in an archaeological sense seems to have been in late seventeenth century Germany, and in England not much later.

Now let us turn to the first usages of Celt and Saxon in respect of the early inhabitants of the British Isles. There is no difficulty about the Saxons, always recognised for what they were. The Latin noun *Saxo* appears in one of Claudian's panegyrics at the end of the fourth century, and thence continues in medieval Latin and finds its way into Old and Middle English. But Celts are quite another matter. The earliest use of the name, in its Greek form *Keltoi*, dates back to Hecateus in about 500 BC, thence continuing in Herodotus and numerous later writers as descriptive of barbarian people on the European continent. The word itself, Professor Kenneth Jackson informs me, makes no sense linguistically as Celtic, and is probably a corruption of a word better represented by the Greek alternative *Galatoi*. In Latin the corresponding alternatives *Celtae* and *Galatae* exist, the earliest usage of the former probably being in the *Ora Maritima* of Avienus, which although composed in the fourth century AD derives largely from a lost Massaliot *Periplus* of the sixth century BC. Schulten, editing Avienus, accepts the mention of *Celtae*, located somewhere by the North Sea, as in the original source of the poem, not an introduction by Avienus or an earlier Latin redaction he is sometimes thought to have used. At all events the word becomes freely used by writers from the first and second century BC onwards, such as Caesar, Mela and Pliny, in some cases deriving from the Greek text of Posidonius. The best known occurrence is that at the very opening of Caesar's *Gallic War*, with its famous tripartite division of Gaul into Belgae, Aquitani and *qui ipsorum lingua Celtae, nostra*

Galli appellantur—those who in their own language are called Celts, but Gauls in ours. But in all the classical references to *Keltoi* and *Celtae*, or *Galatoi* and *Galatae*, they are never located in the British Isles. They were brought here by the early antiquaries in curious and complicated circumstances which we will now examine.

What may appear at first sight to be a fairly simple lexical enquiry turns out on examination to have unexpected dark corners. For instance, in William Harrison's description of Britain prefaced to Holinshed's *Chronicle* of 1577, we read 'In the diligent perusal of their treatises, who have written on the state of this our island, I find that at first it seemed to be a parcell of the Celtike Kingdom'. Out of context this sounds straightforward enough, but when we read further we find that the kingdom was named from its king, Celtes, a descendant from Noah and Japhet through King Samothes and King Bardus. The inhabitants of this kingdom were later conquered by the giant, Albion, and then again by Brutus, from whose name they were called Britons. Clearly we are not within any historical framework recognisable to us today, and we have to dig deeper.

We should glance in passing at what one might call the logical and sensible early use of the word 'Celt' in English. In variant forms it was in use during the sixteenth century, and probably before that, though I have made no exhaustive search. Fleming translating Aelian in 1576 uses a curious form—'no Indian, no Celtan, no Aegiptian harboured so hellish an opinion'—perhaps comparable with the use of 'Druydans' for Druids in Barclay's *Shyp of folys* of 1509. Clement Edmonds, translating and commenting on Caesar in 1604, gives the phrase I have already quoted as 'the *Celtae*, whom we call the *Galli*', leaving the Latin words untranslated; by 1655 a new edition of the book has a fresh translation into 'those which they call *Celtes* and we *Galles*'. A year later Blount in his dictionary glossed 'Celt' as 'one born in Gaul'. By the end of the seventeenth century, as we shall see, 'Celtic' was being used in a linguistic sense more or less as it is today. But what of King Celtes, Samothes and his kin?

For a moment let us leave the early part of the pedigree through Japhet and Noah to Adam, though we must shortly return to it, as it is crucial to early thought about Celtic and Saxon origins. But the Celtic kings descended from Samothes do not derive from Holy Writ: on the contrary, they were invented as part of a literary forgery which Kendrick has described as 'undoubtedly the most mischievous study of the remote past published during the Renaissance'. Brought out in Italy by Annius of Viterbo in 1498, it purported to be a history of the peopling of the world after the Flood written by a Chaldean priest, Berosus. Now Berosus was a genuine Babylonian priest and historian who wrote, about 275 BC, in Greek, a history of Babylonia from the earliest times to Alexander, which survives in excerpts and paraphrases. Annius however wrote a bogus commentary on a bogus text, and proceeded from the Biblical story by inventing a family descended from Japhet (to whom Europe had been allotted after the Flood), who were rulers of the Celts. These he named by collecting words or titles from the classical texts on the Druids, and turning these into personal names. To confuse things utterly, two of them are based on misreadings of the original sources. Samothes, founder of the line, is one of these, from a word *semnotheoi* in Diogenes Laertius quoting the Pseudo-Aristotle: the word is obscure and a hapax. His son Magus is from Pliny or some other source talking of *magi*; Sarron, who follows, results from following a copyist's error in a Renaissance Latin translation of Diodorus Siculus, whereby the original *drovidas* has become *sarronidas*. Dryius, Bardus and Celtes himself are obvious enough.

It all seems very naive and unconvincing, but this nonsense was widely and eagerly accepted. It was given circulation in Britain by John Bale, Bishop of Ossory, in books of 1548 and 1557; it was taken up by others such as John Caius of Cambridge and John White of Basingstoke, who improved things enormously by grafting on to the pseudo-Berosus another famous forgery, the *Historia Regum Britanniae* of Geoffrey of Monmouth. The British History, with its fabricated Celtic past of Britain, its fabulous king-lists, and its idealisation of Arthur, had been under attack from the time of John Major and Polydore Virgil early in the sixteenth century, and although its defenders fought back hard, by the end of the century it was hardly taken seriously by any reputable scholar. Camden ignored Geoffrey and Samothes and John Speed in his *Historie* (1611) dismissed as fictitious the alleged line of Celtic kings, 'now universally rejected by all skillfull *Antiquaries*'. The facts, he decides, 'doe warrant us (me thinkes) to come from the *Cimbrians*, whose sonnes, and our fathers, were the *Celts* and *Gaules*'.

These Cimbrians, you may be surprised to hear, take us in fact to the Biblical story and its exegesis. We must remember at the outset that with rare and hesitant exceptions, until the later eighteenth century the monogenetic origin of mankind from Adam was unquestioned doctrine, as was the peopling of the world after the Flood by the descendants of Noah, who would have spoken the original language of mankind, Hebrew. The close relationship of Hebrew to Welsh was argued by Charles Edwards in 1675 and by many subsequent writers. Behind all antiquity lay Ararat and the Ark: Shem, Ham and Japhet. History and philology could go no further than the tenth chapter of Genesis, and in the eighteenth century William Cowper laughed at

> those learned philologists who chase
> A panting syllable through time and space,
> Start it at home, and hunt it in the dark,
> To Gaul, to Greece, and into Noah's Ark.[3]

In such a framework, pedigrees of peoples and nations as well as of families were fabricated, assembling long lines of highly respectable ancestors. It is characteristic that one of the most gloriously crazy of these was by an eccentric Scot, Sir Thomas Urquhart of Cromarty, who in 1652, the year before his famous translation of Rabelais appeared, published his *Pantochronokanon or Peculiar Promptuary of Time*, in which he derived his family, and himself, not only from the 'Ionian Princes of Achaia', but eventually from 'Adam, surnamed the Protoplast'.[4]

But we are concerned not so much with Adam as with Noah. The tenth chapter of Genesis sets out the inescapable story that had to stand at the head of any enquiry into early peoples. Noah's three sons, Shem, Ham and Japhet, have themselves numerous sons born to them after the Flood: 'The sons of Japheth; Gomer and Magog, and Madai and Javan', and so on. 'By these' it goes on 'were the Isles of the Gentiles divided in their lands'—*divisae sunt insulae gentium*, in the Vulgate. Of the numerous sons of Japhet, Gomer is the one of importance for us, by a curious but not inexplicable line of reasoning.

Gomer in Gen. X, 2 is taken by the historians of ancient West Asia to be the equivalent of the people called *Gimirrai* in Assyrian documents of around the eighth century BC—they are defeated for instance by Sargon in 720, in Urartian territory.

The *Gimirrai* in turn are equated with the Greek *Kimmerioi*, the Cimmerians. About 670 these people moved west into Asia Minor, broke up Phrygia, sacked Sardis, defeated Lydia and attacked the Greek colonies on the west coast. Now the historian Josephus, writing in the first century A D, refers to an individual also called by him *Gomer*, who 'founded those whom the Greeks call Galati, but were then called Gomerites'. This appears to contain a genuine tradition of Cimmerians establishing themselves as a power in Asia Minor, but given an anachronistic twist by equating them with the Celtic *Galatae*, the foolish Galatians who by Josephus' day had been settled in Asia Minor for nearly 300 years and had been formed into a Roman province in 25 B C. As we saw, *Galatae*, *Celtae* and *Galli* were constantly muddled and virtually interchangeable even in antiquity, so it is little surprise to find Nennius in the eighth century writing of *Gomer, a quo Galli*. The identification of Gauls and Celts as the sons of Gomer is complete, and eventually even the ancient Britons were provided with an authentic Biblical pedigree. But we approached Gomer through John Speed's Cimbrians: how do they come into the story?

The historical Cimbri were a tribe from North Jutland who, joining with the Teutones and Ambrones, raided far south and west and into the Roman Province in the second century B C, until finally defeated in 101 in the Po valley. The classical writers themselves confused them on occasion with both the Celts and the Gauls, and all three with the Hyperboreans, as a rabble of northern barbarians. Let us now hear how the early antiquaries dealt with them in the words of what Kendrick truly called an 'enchanting but bafflingly muddle-headed book', the *Britannia Antiqua Illustrata* of Aylett Sammes, published in 1676. 'The Britains', says Sammes, 'call themselves *Kumero*, *Cymro*, and *Kumeri* . . . the truth is, the similitude of Name between these *Cymri* of Britain, and the Ancient people, the *Cimbri* of the Continent, in things so distant, doth give sufficient ground for a Reasonable conjecture' that 'the *Cimbri*, were the Forefathers of these *Cymri*.' But he does not regard them, he goes on, as descendants of Gomer, but 'the Relicks of the Ancient *Cimerii*', who had migrated northwest from the shores of the Black Sea, and had become known indifferently as Germans, Celts or Gauls. Camden was wrong about the languages, says Sammes, 'the *Cimbrian* tongue is made the same as the

Celtic, the *Celtae* being a promiscuous Name of the *Germans* and *Gauls*; the *Celtic* language is as much the *German* language as the *Gaulish*'. We will later return to these early efforts to make Celts and Saxons one and the same people, but we may notice in passing Cluverius's division of ancient European peoples in 1616, into Celts and Sarmatians, the former comprising Gauls, Germans, Britons, Saxons, Hyperboreans and Scythians; the latter, the Slav peoples. This view was also adopted by Keysler in 1720 and by Pelloutier in 1750, while Bishop Percy still thought it worth while attacking when he published his English translation of Mallet's *Northern Antiquities* in 1770.

By the middle or late seventeenth century the Gauls at least were firmly established as the descendants of Gomer, Japhet and Noah. Even if Sammes thought the Welsh were *Cimbri*, descendants of Cimmerians, there were others then or later who would happily accept them as the sons of Gomer on the grounds of the assonance *Cumri-Gomeri*. The use of 'Celtic' to denote Gallo-Brittonic unity was however shortly to come into general use—Sammes as we just saw used it in a linguistic context, however oddly, but Milton, in *Paradise Lost* of 1667, employs it in a vague geographical sense. He is bringing in the tail end of the fallen angels, 'with looks Down cast and damp', and among them Titan's brood and those

> who with *Saturn* old
> Fled over *Adria* to th' *Hesperian* fields
> And ore the *Celtic* roam'd the utmost Isles.

But more precise linguistic usage was on its way before the end of the century and had indeed been hinted at by George Buchanan in 1582. Professor James Garden of Aberdeen had been reading an edition of Maimonides, *De Idololatria*, by Dionysius Vossius. In 1693 he wrote to John Aubrey about recumbent stone circles, and notes that Vossius thought 'that Druid is a word of Celtick extract, and that the origin thereof is to be sought for in the Celtick tongue such as both the old Gallick and the British tongues were.[5] Garden does not seem to have known Edward Lhwyd, 'our exquisite antiquary Mr. Lhuyd of Oxford', though of course Aubrey did, and it is interesting to find Lhwyd writing about the 'Celtic languages' as such when in the late 1690s he was about to enter into a correspondence with a Frenchman who was to be one of the most influential in making Celtic Britain such by name. Paul-

Yves Pezron was a Cistercian monk and a Breton, 'Gallican, patriotic and imperialist' in feeling.[6] In 1703 he published *L'Antiquité de la Nation et de la Langue des Celtes*. 'He has infinitely outdone all our Countrymen as to national zeal', wrote Lhwyd to a fellow Welshman. 'He proves that they and we have the honour to have preserv'd the language of Jupiter and Sadurn, whom he shows to have been Princes of the Titans, the Progenitors of the Gauls, and to have an Empire from the Euphrates to Cape Finister in ye time of Abraham'.[7] Three years later David Jones published an English translation of Pezron as *The Antiquities of Nations: More particularly of the* Celtae *or* Gauls, *Taken to be Originally the same People as our* Ancient Britains. The title makes the assumption that Britons and Gauls are the same, and both Celts.

Though not widely popularised before, the idea was not altogether new, for Camden, in his *Remaines*, discussing the Welsh language, thought it had 'great affinity with the old *Gallique* of *Gaul*, now *France*, from whence the first inhabitants in all probability came hither', and Richard Verstegan in 1605 had recorded his belief that 'Britains were anciently indeed a people of the Gauls', but no one had really called them Celts. In Pezron the reader would find the familiar descent of Celts or Gauls from Gomer, and also of Teutones assigned Gomer as a grandfather through his son Ashkenaz. Some Gauls (also known as Galatians, said Pezron) moved north to become Cimmerians or Cimbri; the Gauls in Phrygia adopted the title of Titans, having as kings successively Saturn and Jupiter. Here was something exciting for everyone, and if readers had not come across it before, an origin for the Anglo-Saxons in the same Gomerian family—this idea was not new either, for Verstegan had also held that 'according to the opinion of sundry very learned and judicial Authors', Ashkenaz was the father of Tuisco, founder of the Teutonic peoples (and in origin the Germanic god Tiwaz or Tiw). We have reached the position of Anglo-Celtic consanguinity by another route.

Lhwyd had laughed at Pezron, and with justice: in addition to his incredible farrago of nonsense about origins, the 'Armorique Britan', as Lhwyd called him, was under the impression that the Breton language was an indigenous survival of Gaulish. It is salutary to remember that in the year of the publication of Pezron's book, Lhwyd was feeling towards the real roots of the problem when, struck with the two types of Celtic place-names in Scotland, Gaelic and Cumbric, he 'became troubled with an hypothesis of C Britons and P Britons', emigrants from Gaul to Britain, with his 'C' (our 'Q') group the earlier arrivals. Now, at the beginning of the eighteenth century, the words 'Celt' and 'Celtic' had taken on more or less their present popular usage, but the Celtic Druids are still waiting in the wings to be brought on to the stage by William Stukeley and his followers.

The Anglo-Saxons did not present to antiquaries the complex problems that enmeshed Britons, Gauls and Celts. They were after all an historically documented people, known as such since the early middle ages, who had invaded Britain in circumstances described in Bede, Gildas and many others. While the precise date and character of the *adventus Saxonum* might well admit of discussion, as indeed it still does today, there was never any question but that Anglo-Saxons had, since the fifth century A D, formed the English-speaking component of the peoples of Britain. As to their ultimate origins, they had of course to be descended from Noah and Japhet and while some might favour the equation of Cimbri-Cimmerians-Gomerians, an alternative pedigree for the northern nations could, as we saw, be devised via Ashkenaz and Tuisco. This was set out in a charming and entertaining little book published in 1605, the *Restitution of Decayed Intelligence in Antiquities concerning the most Noble and Renowned English Nation*, written by Richard Verstegan. His grandfather was a Dutchman from Antwerp, who had emigrated to England as a young man, where his grandson took the name of Richard Rowlands, but returning to Antwerp as a Catholic exile, he re-assumed his Dutch name on taking over the family printing business. He was passionately Anglophil—England was 'my most noble nation, most dear unto me of any Nation in the world'—but he was anxious as a Dutchman to demonstrate the glories of its Saxon, rather than its Celtic, past, and to link its origins with the lineage of Tuisco. The Anglo-Saxons had not had a fair deal in the past, Verstegan thought—'Divers Foreign Writers do I also find foully to err, in not knowing rightly to attribute things to the ancient *Britains*, that properly concern them, and things unto the *English* that rightly unto them appartain'. Britain, he said, was originally Albion, and then named Britain from the conquest by Brutus, who was not however a Trojan as described in the British History, but a

Gaulish prince: the Gauls of course were sons of Gomer and so collaterals of Tuisco. The Scots came from Scythia, as their old writers had declared, and Scythia was part of the northern world of continental Europe, while the Picts too were 'first out of the German Scythia' on the shores of the Baltic. By and large the enthusiastic author managed to make all the peoples of Britain Germanic in various degrees. His friend the geographer Abraham Ortelius thought well of the hypothesis that Cimbric, ancestral to the language of the Saxons, was spoken by Adam and Eve in the Garden of Eden.

Verstegan was a student of Christ Church, where he acquired a knowledge of Old English in the circle of Anglo-Saxon scholars which had been growing up in England since the middle of the sixteenth century. Part of the background of these remarkably precocious linguistic studies goes back to Leland and his collection of manuscripts for a history of English authors before his death in 1551, part lies in the political and ecclesiastical temper of the times, when Church and State alike in England searched the records for precedent and authority for the new fabric of government and society which was coming into being with the advent of the Protestant church. It is sometimes forgotten how early and how rapidly Old English scholarship blossomed. The language was attacked by means of the extant glosses, or the vernacular translations of known Latin texts; manuscripts were assiduously collected, and translated, by such as Archbishop Parker and Sir Robert Cotton, Lawrence Nowell and William Lambarde. Parker caused Saxon type to be cut, and an Old English sermon was printed in 1566, the Gospels in 1571. In the 1560s Nowell not only compiled a Saxon Dictionary, but utilised the Old English place-names to make a map of Saxon Britain; Lambarde compiled an Anglo-Saxon topographical dictionary. That great antiquary, William Camden, whose epoch-making *Britannia* was first published in 1586, decided, in planning his research, that a knowledge of Old English was a necessary part of his training. His friendship with Cotton would have helped him in his task for, as his biographer put it, 'A Language then, which had lain dead for above four Hundred Years, was to be reviv'd; the Books, wherein it was bury'd, to be (as it were) rak'd out of the ashes; and (which was still worse) those Fragments, such as they were, exceeding hard to be met with'. It is eloquently put, but the simile of raking the ashes gives one today an uncomfortable *frisson* with its un-conscious anticipation of the disastrous fire among the Cottonian manuscripts in 1731.[8]

Camden, characteristically, also realised that a knowledge of some Celtic language, side-by-side with Old English, would be necessary. Samuel Butler, the author of *Hudibras*, told John Aubrey that 'Mr. Camden much studied the Welsh language, and kept a Welsh servant to improve him in that language, for the better understanding of our antiquities'. Camden tells us that he found Welsh 'very significative, copious and pleasantly runninge upon agnominations, although harsh in aspiration'. Welsh was in fact the only accessible Celtic language in six-teenth-century England, not only because of the prestige of a Tudor dynasty, but because, since the Edwardian conquest, Wales had become (with Cornwall) the only assimilated Celtic-speaking region of the British Isles. Camden saw this when he wrote of 'The Welchmen our neighbours, or rather our in-corporate countrymen, both by approved allegance and law'.

But to Elizabethan Englishmen, Scots and Irish were bar-barian foreigners. As Margaret Hodgen remarked, at this time 'the epithets used to describe the folk on Britain's Celtic border were interchangeable with those applied to the Negroes in Africa or to the Indians across the Atlantic. While sovereigns of the realm were struggling to pacify the tribal Celts, and the Puritan colonists in North America were wrestling with the Red Indian for his soul and his land, all frontier antagonists looked more or less alike'.[9] David Quinn has shown that the early 'plantations' of Ireland, such as that of Munster, can best be understood in the context of the English temper of thought that was also responsible for the first colonisation of the Americas.[10] In such circumstances the study of the Celtic languages enjoyed none of the advantages of Old English scholarship. The texts were very hard to discover, even in Welsh: Irish manuscripts were virtually inaccessible, in a foreign island of bare-footed savages. There were no incentives from Church or State to seek for precedents in texts as obscure as in fact they were irrelevant for such purposes; the old forms of the languages involved were exceedingly difficult to master and translate.

It is all the more heartening and surprising to think of Camden acquiring enough Welsh to quote a 'British old book of Tripli-cities'—some of the Triads, and to cite them as authorities on three occasions. Later, when one reads Edward Lhwyd's letter of 1702 describing his recent work to a friend, one re-lives the excitement of his discovering, in the margin of the Cambridge University Library Juvencus MS., the three early ninth-century stanzas that represent the most ancient surviving contemporary manuscript of Welsh poetry. He made a fairly accurate transcript, but could not translate them: he submitted them to William Baxter who, says Lhwyd, 'declares it is to him a very plain prediction that our gracious Queen shall have another prince who shall reign after her'. The late Sir Ifor Williams puzzled for ten years over these nine lines before producing a translation which satisfied him. Even if in the end it contained nothing about the gracious Queen, it emphasises the difficulty of the texts the early scholars encountered. But they turned to them when they could, as did Henry Rowlands, an Anglesey antiquarian vicar, in 1723, quoting in his *Mona Antiqua Restaurata* and in the original Welsh, some of the twelfth century 'Mountain Snow' stanzas then attributed to Llywarch Hen.[11] As the century ran its course, the Welsh poetry became better known, but increasingly transmuted into fantastic and allegorical English versions bearing little or no relation to the actual meaning.

By the seventeenth century the Celts and Saxons were firmly established as a part of the British past. Celts of course were senior, for were they not the Ancient Britons, not only here when the Saxons arrived, but in undisputed possession of the island at the Roman Conquest? Their origins lay in the fog beyond written records, but we must now turn to consider how the early Britons or Celts were visualised by the antiquaries and historians of the seventeenth century. The sources available to them were in fact only the classical texts, for what we would now call archaeological evidence was only appreciated by a few exceptional persons, notably John Aubrey in the seventeenth, and William Stukeley in the eighteenth century. But the classical sources, by the sixteenth century, were being interpreted in the light of a novel and disturbing intellectual experience—the discovery of primitive peoples in the Americas.

The earliest visual portrayals of Ancient Britons date from about 1575, when a Dutchman, Lucas de Heere, in a Description of Britain, made two versions of a drawing of a couple of long-haired naked men, tattooed or woad-painted, carrying long shields, spears and a sword, labelled 'Les premiers Anglois comme ils alloyent en guerre du temps de Julius César'. Now these are closely related to contemporary and rather later drawings of American Indians, and in particular to those by John White, who accompanied Raleigh on his 1585 Virginia expedition, and not only drew Indians, but a series of ancient Britons, Picts and 'Neighbours unto the Picts', whose characteristics were profoundly influenced by the New World peoples he had seen and drawn with such brilliance. By the intermediary of the engravings in de Bry's *America* of 1590, four of these representations of the early, non-Saxon, inhabitants of Britain appear as illustrations to Speed's *Historie* of 1611, one dressed up to represent Boadicea, and there is a splendid shaggy Briton at the top of the title-page of his *Theatre of the Empire of Great Britaine* of the same year, sharing that empire with a Roman, a Saxon, a Dane and a Norman, all tricked out, in Kendrick's phrase, in 'baroque plumes and swagger clothes'.

Speed in his text reconstructs the Ancient Britons from the classical texts alone, but Samuel Daniel a year later drew a parallel between the tribal organisation and warfare of the North American Indians and that of Celtic Britain, while during the seventeenth century several scholars, including William Dugdale, Robert Plot and Edward Lhwyd, compared British flint arrow-heads and axes with those still in use across the Atlantic. John Aubrey, in 1659, wrote an essay on prehistoric Wiltshire. Having described the primitive woodland environment he goes on to the inhabitants, skin-clad and savage, whose warfare and Druidic priesthood were described by Caesar. Their temples, he suggests, may have been monuments such as Avebury and Stonehenge, and they had the use of iron. As a final estimate of their cultural status he adds, 'They were 2 or 3 degrees I suppose less savage than the Americans'. This disconcerting usage to denote the indigenous inhabitants rather than the colonists appears until well into the eighteenth century—'I have conversed with Americans', writes Johnstone in the 1760s, 'who are far from being such fools as they are too generally thought to be'. But the importance of Aubrey's view is that it is objective, realistic, and devoid of romantic or sentimental overtones, and in its factual approach very different from other views of the early British past to be held within the next century. It is perhaps no coincidence that Aubrey had known Thomas

Hobbes 'from my childhood, being his countreyman and borne in Malmesbury hundred and taught my grammar by his schoolmaster', and he wrote Hobbes's life. Hobbes's famous description of primitive society, living in 'continuall feare, and danger of violent death; And the life of man, solitary, poore, nasty, brutish and shorte', represents the same attitude to uncivilised peoples as that behind Aubrey's concept of the earliest Wiltshiremen.[12]

Historians of ideas who have examined the question have coined a rather unsatisfactory word—'primitivism'—for the attitude of civilised societies to savage or barbarian peoples, whither contemporary or in the past, and have seen two contrasted modes of apprehension. The unfavourable, or at least empirical and unromanticised view, as in Hobbes and Aubrey, represents 'hard' primitivism; the idealisation of the Noble Savage, 'soft'. These two attitudes were from the first mixed in relation to the American Indians and other peoples at a low level of material culture encountered by Europeans from the sixteenth century onwards. On the one hand we have the hideous heathen, disturbingly difficult to accommodate in terms of Noah's progeny, sunk in 'dayly tumultes, fears, doubts, sispitions and barbarous cruelties'; on the other, the testimony of such as Arthur Barlowe, writing of one of the Roanoke voyages in 1584–5: 'we found the people most gentle, loving and faithful, void of all guile and treason, and such as live after the manner of the Golden Age'. Between these two poles of emotion the attitude not only towards contemporary barbarians, but those of the Celtic past, was to veer and change for a couple of centuries, with soft primitivism coming into its own with the Romantic Movement.[13]

We will look at this fascinating phenomenon in a moment: in the meantime Camden can be our spokesman for an Elizabethan estimate of the respective qualities of Celts and Saxons. The Ancient Britons are of course notable for their 'valour and prowess' in opposing the Roman Invasion—'the most puissant Roman forces, when they were at the highest, could not gain of them (being then a half naked people) in thirty whole years the countries from the Thames to *Striviling*'. But they are, as in White's or Speed's illustrations, no more than imperfectly dressed savages, and so I fear Camden thought of the Scots and Picts. 'After the Scottishmen' he then goes on enthusiastically

7. '*A Britaine*' *from Speed*, Theatre of . . . Great Britain, *1611*.   (69

'the Angles, Englishmen or Saxons, by God's wonderful providence were transplanted here out of *Germany*. . . . This warlike,
victorious, stiff, stout and vigorous Nation . . . spread its
branches far and wide, being mellowed and mollified by the
mildness of the soyl and sweet air, was prepared in fullness of
time for the first spiritual blessing of *God* . . . which *Beda* our
Ecclesiastical Historian recounteth in this manner, and I hope
you will give it the reading'. Descended from the German
nation, 'the most glorious of all now extant in *Europe* for their
moral and martial vertues', the pagan Saxons became Christian
Englishmen, and from them came Camden and his contemporaries. The Saxons were too well documented historically to
be fit subjects for really imaginative and romantic idealisation.

During the eighteenth century there was much confusion
between what was Celtic and what Saxon. When Thomas Mason
was writing his Celtic drama *Caractacus* he was being helped by
Gray, and in 1757 the poet sent him some books, with words of
advice on amplifying the Druid scenes. 'I told you before' he
writes, 'that (in a time of dearth) I would borrow from the
Edda, without entering too minutely on particulars'. He erred
in good company in recommending this Old Norse source for
the Druids, for Edward Gibbon described the Edda as 'the
sacred book of the ancient Celts', and Mallet thought the Eddas
contained Druidic poetry, as did others of his time. William
Blake, with at least the prerogative of a great poet, turned the
Druidic holocaust into 'The Wicker Man of Scandinavia'. The
later Anglo-Saxons suffered for long from a misunderstanding
of their architecture: before the middle of the nineteenth century
'Saxon' usually designated not only pre-Conquest but also
post-Conquest buildings. Thomas Warton (rather unexpectedly
in his Observations on Spenser's *Fairy Queen* in 1763) classified
the styles as successively Saxon, Gothic Saxon, Absolute Gothic
and so on, Saxon being specified as buildings erected by the
Normans.[14] It was all very confusing.

The Celts, by the eighteenth century, were to enjoy a happy
phase of soft primitivism. The story is an involved one, and we
have no time for more than a brief outline here. I have made a
full-length study of William Stukeley and his part in it, and of
the idealisation of the Druids, also set out in entertaining detail
by A. L. Owen, while Lois Whitney, Henry Fairchild and
Margaret Hodgen have discussed the general temper of eigh-

teenth century primitivism.[15] Behind Stukeley lies Aubrey, who as we saw made the tentative suggestion of 'restoring' as temples to the Druids such monuments as Stonehenge and Avebury. His main statement on this was in the *Templa Druidum* chapter of his still unpublished *Monumenta Britannica*, though Edmund Gibson printed extracts from it in his 1695 edition of Camden's *Britannia*. Aubrey linked field monuments to the classical texts — hill-forts, linear earthworks, barrows and of course stone circles — and was the unacknowledged archaeological godfather of Stukeley, who saw and transcribed a copy of the *Monumenta* MS. in 1718. This fired him with a passion for archaeological field-work in Wiltshire, and it is worth while remembering that he there encountered and surveyed in the early 1720s three of the most extraordinary and impressive prehistoric monuments in Britain — Stonehenge, Avebury and Silbury Hill. It would indeed be difficult, after studying these, to think that their builders were no more than two or three degrees less savage than the American Indians. By 1723 Stukeley was drafting a book *The History of the Temples of the Antient Celts*, which ultimately, in revised form, was partly incorporated in his volumes on *Stonehenge* (1740) and *Abury* (1743), the only published parts of a vast projected work entitled *Patriarchal Christianity, of a Chronological History of the Origin and Progress of true Religion, and of Idolatry*.

The Druids were the unwitting instruments in bringing about the romantic idealisation of the Celts in the eighteenth and nineteenth centuries. Soft as well as hard primitivism existed in the classical sources, particularly in the later writers on Druids, and this was eagerly taken up and developed by the early antiquaries and the imaginative writers in prose and verse. Milton had taken a hard line with the Druids — 'Philosophers I cannot call them, reported men factious and ambitious' — but before him in 1622 Drayton in his *Polyolbion* had made them 'sacred bards' and sages 'Like whom great Nature's depths no man yet ever knew'. Going back to the pseudo-Berosus and the descent from Japhet, Dickinson in 1655 was able to point not only to Abraham, but to the oak trees of the Plain of Mamre, and exclaim 'Lo the *Oke Priests!* Lo the *Patriarchs* of the *Druides!* For from these sprang the *Sect* of the *Druides*, which reached up at least, as high as *Abraham's* time'. He was endorsed with much apparent erudition by John Smith in 1664, but Sammes in 1676 makes much of the Druid's idolatry and holocausts in wicker images (with a stirring picture of one), and Henry Rowlands in 1723 moves only tentatively to a more favourable view.

In a retrospective journal written about 1750 Stukeley said that by 1726, three years before he retired from medical practice and took Holy Orders, he was deciding that the Druids' beliefs were 'near to the Christian doctrine' and certainly in a few years' time he had no doubts. They were 'of *Abraham's* religion intirely' and had arrived at 'a knowledge of the plurality of the persons in the Deity', so that their faith was 'so extremely like Christianity, that in effect it differ'd from it only in this; they believed in a Messiah who was to come into this world, as we believe in him that is come'. After all this he shows wise caution in writing 'we cannot say that Jehovah appeared personally to them'. In the 1760s, now a London parson, he preached and published what were known as the Vegetable Sermons, endowed to demonstrate the wonderful works of God as shown by vege-tables. They were very odd. 'Christianity is a republication of the patriarchal religion' he announced in his preface. 'I have not scrupled to introduce Druids before a Christian audience. They were of the patriarchal religion of ABRAHAM ... and have a right to assist at a Vegetable Sermon.' Druids, mistletoe, and Balaam 'who was really a Druid' duly appear, as do Avebury and Stone-henge. His doxology begins 'As once of old in groves, so here in their representative fabrics, we adore the three sacred persons of the deity'. The ancient Celts had been provided with pre-Christian Christian patriarchs, who themselves had been assigned temples at Stonehenge, Avebury, Long Meg, Caller-nish and elsewhere. Nothing could be more exciting, comfort-ing, and romantic.

Stukeley's beliefs, if eccentrically presented and based on the unexpected evidence of archaeological field-work, were not so unusual as they may appear to us today. Although his intention was to 'combat the deists from an unexpected quarter' his views are only the usual attack on the deistic concept of Natural Religion current at the time as expressed so well in the title of Matthew Tindal's book of 1730, *Christianity as Old as the Creation, or the Gospel, a Republication of the Religion of Nature* —indeed we saw how Stukeley used almost the identical phrase about 'republication'. Groves, Druidic or otherwise, were of course part of the stage properties of Natural Religion—why, asked John Warton in 1740, should men prefer

> To dwell in palaces and high-roof'd halls
> Than in God's forests, architect supreme?

Stukeley was eagerly followed, adapted, improved upon and even outdone as English taste moved towards new ideas of romanticism and the idealisation of a hypothetical simplicity among primitive peoples. Some were looking further afield for Celtic origins. By 1730 Strahlenberg was deriving the Celts from the Siberian Tungus peoples, and the idea was found attractive on the Continent and in Ireland, where by the 1840s Ossian was to become a prepresentative of 'that interesting Siberian tribe the U-Sin, one of the principal tribes of the White Tartars'. And as if Geoffrey of Monmouth and Annius of Viterbo had not done enough in fabricating a fictitious Celtic past, yet further literary forgeries appeared. In 1750 the first part of James Macpherson's *Ossian* poems appeared, a forgery accepted with so much enthusiasm that the poems were seriously and elaborately compared to the *Iliad*, and were on occasion thought to excel Homer. John Smith in 1780 published a collection of Gaelic poems with translations, as editor claiming them to be of high antiquity and containing many references to Druids. 'There can be no better authority', Owen mordantly remarks, 'for he had himself first written the poems in English, and after translating them into Gaelic, he then published the translations as originals, and the originals as translations'. And even if poems were not forged, they were mistranslated into fantastic and even comic travesties of the originals, as when in 1809 Edward Davies brings Merlin to the mystic apple trees, 'guarded by one maid with crisped locks: her name is Olwedd, of the luminous teeth'.

But all this was not happening in an antiquarian vacuum. Among significant dates in the history of ideas at this time we may remember first Montesquieu's *Esprit des Lois* of 1748 and Rousseau's *Discours sur l'Inégalité* of 1753, and later, the Scottish primitivists such as Lord Kames and Professor Blackwell, and of course Lord Monboddo. All these were concerned with enquiries into the origin of man in a context no longer always dominated by the literal text of Genesis; the nature of primitive society, the beginnings of language and literature, the existence of natural law and the earliest development of institutions.[16] Behind much of this, as with the formation of the popular romantic image of the Celts and Druids, was the rediscovery of the Noble Savage, in the person of a South Sea Islander. Between 1756 and 1799 at least ten books presented to an eagerly receptive public the picture of a Polynesian paradise. George Richards, in an Oxford Prize Poem of 1791 entitled *The Aboriginal Britons*, significantly opens with 'An address to the first Navigators of the South Seas', and explicitly compares his Aboriginal Britons with the Polynesians. The Rev. John Ogilvie, Minister of Midmar, in his *Fane of the Druids* (published anonymously in 1788) after a description of a Druidic ceremony in an Aberdeenshire stone circle, turns to ask

> Ye days of quiet, now beheld no more!
> Where are ye fled, To what far distant shore?

and where too has gone the ancient goddess of the Druidic simple life?

> Ah! In the depths of Tahaiteean groves
> She dwells with swains that take unenvied loves
> Or joins in social isles the mirthful band,
> Or leads the dance on Monotoopa's strand . . .
> There soothes to rest, and pleas'd with artless strains
> Restores a golden age on Indian plains.

We are back to Barlowe and his golden age among the Virginian Indians two centuries before, and Ancient Celts and South Sea Islanders are sharing not only savagery, but unquestioned nobility.

And at this point the story must be left, with the shadows of the Celtic Twilight closing in upon us. Nor that the story itself ends, for fresh fantasies were devised with unabated ingenuity through the later eighteenth century and into the nineteenth century and our own time. New forgeries were produced to add to Geoffrey and Annius, Macpherson and Smith, by Edward Williams, who gave himself the 'Bardic' name of Iolo Morganwg and who not only fabricated a remarkable corpus of alleged early Welsh poetry, but invented the Gorsedd Circle in a fictitious ceremony on Primrose Hill in 1792, and later grafted it on to a revived and romanticised Eisteddfod. Patriarch Druids, Oak Groves, Stonehenge and Avebury all figure in word or picture in the *Prophetic Books* of William Blake: 'All things Begin and End' he announced 'on Albion's Ancient Druid Rocky Shore'. As late as 1865 a Gloucestershire vicar, the Rev. Samuel Lysons, in *Our British Ancestors*, argues at great length that, as the historian Freeman wrote in an amusing review, 'English is

Welsh and Welsh is Hebrew' on the evidence of English place-names. We have seen how some of these ideas originated, from the Renaissance onwards, and how persuasive they have been to generation after generation. O'Donnell wished the lectures he endowed to demonstrate the survival of Celtic elements in England, and the early antiquaries we have been discussing brought into being the most potent survival of all, still with us today at Stonehenge at sunrise or the Eisteddfod in the rain, and cosily at home among the Comforts of Unreason in popular belief, the dream-world of Celtic nonsense.

NOTES

1 Where not otherwise specified, the documentation of my sources will mainly be found in T. D. Kendrick, *British Antiquity*, London 1950, and A. L. Owen, *The Famous Druids*, Oxford 1962, or in the original texts.

2 J. Evans, *The Ancient Stone Implements . . . of Great Britain*, London 1872, 55.

3 *Retirement*, 691-4, quoted by J. S. Slotkin, *Readings in Early Anthropology*, London 1965, 235.

4 For Urquhart, cf. *Proc. Soc. Ant. Scot.* LXI, 1926-7, 181-91; F. C. Roe, *Sir Thomas Urquhart and Rabelais* (Taylorian Lecture), Oxford 1957.

5 C. A. Gordon, *Third Spalding Club Miscellany* III, 1960.

6 R. Heppenstall, *Times Lit. Supp.* 17 Oct. 1958.

7 E. Lhwyd to J. Lloyd, 29 Sept. 1703; R. T. Gunther, *Life and Letters of Edward Lhwyd*, Oxford 1945, 489.

8 For Saxon scholarship at this time, cf. D. C. Douglas, *English Scholars*, London 1939; R. Flower, *Proc. Brit. Acad.* XXI, 1935, 47; S. Piggott, 'William Camden and the Britannia', ibid., XXXVII, 1951, 199, No. III above.

9 M. T. Hodgen, *Early Anthropology in the Sixteenth and Seventeenth Centuries*, Philadelphia 1964, 364.

10 D. B. Quinn, *The Elizabethans and the Irish*, Cornell 1966.

11 Lhwyd in Gunther, op. cit., 476; I. Williams, *Lectures on Early Welsh Poetry*, Dublin 1944, 28; K. H. Jackson, *Early Celtic Nature Poetry*, Cambridge 1935, 58, 76; R. Bromwich, *Bull. Board Celtic Studies* XXIII, 1968, 14; ibid., '*Trioedd ynys Prydain*' in *Welsh literature and scholarship*, Cardiff 1969.

12 J. Aubrey, Introduction to *An Essay Towards the Description of the North Division of Wiltshire*, London 1659; A. Clark (ed.), *Aubrey's Brief Lives*, Oxford 1898, I, 17, 321; T. Hobbes, *Leviathan*, 1651, 97, No. I above.

13 A. O. Lovejoy and G. Boas, *Primitivism and Related Ideas in Antiquity*, 1935; L. Whitney, *Primitivism and the Idea of Progress in English Popular Literature in the Eighteenth Century*, Baltimore 1934; H. N. Fairchild, *The Noble Savage: A Study in*

Romantic Naturalism, 1961; M. T. Hodgen, op. cit. For Barlowe, D. B. Quinn (ed.), *The Roanoke Voyages* (Hakluyt Soc. 2nd ser. 104), 1951, 108.

14 A summary of the earlier views on the sequence of English medieval building styles is given by J. Britton, *Architectural Antiquities of Great Britain*, v, 1820, 31, No. VI below.

15 S. Piggott, *William Stukeley: An Eighteenth Century Antiquary*, Oxford 1950; *The Druids*, London 1968; other works already cited.

16 Cf. S. Piggott, *Antiq.* XXIX, 1955, 150; No. VII below.

V.

BACKGROUND TO A BROADSHEET.
WHAT HAPPENED AT
COLTON'S FIELD
IN 1685?

In 1685 an anonymous folio broadsheet was published in
London, 'printed for *W. Budden*; near *Fleet-Bridge*'. Entitled
'A Strange and Wonderful DISCOVERY Newly made of Houses
Under Ground, At Colton's-Field in Gloucester-Shire', it
relates a remarkable story of archaeological discoveries made
near Cirencester. The Bodleian Library contains two copies,
one bound by John Aubrey into his *Monumenta Britannica* MS.
and the other at the end of a volume of antiquarian notes on
Gloucestershire parishes made by Dr Richard Parsons, who
became Fellow of New College in 1657 and was Chancellor of
the Diocese of Gloucester from 1669 until his death in 1711.[1] A
more or less accurate transcript of the Parsons broadsheet was
printed by Samuel Rudder in 1800;[2] this was partly reprinted
and paraphrased by Beecham in 1887,[3] and the writer briefly
commented on Aubrey's copy in 1945.[4] The implications of the
bizarre narrative are such however as to merit a more careful
scrutiny.

The account opens with a paragraph saying that, as it is
generally agreed that new geographical discoveries are still to
be made, and that also parts of the earth can be lost (as with
sunken islands), 'These Considerations will, I hope, render the
following Account more Credible in it self'. The 'Strangeness
and *Novelty* of it' might otherwise make it hard to accept
'amongst the ignorant and unlearned parts of Mankind'. The
narrative then opens by describing how 'in a piece of Ground
within two Miles of *Cirenchester* . . . commonly known by the

Name of *Colton's-Field*' two labourers in a gravel pit at the foot of a hill, and a depth of four yards, 'discovered an Entrance into the Belly of the Hill . . . rather the Work of Art than Nature', and explored this with a lantern. They first entered what 'appeared to have been a Hall, which was large, and in it two long Tables with Benches on each side' which crumbled to dust at a touch, and thence went into 'another Room, which by the Furniture had been a Kitchin' with rusted and corroded 'Pots, Kettles, &c' of 'Brass or Iron'. Beyond this again was 'a Parlour, furnish'd according to the fashion of those Times' with carpets and furniture which again crumbled away, but going back, a passage from the hall 'led them into a square Room, curiously beautified with Carved Work' and with images in the wall suggesting it was a place of 'Worship and Devotion'. Here too were 'several Urns, some of which had only Ashes in them, others were filled with Coyns and Medals of Gold, Silver and Brass, with *Latin* Inscriptions, and the Heads of several of the *Roman Emperours*'. An iron-bound door of rotted wood in one wall they then broke open, 'and looking in, to their great Astonishment they saw the Image of a Man in full proportion with a Truncheon in his hand, and a light in a glass like a Lamp burning before him'. Thinking that if not the Devil, this might be the guardian spirit of treasure, one man went in, whereat the figure seemed to strike at him, and he and his companion fled, snatching 'many of the Medalls and Coyns' from the urns as they went.

That night they informed 'a Gentleman who is a famous Antiquary', showing him the coins; he told them to keep quiet but went with them to the site next morning, where 'with wonder and delight' he saw the outer rooms and then 'the place where the Image was, which he supposed might, by some great Artist, be made to strike at certain times'. At his first step the automaton once again made as if to strike; at the second it repeated the gesture more violently, and 'at the third step it struck a violent blow on the Glass where the Light was', extinguishing it and leaving them in darkness save for their lantern. The figure they thought must have been 'the Effigies of some *Roman* General, by those Ensigns of Martial Honour which lay at his Feet. On the Left Hand lay two Heads embalm'd, the Flesh was shrievel'd up and looked like Parchment scorched, of a dark Complexion, they had long hair on the Chin, one seem'd to be Red, the other Black'. They saw too that there were still more passages to explore, 'but a hollow Noise like a deep Sigh or Groan prevented any further Discovery, our Adventurers hastily quitting those dark Apartments, which they had no sooner done, than the Hill sunk down and buried all the Rarities'. The coins alone survived as witness: they were 'now shewn for the satisfaction of Curious and Ingenious Persons, who in great numbers flock to see them, and purchase them at great Rates, as the most valuable *Relicks of Antiquity*'.

So ends the printed account, but before we turn to examine this extraordinary narrative in detail, additional information is provided by a MS. note by John Aubrey in the bottom margin of the verso of his copy, which runs:

This Paper I had from Mr Tho. Pigot M.A. of Wadham
coll Oxon. who went to see it.

Quaere Mr Edw. Stephens of Cheriton + de hoc.

It is convenient to deal first with Mr Stephens, from whom Aubrey thought of obtaining further information. Edward Stephens of Norton and Cherington, Glos., was the son-in-law of Sir Matthew Hale, Lord Chief Justice, of Alderly in the same county, and an acquaintance of Aubrey's to whom he might naturally turn for local confirmation.[5] But Thomas Pigot is a far more significant figure, for he can only be the 'Gentleman who is a famous Antiquary' who in the broadsheet narration allegedly visited the site. Of a Rochdale, Lancs., family, he was born in 1657, was Fellow of Wadham in 1677, and elected Fellow of the Royal Society two years later. He held the living of Yarnton in Oxfordshire, concurrently with being domestic chaplain to James Earl of Ossory, from 1681 until his unexpected early death in 1686 at the age of 29. In the manner of the period he was interested in both science and antiquities. Anthony Wood records that in 1673 he 'made a new discovery of certain phoenomenas in music', but thought that in fact he had got his ideas from William Noble of Merton, a modest man and a better musician, but 'Pigot being a more forward and mercurial man got the glory of it among most scholars'. He published an account of an earthquake near Oxford in 1683, and for Aubrey he was 'my worthy friend', who provided him with information on a Roman pavement found at Badminton, which he transcribed into his *Monumenta* a couple of pages before the Colton's Field account, in the section headed 'Roman Pavements and Opus Tessellatum'.[6]

On the face of it we have a circumstantial account of a sensational archaeological discovery near Cirencester, with a field name (though unfortunately no parish or other identification beyond this) and, according to Aubrey's memorandum, a named and an identifiable witness. It can however be shown to be a complete fabrication, utilising traditional folklore and popular tales of a very interesting kind which richly repay detailed examination, not only in themselves, but as part of the intellectual background of the seventeenth century. For this is not a write-up of the gossip of Gloucestershire yokels in a local ale-house, but a learned hoax with a long literary history. As such however it falls neatly into place within a class of folk-tales, recently defined by Stewart Sanderson in a completely modern context, which he described as

a new folktale repertoire which circulates in oral transmission in modern society . . . mainly among people of a fairly high level of intelligence, education, and, to use current jargon, economic and social status . . . doctors, lawyers, university teachers and the like.

Such stories are accepted as true (if strange) and are 'supplied with such supporting credentials as details, names and dates'.[7] I hope to show that the Colton's Field story is just such a folk-tale, circulating in various forms for centuries before being produced with new credentials in exactly such a social and intellectual setting in the late seventeenth century.

The production of the story may of course have been prompted by some genuine if less spectacular archaeological find in the locality. Roman coins certainly seem to have existed, and, their value enhanced by the romantic story of the discovery, may indeed have sold 'at great Rates' to 'Curious and Ingenious Persons'. Perhaps the labourers found pottery too, and may have broken into the stone-built burial chambers of a Cotswold neolithic long barrow, or into one of the enigmatic stone corbelled structures traditionally known as 'Shepherds' Cots'.[8] Cotswold long barrows were certainly dug into late in the seventeenth century, since Dr Parsons records, in the papers accompanying his copy of the broadsheet, that the West Barrow at Leighterton was

opened out of Curiosity about 20 years since. There were found 3 Artificial Vaults arched over like Ovens at the Entrance of Each an Earthene Urne where was Ashes &

some mens Bones imperfectly burnt & broken.[9]

Parsons died in 1711 and his parochial notes were clearly assembled over several years, but at latest this entry should refer to an event around 1690. Aubrey knew of the barrow and recorded it in his *Monumenta* probably in the 1670s, with no mention of excavations. It cannot be Colton's Field, as it lies 15 miles S W of Cirencester, but if it were dug into in 1685 or shortly before, it could have been an item to prompt the fabrication. The Querns long barrow in Cirencester itself can hardly be a claimant, and when Samuel Rudder printed the text of the broadsheet from Parson's copy in 1800, he could suggest no convincing location. The circumstantial place-name in fact seems to have been an invention, and cannot be traced in local records.[10]

The general background to the folklore embodied in the story is familiar and widespread within what Kenneth Jackson has called the International Popular Tale repertoire,[11] conflating several motifs associated with the general theme of supernatural dwellers under hills which may be natural features or prehistoric burial mounds.[12] The belief is strongly represented in the two main strains of ancient western European folklore, Celtic and Germanic. The hero-gods of early Irish mythology are the *aes síde*, those who dwell in the Underworld beneath the great *síde* or burial mounds,[13] and in old Norse tradition there are those who live under mounds which are entered from time to time by the saga heroes,[14] and I have suggested that these stories 'may go back to aetiological myths invented to explain the phenomena encountered when breaking into chambered tombs, with their collective burials ranged round the stone-built vault'.[15] Thomas of Ercildoune and the Pied Piper of Hamelin belong to this world, which was that of the fairies; in the Downie Hills visited by Isobel Gowdie of Auldearne in 1662, or under barrows as was thought by John Walsh in Dorset in 1655, and by a peasant in Yorkshire in 1653.[16] The Reverend Robert Kirk of Aberfoyle in 1691 asked, reasonably enough in terms of the concepts of the plentitude of the Creation and the Great Chain of Being, that in the sequence from the angels of the empyrean through terrestrial life and thence to the fallen angels in Hell, 'can wee than think the midle Caveties of the Earth emptie ?'.[17] But more specific variants of the theme bring us closer to Colton's Field.

This group, which also embodies the motif of cave-sleepers (as at Ephesus), was defined by E. K. Chambers in connection with the legends of the return of Arthur[18] as the 'Hollow Hill' theme, where Arthur and other heroes of antiquity await a second coming in a room, palace or otherworld under a hill. Arthur was thus located under Etna as early as the late twelfth century, and the legends about his dwelling underground continued until they found their way into modern folklore. It is here that we encounter another set of beliefs, recently examined by Norman Cohn, that of the sleeping Emperor of the Last Days, who in a medieval eschatology will rule Christendom, destroy the heathen and convert the Jews in a final Golden Age. In an apocalyptic Three Ages system there follows the brief reign of Antichrist, cut short by the Archangel Michael, who by destroying him prepares the way for the Second Coming.[19] The concept of the emperor thought to be dead but sleeping goes back to the late seventh century, and by the eleventh and twelfth centuries not only Arthur, but many other heroes were competing. By the eleventh century Charlemagne sleeps in a vault either at Aachen or under a mountain—the Underberg near Salzburg is one claimant, the Odenberg another. Germany is rich in such locations. Both Frederick I and II sleep in more than one mountain, the latter having been seen to vanish into Etna with an army, as did Emico, Count of Leiningen, this time into a hill near Worms. Barbarossa sleeps sitting at a stone table under the Kyffhaüser in Thuringia, where his beard has grown twice round the table. He will arise, the early fourteenth-century story goes on, when the third circuit is completed, but in the meantime he once spoke to a shepherd who entered the mountain and piped to him, and rewarded him by giving him the stand of a gold basin.

But the most specific of all such medieval tales, and the one which seems to be of cardinal importance in our Colton's Field enquiry, is that related by the great English medieval historian, William of Malmesbury, of a far greater figure of the Middle Ages, Gerbert of Aurillac, who ended his life as Pope Silvester II from 999 to 1003. I have deliberately deferred reference to it, so that it can be seen in its proper setting of the popular tales of the time. Such wonder-tales were popular with all social classes, and not merely the peasantry. 'Before the Renaissance', Kenneth Jackson has written:

the stories genuinely popular and current among the upper classes had a great deal in common with those popular with the unlettered peasantry, and their plots were very often the same. The same tales would entertain princes and paupers, the Knight and the Miller.

And Comparetti wrote, of the legends which turned Vergil into a magician and originated in Naples around the twelfth century, that they are 'found in literary works which were in no way popular in origin or intention but were written in Latin by persons of education and destined to be read by the highest classes of society'.[20]

Gerbert was one of the most outstanding and many-sided scholars not only of the intellectually impoverished tenth century, but of earlier Medieval Europe at large. We can see him today, wrote Raby, 'as a mathematician and astronomer who attempted to solve the riddles of nature; as a man of high purposes and great religious ideals — in short, as a rare genius in an age of darkness and confusion'.[21] He became acquainted with Arabic science and mathematics during residence in Spain between 967 and 970; he materially advanced the study of Aristotelian logic and dialectic; he interested himself in such curious by-ways as the manuscripts of the Roman land surveyors, the *agrimensores*, when Abbot of Bobbio in the 980s.[22] He 'was a portent, both in his interest in science and in his approach to dialectic'.[23] Legend endowed him with a practical knowledge of mechanics, and in the early twelfth century a clock and a water-organ were attributed to him in the Cathedral of Rheims, where he had been Archbishop from 991 to 997; another clock was shown at Magdeburg. But the scientist and philosopher was soon seen and suspected as a magus who had gone beyond the bounds of permitted knowledge; had sold his soul to the Devil and practised the magic arts; had made, like Roger Bacon, Albertus Magnus and the medieval magician, Vergil, a speaking head; and had died an unedifying death.[24]

William, a monk of Malmesbury, lived between the 1090s and the 1140s and wrote at least three other historical works in addition to the *Gesta Regum Anglorum*, completed in 1125 and containing a biography of Gerbert. He is an attractive and lively writer — he has been described as a 'cultivated and ambitious stylist' — and his historical reputation, Galbraith has written 'probably stands higher today than ever before'. He made good and critical use of his sources, but Galbraith goes on:

> In the absence of authentic record what was there to be done
> with the luxuriant undergrowth of legend and miracle which
> ran riot in that oral society, and is still respectfully labelled as
> 'tradition'? We shall greatly wrong the medieval historian
> if we ignore the climate of opinion in which he worked and
> lived'.[25]

So in his section on Gerbert we not only have a factual account
of his career and intellectual attainments, but also the legends
which were used in the subsequent denigration of him in the
character of a papal Faustus, and of these the most considerable
is the relation of his discovery of treasure underground in
Rome—*Quomodo Gerbertus thesauros Octaviani invenit*—by
the exercise of his necromantic arts. I suggested in 1945 that
this tale should be related to that of Colton's Field, and I now
propose to develop the theme in more detail.

In the Campius Martius in Rome stood a statue with a pointing finger, inscribed *percute hic*. Many had struck the figure, but
Silvester II marked where the shadow of the finger fell at noon-
day, and at night came with a servant bearing a lantern. 'The
earth opening by means of his accustomed arts', an entrance
appeared, leading them underground into a palace where all
was gold—'*aureos parietes, aurea lacunaria, aurea omnia*'—and
where golden figures of soldiers seemed to be playing with gold
dice, and a golden king and queen sat at table with vessels and
attendant servants of all gold. An inner chamber was internally
lit by a carbuncle—'*in interiori parte domus carbunculus, lapis
inprimis nobilis est et parvus inventu, tenebras noctis fugabant*'—
while in the corner was the figure of a boy with a drawn bow.
They marvelled at the artifice, but if they moved to touch anything the automata began to rush forward. The servant could
not resist temptation, and made to take a knife from a table,
whereat the figures rose with a loud noise, and the archer dis-
charged his arrow into the carbuncle, leaving them in darkness
—'*verum mox omnibus imaginibus cum fremitu exsurgentibus, puer
quoque, emissa arundine in carbunculum, tenebras induxit*'. They
escaped by lantern-light, and it was generally agreed that Gerbert 'performed such things by unlawful devices'.

Before commenting on this story we must glance at a second
tale of how someone else looked for Octavian's treasure, given
immediately after the Gerbert episode. It was told to William

by a member of the Malmesbury community who was a native of Aquitaine, who said that he as a boy in Italy had been shown a 'tunnelled hill'—*montem perforatum*—said to hold the treasure of Octavian. With a band of a dozen friends he went into the caves beneath the mountain with lanterns, encountering in the dark all the terrors of bats, skeletons and rotting corpses until they came to a lake crossed by a bronze bridge. They saw across the bridge, as in full sunlight, gold figures of horses and riders 'and all those other things which are related of Gerbert', but they could not reach them, as the bridge was devised to operate an automaton at the far end, so that when one put a foot on the near end, 'wonderful to hear, it became depressed, and the further end was elevated, bringing forward a rustic (*rusticus*) of bronze with a bronze club' with which he then threshed the waters of the lake into a blinding spray. The boys returned to the outer world, having picked up en route a silver dish (*pateram argenteam reperimus*) which they shared by breaking into pieces, as testimony of their adventure.

Very comparable stories were told in the Middle Ages of Vergil, in his legendary character of magus; an ever-burning asbestos torch appears as early as the twelfth century in the *Miribilia urbis Romae* in what was said to be the *Mutatorium Caesaris* on the site of the church of St Balbina, and by the next century several sources, such as the *Image du monde* of 1245, describe the discovery of Vergil's tomb near Naples, and of St Paul's visit to it. He approached through unnatural winds and horrible noises to an underground vault guarded at the door by 'two bronze men who kept plying two steel hammers' to prevent access, and beyond them in the chamber sat Vergil under an ever-burning lamp with his magic books, with the figure of an archer who, when the apostle had stopped the hammering automata, 'shot out the light, leaving everything crumbling to dust in the darkness.[26]

The relevance of these tales to Colton's Field is clear, but we can also see how they fit the general pattern of folktales of the 'Hollow Hill' type outlined above. The taking of the silver dish as tangible evidence of underground treasure belongs to the group of tales about precious cups or drinking-horns taken from or given by dwellers under barrows, well known in Nordic folklore and going back in England to the twelfth century, when William of Newburgh gave a circumstantial account of a strange vessel—*vasculum materiae incognitae, coloris insoliti*—given to a Yorkshire peasant by the supernatural denizens of a barrow which can be identified as Willy Howe near Scarborough, where the legend survived until the last century.[27] The gold object given to the peasant by Frederick Barbarossa is a comparable variant, as so presumably in diminished form, the coins at Colton's Field. The *aurea omnia* theme is of course an ever-present motif of folktale, but a curiously close parallel to the golden soldiers playing dice occurs in the twelfth century Welsh tale of the *Dream of Macsen* in the Mabinogion, with the golden-haired youths playing with gold and silver pieces on a golden gaming-board in a golden hall.[28] The presence of metal automata in the Gerbert, Monk of Aquitaine and Vergil stories is another interesting detail: the golden king, queen, soldiers and horsemen in the first two; the archer in the first and third; the club-bearing or hammer-wielding men in the last two.[29] In all, their movements are deterrent, and the archer extinguishes the light, and in the Gerbert context automata are appropriate to the mechanical contrivances—clocks, water-organ and speaking head—attributed to him as practical expressions of his scientific expertise. The carbuncle as illumination we shall meet again in a later context, and etymologically the stone has the quality of a 'little fire' or of incandescence; it was one of the precious stones in the Garden of Eden and on Aaron's breast-plate. In medieval lapidaries it was assigned to the Archangels, and astrologically to the Sun, but as Joan Evans noted, by the early seventeenth century at least doubt was being cast on its phosphorescent qualities.[30] Internally-lit rooms will engage us shortly, and the legend of Merlin's illuminated tomb or cave in Arthurian romance might be a contributory factor in the legends, though it appears to be a late addition to the basic Merlin story, in which he sleeps in an enchanted castle.[31]

The common elements in these twelfth century narrations, and in the 1685 broadsheet, are curiously specific. The obviously fairy-tale gold is removed, but we still have the underground building with an outer hall with tables and benches leading to an inner room containing an ever-burning light and an auto-maton activated by a mechanism set in motion by the intruders —an archer under the Campus Martius and with Vergil, but a man with a club, more like the figure in the Monk of Aquitaine's story, at Colton's Field. The overtly supernatural element of the original tales is removed, and we are left with a piece of mechanical ingenuity, though the macabre detail of the two shrivelled human heads appears for the first time in the 1685 narration. If the other parallels are to be thought significant, however, can we in any way bridge the gap between the twelfth and the seventeenth centuries?

It seems that we may, in very curious circumstances, take back a version of the story to at least the beginning of the seventeenth century, but before considering this context we must glance at a new contributory fiction, known from the twelfth but revived in the sixteenth century, that of ever-burning lamps in ancient tombs.[32] Characteristically William of Malmesbury supplies our earliest example, recording, in the time of Pope Gregory VI (1045) the discovery at Rome of the tomb of the legendary Pallas, son of Evander: the corpse was uncorrupted, with 'a burning lamp at his head, constructed by magical art; so that no violent blast, no dripping of water could extinguish it'. The most famous discovery was however that alleged to have taken place in the reign of Pope Paul III (1534–49), when the tomb of Cicero's daughter Tullia was said to have been discovered on the Appian Way, containing a still burning light. This came aptly after the popularisation of the Merlin's Tomb motif, from Arthurian romances as already mentioned, by Ariosto in his *Orlando Furioso* of 1516, made available to English readers by Sir John Harington's brilliant translation published in 1591. The last lines of Canto 15 of Book III, describing the tomb, run in this version

> The verie marble was so cleare and bright
> That though the sunne no light unto it gave
> The toombe it self did lighten all the cave.

Harington noted that 'the fiction of the tombe is taken of a former fiction in king *Arthur's booke*', and it was an arresting image, giving rise eventually to J. M. Gandy's haunting painting exhibited at the Royal Academy in 1815.[33]

Tullia's lamp caught the imagination of the poets and aroused the scientific interests of men of learning for generations to come. Other finds were soon reported: the story of the tomb of Pallas was quoted, and a similar find in that of Olibius near Padua. Actual lamps, said to have been found still alight in ancient tombs, were treasured in Renaissance cabinets of rarities such as that of Ulisse Aldrovandi in Bologna, or in the museum formed around 1589 in the University of Leyden.[34] John Donne turned the story into the magic lines

> Now as in Tullia's tombe, one lampe burnt cleare
> Unchang'd for fifteen hundred yeare

in his 1613 *Epithalamion*, and Samuel Butler in 1664 treated the theme more lightly (*Hudibras* II, I.309):

> *Love* in your heart as idly burns
> As Fire in antique *Roman*-Urns
> To warm the *Dead*, and vainly light
> Those only, that see nothing by't.

The scholars approached the subject with an interest part antiquarian, part scientific—what was the chemistry behind an ever-burning lamp, and could one recover the secrets of the Ancients and construct one today? The question was not wholly academic, for from the Renaissance onwards mining technology was being rapidly developed, and ever-burning lamps for miners would be a sound commercial proposition. So in 1599 Guido Panciroli in his *Rerum memorabilium deperditarum* has a chapter *De oleo incombustibili veterum*, including Tullia's tomb; Fortunio Liceto in 1621 published a formidably learned *De lucernis antiquorum reconditis libri quatuor*[35] introducing every possible claimant. He incidentally mentions the carbuncle as a light-emitting stone, and also draws attention to the Merlin's tomb passage in Ariosto. It is interesting that in the stanza following that just quoted, the poet takes a detached scientific view of the phenomenon and concludes that the effect might have been achieved 'by helpe of Mathematike skill' and appropriate contrivances to bring in sunlight from outside. Sir Kenelm Digby noted 'lamps pretended to have been found in Tombes with inconsumptive lights' in 1644, and Abraham Cowley wrote of '*Lamps* burning in the *Sepulchres* of the Ancients' as a matter of course in 1656. Sir Thomas Browne in his *Vulgar Errors* of 1646 toyed with the idea of naptha as did others later; Robert Kirk in 1691 observed that the fairies living in their hills had for 'light continuall lamps, and fires, often seen without fuel to sustein them', without further comment.[36] The subject was found perennially interesting throughout the century, and seems to have been taken as a matter of course. A sober and factual account of a Roman find near Coggeshall in Essex published in 1658 describes 'an Hypogaeum or Grot, with arched work' and 'some Urnes, or Crocks, which contained in them ashes and bones' and goes on 'There was a Lamp yet burning still in a glasse Vial, covered with a Roman Tile', and expresses no surprise. In 1684, the year before the Colton's Field broadsheet, Dr Robert Plot read to the Royal Society 'A discourse concerning the *Sepulchral Lamps* of the *Ancients*'.[37] At all events, by the beginning of the seventeenth century tombs or vaults underground lit by ever-burning lamps were already well established in literary tradition, and by later in the century they were a commonplace.

By the end of the Middle Ages, with the Renaissance and on the eve of the Reformation, the Gerbert story had become a part of the corpus of legend surrounding the medieval papacy, copied, borrowed or adapted by more than one writer, such as Vincent of Beauvais in his *Speculum historiale* of the mid-thirteenth century, and others later. The original source, the *Gesta regum anglorum* of William of Malmesbury, was first printed in part by Jerome Commelin at Heidelberg in 1587[38] as the work of an anonymous 'continuator of Bede', and the portion printed (Books I–III) contained the stories of Gerbert and of the Monk of Aquitaine. The first English edition, with the authorship correctly attributed, was by Sir Henry Savile in 1596.[39] For what it may be worth, William of Newburgh, with the story of the magic cup taken from a barrow-dweller, was printed in 1567[40] and again by Commelin. One assumes that by the Renaissance the Vergil legends would have been forgotten in the face of the rediscovery of the real poet, but folktales of heroes sleeping in vaults under hills awaiting the call of destiny had circulated for centuries and were still told. Poetic imagery and scientific speculation were drawing attention to under-ground tomb-chambers lit by ever-burning lamps. The time was ripe for the re-invention and acceptance of a new and circumstantial folktale among educated men, embodying these learned and popular elements of long standing, and this is just what seems to have happened in the deliberately mystifying and confused circumstances of the Brotherhood of the Rosy Cross in Germany at the beginning of the seventeenth century.

The complex story has recently been examined by Dr Frances Yates.[41] The setting is one of the late Renaissance 'hermetic philosophy' and magic deriving from Giordano Bruno, Ficino and Pico della Mirandola in the fifteenth century, and now com-bined with the alchemical mysticism of Paracelsus (1490–1551)

to bring together the study of 'Magia, Cabala and Alchymia' —
astrology and astronomy, mathematics and mechanics, and
chemistry and medicine in alchemical guise. Many seem to have
contributed to the climate of thought and emotion in early
Protestant Germany which prompted the appearance of three
extraordinary publications advertising the existence of a secret
Brotherhood originally founded by one Christian Rosenkreutz.
The first two were in Latin, with long titles conveniently
abbreviated to the *Fama* and the *Confessio*, and were published
at Cassel in 1614 and 1615. The third was an allegorical alchemical fantasy in German, the *Chymische Hochzeit*, the
Chemical Wedding of Christian Rosenkreutz, published in
Strasburg in 1616. The questions of the existence or non-
existence of an actual Brotherhood, and the attendant implications discussed at length by Dr Yates need not concern us here,
but the essential point for our purposes is that the core of the
Rosicrucian myth was the discovery of the body of the founder
in an underground vault, 120 years after his death (at the age of
106) in 1484.

Christian Rosenkreutz, the *Fama* relates, was a monk who
had travelled widely·and studied the wisdom of the Arabic
world in the Levant, North Africa and Spain, devoting himself
to science, philosophy, magic and alchemy, and 'spent a great
time in the mathematics, and made many fine instruments'.
After his death his tomb was lost, its location unknown, until in
1604 a hidden door in the house he had bequeathed to the
fraternity he founded was broken open, and 'a vault of seven
sides and corners' was entered. 'Although the sun never shined
in this vault, nevertheless it was enlightened with another sun,
which had learned from the sun, and was situated in the upper
part of the centre of the ceiling'. This illuminated vault contained the mystical books of the Fraternity, and elsewhere were
other wonders including 'burning lamps'. Behind an altar was
the uncorrupted body of Brother Rosycross 'with all his ornaments and attires', holding the greatest of all the Rosicrucian
magic texts, like the legendary Vergil.[42]

If the *Fama* is allegorical, the *Chemical Wedding* is even more
obviously a mystical romance, written by Johan Valentin
Andreae (who appears not to be the author of the anonymous
Fama and *Confessio*). Its hero is the same Christian Rosenkreutz
in life, who spends a symbolic seven days attending a mysterious

Royal wedding in a castle. On the fifth day he discovers a door with a mysterious inscription in the castle cellars; 'when it opened', Dr Yates paraphrases, 'a vault was disclosed, in which the light of the sun could not penetrate; it was lighted by huge carbuncles. In the midst of it was a sepulchre covered with many strange images'.[43] The 'sun enlightened with another sun' in the *Fama* is surely an alchemical periphrasis for a carbuncle, and we seem to have come back to the Campus Martius by way of Merlin's tomb.

Dr Yates has pointed out that 'the opening of the magic vault . . . was not intended to be taken as literally true' but was based on 'legends of buried treasure such as were particularly prevalent in the alchemical tradition'. But is it not possible to be more precise, and to see the writers consciously looking back to and hinting at the Gerbert/Vergil tradition itself? It must be remembered that the Rosicrucian episode was set in Protestant Germany, and indeed anti-Jesuit overtones have been detected in the *Fama*. From the 1570s at least the Gerbert legend was revived by religious controversialists anxious to denigrate the Papacy by pointing to its more unworthy members, and Pope Silvester II with his magic arts and Satanic pact was set alongside the scandal of Pope Joan. The first printing of William of Malmesbury at Heidelberg in 1587 and in England nine years later rendered the original legend available to a wide public.

But on the other hand Gerbert had his apologists, especially in France in the controversy between Gallicans and Ultra-montanists and if we are to see a possible connection with the fables of the *Fama* and the *Chemical Wedding* there is another aspect of Gerbert to consider. 'Rehabilitated by history' wrote Raby, 'he now appears as a humanist who sought after the learning of the ancient world with the ardour of the Renaissance scholar'. Leff goes further: 'Altogether he presents the classic picture of the renaissance man, which is usually reserved for the fifteenth and sixteenth centuries'. The character of Gerbert could be seen as something akin to that of Christian Rosen-kreutz, and the tenth century French magus, misunderstood and calumniated by his own ignorant church, could be revisual-ised as a hermetic scientist-philosopher in seventeenth century Protestant Germany, in a context too with reminiscences of Vergil and his magic books and reinforced by the messianic overtones of the sleeping Emperor of the Last Days anticipating

Overleaf. 8. *Page of broadsheet of 1685.*
9. *Extract from* The Chymical Wedding, *1690.*

A Strange and Wonderful
DISCOVERY
Newly made of
Houſes Under Ground,
At *Colton's-Field* in *Gloucester-Shire.*

THat there is yet a great part of the Earth undiſcovered, is both the Opinion of the moſt famous Geographers (as appears by their vacancies in the Globe) and the Belief of the Learned of this and former Ages; And as *New Iſlands* have been found which were never known to our Anceſtors, ſo ſeveral parts of the Earth which were known, have been Loſt, as that Iſland near *Ireland,* which is deſcribed in the Maps, but cannot now be found by all the induſtrious Search made after it, which no doubt hath been ſwallowed up, as ſome Parts of *Zealand* are, by the Sea, the tops of whoſe Steeples are yet ſeen by Mariners as they Sail by 'em. Theſe Conſiderations will, I hope, render the following Account more Credible in it ſelf, and give it a better appearance of Truth, and Acceptance in the World, than probable the Strangeneſs and *Novelty* of it would admit of amongſt the ignorant and unlearned part of Mankind The Relation is thus:

In a piece of Ground within two Miles of *Cirencheſter,* (in the County of *Gloucester*) commonly known by the Name of *Colton's Field,* as two Labourers were digging a Gravel-Pit at the foot of a Hill (which they had now ſunk four yards deep) they obſerved the Ground on that ſide next the Hill to be looſe, and preſently diſcovered an Entrance into the Belly of the Hill, which appearing very ſtrange to them, and rather the Work of Art than Nature, one of them ventur'd a little way in, and by the Light from the hole, diſcovered a large Cavity; whereupon they got a Lanthorn and Candle to make a further Search into it. By the Advantage of this Light the firſt place they entred appeared to have been a Hall, which was large, and in it two long Tables with Benches on each ſide, which they no ſooner touch'd to feel their ſubſtance, but they crumbled into Duſt; from thence they ſaw a Paſſage into another Room, which by the Furniture had been a Kitchin, ſeveral Utenſils proper to it, as Pots, Kettles, &c. being of Braſs or Iron, continued firm, but eaten through with Ruſt and Canker. Beyond the Hall they went into a Parlour, furniſh'd according to the faſhion of thoſe Times, with Carpets richly wrought, and other Furniture agreeable; theſe alſo fell to pieces upon their touching 'em. At one Corner of this Room there appeared to have been a pair of Stairs, but the Earth had fallen in, and ſtopt the Aſcent. Going back, in the Hall, they obſerv'd

another

The fifth Day.

The night was over, and the dear wished for day broken, when hastily I got me out of the Bed, more desirous to learn what might yet insue, than that I had sufficiently slept; Now after that I had put on my Cloaths, and according to my custom was gone down the Stairs, it was still too early, and I found no body else in the Hall, wherefore I intreated my Page to lead me a little about in the Castle, and shew me somewhat that was rare, who was now (as always) willing, and presently lead me down certain steps under ground, to a great Iron Door, on which the following Words in great Copper Letters, were fixed.

* * * * * * * *

This I thus copied, and set down in my Table-Book. Now after this Door was opened, the Page led me by the hand through a very dark Passage, till we came again to a very little Door, that was now only put too, For (as the Page informed me) it was first opened but yesterday when the Coffins were taken out, and had not been since shut. Now as soon as we stepped in, I espied the most pretious thing that Nature ever created: For this Vault had no other light but from certain huge great *Carbuncles*; And this (as I was informed) was the *King's Treasury*. But the most glorious and principal thing, that I here saw, was a *Sepulcher* (which stood in the middle) so rich that I wondred it was no better guarded ; whereunto the coming of a new enlightenment which was also a *renovatio*.

The legend of Brother Rosenkreutz, intrinsically intriguing and rendered irresistably attractive by its association with a mysterious secret society, was familiar to English scientists and antiquaries in the seventeenth century. The *Fama* and *Confessio* were translated by Thomas Vaughan, brother of the poet Henry, and published in 1652; Newton, deeply interested in the hermetic tradition, had a copy in his library. Elias Ashmole had made a MS. transcript of another English translation, and quoted the *Fama* in his alchemical collection, the *Theatrum Chemicum*, also in 1652. The *Chymische Hochzeit* was itself translated, by Ezechiel Foxcroft, a Fellow of King's College, Cambridge, a mathematician with theological propensities, who died in 1674. The translation was published posthumously, as *The Chymical Wedding*, in 1690, but there is evidence that MS copies were earlier in circulation. The ever-burning lamp theme was as we saw arousing the nascent scientific interests of the seventeenth century, and John Wilkins, discussing underground lamps, noted that one 'is related to be seen in the sepulchre of Francis Rosicrosse, as is more largely expressed in the Confession of that Fraternity'. This was in his *Mathematical Magick, or, The Wonders that may be performed by Mechanical Geometry* of 1648: Wilkins (who seems to have confused the *Confessio* with the *Fama*) was, with many others of his time, much interested in automata and speaking statues contrived by scientific means, and we can scarcely avoid hearing echoes of Gerbert's speaking head and the mechanical figures guarding the treasures of Octavian.[44]

But still louder and nearer are the echoes from Colton's Field, as Mr Pigot and the workmen 'quitted those dark Apartments' to the sound of 'a hollow Noise, like a deep Sigh or Groan' in 1685. We have persued some devious but I trust not tedious byways of legend and history in an endeavour to elucidate the narrative William Budden printed with the implication that it was fact. Can we escape from the conclusion that we have been dealing with one of those learned folktales which would be current 'among people of a fairly high level of intelligence . . . doctors, lawyers, university teachers and the like' in the late seventeenth century as much as they can be today? Dr Yates discussed the word *ludibrium*, often used by Johann Valentin Andreae, author of the *Chemical Wedding*, in the sense of a

94

fiction or jest, when writing of the Rosicrucian pronouncements. Can we see the story of Colton's Field as a kind of *ludibrium*, an academic in-joke for the private amusement of those Fellows of the Royal Society who knew of Gerbert, Vergil as magus and Brother Rosycross, or was Mr Pigot using its publication to test Aubrey's credulity? The preamble of the broadsheet stresses that the 'ignorant and unlearned part of Mankind' would find the relation difficult of acceptance. If so, was it the work of the twenty-eight-year-old 'forward and mercurial' Mr Pigot, prompted perhaps by a genuine archaeological find and even Dr Plot's paper to the Royal Society on ever-burning lamps the year before? The questions must be left unanswered, but at the least the main sources of the broadsheet stand confessed. 'Many gullible readers at the time and since' wrote Dr Yates of the Rosy Cross 'have taken the story literally'. Perhaps some believed in Colton's Field.

There remain a tail-piece and a postscript to the story. On 15 May 1712, no. 379 of the *Spectator* contained what looks very like a fill-up to a piece of short copy, by Eustace Budgell, Addison's cousin, who was writing the essays at the time. 'I shall conclude this Paper', he wrote, 'with the story of *Rosicrucius's* Sepulcher'. Digging where 'this Philosopher lay Interr'd' someone found a 'small Door having a Wall on each side of it', broke in and entered 'a very fair Vault' lit by a 'blaze of light'. At the far end sat the figure of a man in armour at a table, with a truncheon in his hand and a lamp burning before him. On the intruder approaching, the figure rose; at the second step it lifted the club and at the third broke the light, leaving the vault in darkness. The 'Country People soon came with lights to the sepulchre, and discovered that the Statue, which was made of Brass, was nothing more than a piece of Clockwork' actuated by springs under the floor of the vault.[45]

And where, we may well ask, did Budgell find this story? A *Spectator* correspondent with the convincing name of Emilia Lovetruth, who had 'just done reading the Rosicrucian story in the Fame and Confession, a book published by the fraternity' compared it with the tale of an enchanted cave in Spain,[46] but she did not say that the *Spectator* account only remotely resembles the version in the *Fama* and comes far closer to Colton's Field. Eustace Budgell was at Trinity College, Oxford, Aubrey's college, in 1705, only twenty years after the Colton's

Field broadsheet was printed, and one wonders about copies still in circulation. At all events Samuel Rudder, publishing his *History of Cirencester* in 1800, saw the point, for he printed his transcript of the broadsheet under the heading of 'A Rosicrucian Story', and commenting on it said 'we have found no traces of the facts either in tradition or history' except for the *Spectator* story, which, as he rightly went on, is 'nearly after the tenor of our story, but a little abbreviated'. Unless there is a comparable version with a specifically Rosicrucian attribution to be tracked down, this seems yet another minor mystery emanating from the non-existent Colton's Field.

Good stories die hard, 'supplied' in Sanderson's words 'with such supporting credentials as details, names and dates'. Writing in the *Times Literary Supplement* in 1966, Mr Lawrence Durrell supplied Colton's Field with a postscript.[47] He published in good faith a story transmitted to him as fact by a Mr Sacatos, a Greek resident in Canada, who was told it by the history master of his Cairo school in 1943, a Father Andronicus. In 1898, the story ran, Alexei Ramonsky, Third Secretary in the Russian Embassy, discovered the tomb of Alexander the Great under the Nebi Daniel mosque in Alexandria. He found 'a room fifteen feet by fifteen feet with a ceiling about ten feet in height. On a black basalt base in the middle of the room stood a glass cage'. This was thickly covered with dust, but on clearing part of the glass he saw 'a figure, mummified in the Egyptian fashion ... in a seated position on a kind of throne', with $A\Lambda EXAN\Delta PO\Sigma$ $\Phi I\Lambda I\Pi\Pi OY$ inscribed on the base. The room was filled with 'papyri, vases, and one Roman standard ... also there were a few Macedonian arms and implements'. The Emperor of the Last Days indeed. As I said in a subsequent comment 'the inherent improbabilities in the story, such as Alexander sitting in a glass case like Jeremy Brentham, or the possibility of identifying at sight 'Macedonian arms and implements' are not outweighed by the apparently precise documentation'. Perhaps Mr Pigot of Wadham would have felt more at home.

NOTES
1 Bodleian Library MS. Top. gen. C.25, f. 107; MS. Rawlinson B.323, f. 287 (Parsons).
2 S. Rudder, *The History of the Ancient Town of Cirencester ...*, Cirencester 1800 (and subsequent edd.), 71-5.

3   K. H. Beecham, *History of Cirencester*, Cirencester 1887, 266-7.
4   S. Piggott, *Antiquity* XIX, 1945, 210-11.
5   John Aubrey, *Brief Lives* (ed. A. Clark), Oxford 1898, I, 278;
    DNB XIV, 170.
6   *Brief Lives* II, 155; A. Wood, *Fasti Oxon.* II (Ed. Bliss, Oxford
    1820), IV, 367; M. Hunter, *John Aubrey . . .*, London 1975, 61,
    62; R. Plot, *Natural History of Oxfordshire*, Oxford 1677, 294;
    Thomas Pigot, 'An Account of the Earthquake that happened at
    Oxford . . . Sept. *17, 1683*', *Phil. Trans.* XIII, no. 151, 1683, 311;
    Bodleian MS. Top. gen. C.25, f. 105r. It is with regret that the
    present writer records that he comes from a different family of
    the same name.
7   S. F. Sanderson, *Folklore* LXXX, 1969, 241-52. I am very grateful
    to Mr Sanderson for his help in this investigation.
8   E. M. Clifford, *Proc. Prehist. Soc.* IV, 1938, 214; W. F. Grimes,
    Excav. on Defence Sites 1939-45, London 1960, 25 ff.
9   Bodleian MS. Rawlinson B.323, f. 167; O. G. S. Crawford, *Long
    Barrows of the Cotswolds*, Gloucester 1925, 136, no. 51, cites
    Witts quoting inaccurately and without acknowledgement from
    the Parsons MS. in 1883 and saying the barrow was 'opened
    about the year 1700 by Matthew Huntley', but this must be too
    late.
10 Crawford, op. cit., 129, no. 46; Rudder, op. cit., 75. I am much
    indebted to Mr V. A. Woodman, Divisional Librarian, Glou-
    cester Library, for checking all possible sources of field and
    personal names within a five mile radius of Cirencester, with
    negative results.
11 Cf. K. H. Jackson, *The International Popular Tale and early
    Welsh Tradition*, Cardiff 1961.
12 Stith Thompson, *Motif-Index of Folk-Literature*, Copenhagen &
    Indiana 1955-8, A571; D.1960.2; F.720-5.
13 Cf. M. Dillon and N. Chadwick, *The Celtic Realms*, London
    1967; paperback 1973, 183-6, summarising a large literature.
14 H. R. Ellis, *The Road to Hel*, Cambridge 1943, esp. 90 ff.; 191 ff.
15 S. Piggott, loc. cit.
16 Original sources conveniently set out in M. Murray, *The Witch-
    Cult in Western Europe*, Oxford 1921, App. I, 238-46.
17 R. Kirk, *Secret Commonwealth of elves, fauns and fairies*, 1691,
    ed. S. Sanderson, Folklore Soc. 1976, 88; No. VII below.
18 E. K. Chambers, *Arthur of Britain*, London 1927, 221 ff.
19 N. Cohn, *The pursuit of the millennium*, London 1957; paper-
    back 1972.
20 Jackson, op. cit., 3; D. Comparetti, *Vergil in the Middle Ages*
    (Eng. trans.), London 1895, 257.
21 F. J. E. Raby, *History of Christian-Latin Poetry*, Oxford 1953,
    204; Cf. F. Picavet, *Gerbert, un pape philosophe*, Paris 1897; R.
    Allen, *Eng. Hist. Rev.* VII, 1892, 625-68; G. Leff, *Medieval
    Thought*, Penguin Books 1958, 90-1.
22 O. A. W. Dilke, *The Roman Land-Surveyors*, Newton Abbot
    1971, 128.

23 Leff, op. cit.

24 William of Malmesbury, *Gesta Regum Anglorum*, II, 172 (ed. W. Stubbs, Rolls. S. XC, 1887, I, 193 ff.). For early medieval clocks, cf. Lynn White Jr., *Medieval Technology and Social Change*, Oxford 1962, 120 ff. (At this date presumably water-clocks.) Water-organs go back to Roman times and are described by Vitruvius; a well-known surviving example is that from Aquincum (Budapest). For the Gerbert legend, cf. E. M. Butler, *The Myth of the Magus*, Cambridge 1948, esp. 94-7.

25 V. H. Galbraith, *Historical research in medieval England* (Creighton Lecture 1949), London 1951, 18.

26 The two stories follow one another in the *Gesta*, Book II. For Vergil, Comparetti op. cit. Similar tales, unattributed to specific historical characters, appear elsewhere (e.g. in the *Gesta Romanorum*) and seem to have Oriental counterparts.

27 William of Newburgh, *Rerum Anglicarum* Bk. I, Ch. 28, *De quibusdam prodigiosis* (Ed. H. C. Hamilton, London 1861, I, 76); T. Wright, *Essays on archaeological subjects* I, London 1861, 31; J. Thurnam, *Arch.* XLIII, 1873, 522; L. V. Grinsell, *Folklore* LXXXVIII, 1967, 12.

28 K. H. Jackson, op. cit. for the international folk-tale element in this story.

29 Can there have been a reminiscence of a club-bearing 'wild man' or woodwose here? The legend goes back to the twelfth century: R. Bernheimer, *Wild men of the Middle Ages*, Harvard 1952.

30 Exodus XXVIII, 17; Ezechiel XXVIII, 13; J. Evans, *Magic Jewels of the Middle Ages and the Renaissance*, Oxford 1922, 79, 93.

31 W. E. Mead, 'Outlines of the History of the Legend of Merlin', in E.E.T.S. ed. of the prose *Merlin*, London 1899.

32 There is a good bibliography of ever-burning lamps in D. Murray, *Museums, their History and their Use*, Glasgow 1904, I, 30.

33 *Orlando Furioso translated by Sir John Harington*, ed. R. McNulty, Oxford 1972, 42, 47. For Gandy, J. Summerson, 'The Vision of J. M. Gandy', in *Heavenly Mansions*, London 1949, 111-34.

34 D. Murray, op. cit., 78 ff. Cf. No. VI below.

35 G. Pancirolus, *Rerum memorabilium jam olim deperditarum*, Ambergae 1599; F. Licetus, *De lucernis antiquorum reconditis libri IV*, Venice 1621 and subsequent edd.

36 K. Digby, *Two treatises . . . Of bodies and of man's soul . . .*, Paris 1644, Ch. viii, Sect. 9; A. Cowley, *Davideis*, in *Poems*, London 1656, note to Bk. IV; T. Browne, *Pseudodoxia Epidemica*, London 1646, Bk. III, Ch. 21; R. Kirk, op. cit., 54.

37 W. Burton, *A Commentary on Antoninus his Itinerary . . .*, London 1658, 230; R. Plot, 'A discourse concerning the *Sepulchral Lamps* of the *Ancients*, shewing the possibility of their being made divers waies', *Phil. Trans.* XIV, 1684, 806.

38 H. Commelinus, *Rerum Britannicarum scriptores vetustiores*, Heidelberg 1587.

39 H. Savile, *Rerum Anglicarum scriptores post Bedam*, London 1596.

40 *Rerum Anglicarum libri quinque*, Antwerp 1567.
41 F. Yates, *The Rosicrucian Enlightenment*, London 1972; quotations from paperback ed. 1975.
42 Ibid., 290, 291.
43 Ibid., 96.
44 Ibid., 225, 236, 243.
45 *The Spectator*, ed. D. F. Bond, Oxford 1965, III, 424-5.
46 Quoted by Bond, op. cit. from C. Lillie, *Original and Genuine Letters* . . ., London 1725, II, 252-3.
47 L. Durrell, 'Alexander's Tomb', letter to *Times Lit. Supp.* 7 April 1966, 295; comment by the writer, ibid. 21 April, 352.

10. *Engraving for Gray's* Elegy, *by R. Bentley, 1753.*

VI.

RUINS IN A LANDSCAPE.
ASPECTS OF SEVENTEENTH AND
EIGHTEENTH CENTURY
ANTIQUARIANISM

When seeking for a subject appropriate to a Ford Historical Lecture, as a prehistorian I felt I might reasonably remind an audience of historians that there is a history of prehistory, so that our approach to archaeology today, whether in the non-literate or the literate past, is conditioned by the way in which antiquities have been looked at and thought about during the last three centuries. The circumstances of the emergence of the antiquarian studies which were later to become archaeology are well documented in the seventeenth and eighteenth centuries, and I believe of some interest. It was at this time in Britain that the study of antiquities in the open air, the field archaeology fundamental to any further interpretation or synthesis, was initiated and developed into recognisably modern form. Antiquities and the countryside were seen as part of a common field of intellectual enquiry and aesthetic response, and I offer here a brief survey of some of the aspects of the developing anti-quarianism of this period. In this context, attitudes I take as characteristic of the seventeenth century are hardly recognisable before the 1640s, but continue until the 1730s; the eighteenth century tradition then lasts until the 1830s.

The manner of looking and thinking with which we are first concerned I would call that of the Royal Society, the culmination of the new secular views on all natural and man-made phenomena owing their origins to the attitudes crystallised in the writings of Francis Bacon early in the seventeenth century, and associated with pragmatic observation and experiment, objective record and ordered classification. John Aubrey put his finger unerringly on the point of change. 'Till about the yeare 1649' he wrote '[Experimental Philosophy was then first cultivated by a Club at Oxon], 'twas held a strange Presumption for a man to attempt an Innovation in Learning'.[1] All this is well known, and Dr Michael Hunter has recently discussed the place of antiquarianism in the early Royal Society which embodied this novel approach and, we may recall, though formally founded in 1662, has its beginnings going back to the 1640s.[2] The Fellows, the New Men, (and Aubrey was one of them) were Bacon's 'Men of Experiment', collecting and classifying objects and observations. I would stress classification: to take an outstanding example John Ray, with his friends like Francis Willughby, started from 1658 to construct the first systematic taxonomy in British natural history, and published the beginnings of a scientific flora and fauna.[3] Soon antiquities, as a part of the earth and landscape, followed fossils as subjects for investigation within the same scheme.

We may look with profit (and some pleasure) first at the literal collection of things. I am not going to enter the debate on the social status of early science, and of the Royal Society's first Fellowship, but it may not be wholly irrelevant. Royal or ecclesiastical treasures of precious and curious objects lie behind the Renaissance tradition of the secular and patrician, if not always royal, collecting of works of art, particularly those of antique sculpture. Such collections expressed a veneration of classical antiquity and a correct aesthetic standpoint, reinforced by the experience of the Grand Tour and the comfort of a large rent-roll. It was an essentially expensive pursuit, and as such an appropriate expression of aristocratic status maintained or in the process of establishment. In Oxford we may well remember one of the earliest of these collections in this country, the Arundel Marbles as earlier generations called it, a collection of classical sculpture and inscriptions formed by Thomas Howard, second Earl of Arundel, from 1625 until the eve of the Civil War and his death in 1646. In 1667 such of the inscriptions as had survived neglect and destruction (114 out of an original 250) were presented to the University, and over 100 pieces of sculpture followed in 1755. In 1683 twelve cartloads of very different objects also arrived as a gift, 'Tradescant's Ark' from Lambeth. This collection, through what appear to have been some slightly dubious operations of Elias Ashmole, was to take its place in Oxford in 'the new house by the Theater' as the nucleus of the Ashmolean Museum of today. These two benefactions, one acquired first in 1667 and the other in 1683, represent two parallel and distinct traditions, one the aristocratic art gallery and the other a scientific and mercantile museum, and it is the latter which concerns us here in the study of British antiquities.[4]

Both types of collection have Renaissance origins. The Cabinet of Curiosities, and sometimes of coins (which provided a collection of classical art, but one cheaper than sculpture and so available to the modest purse) was often associated with the formation of ornamental, botanical and 'physic' gardens containing the new exotic plants becoming available for medicine, industry, the kitchen and personal delight as trade developed with the Orient, and increasingly with the Americas. In the wake of botany came ethnography in tangible shape, as examples of the material culture of strange peoples were collected and brought home to be seen by European scholars, and to supplement the travellers' reports of primitive societies which might form a paradigm for those of prehistoric man. To these might be added local prehistoric antiquities themselves, stone arrowheads or axe-blades. It seems in fact that one of the first men to identify European stone artefacts as such, rather than 'formed stones' of natural origin, was Michele Mercati (1541–93), Keeper of the botanical gardens of Pius v and founder of the Vatican museums, although his observations were not published until 1717. There were other great Italian collections such as that of Ulisse Aldrovandi (1527–1605) at Bologna, which did include prehistoric stone axes and flint arrow-heads; that of Giancomo Zanoni (1615–82), also at Bologna, and the ducal 'cabinet or musaeum' seen by John Ray at Modena in 1663. The Elector Augustus of Saxony (1553–86) had a museum at Dresden, and that in the University of Leyden, probably initially made by Peter Pauw, Professor of Botany and Anatomy, about 1589, also contained ethnographical specimens, Egyptian mummies and Roman coins.[5] Ole Worm formed a famous museum in Copenhagen which contained prehistoric stone implements as well as fossils, plants, birds and animals, and ethnographica, the catalogue of which was published in 1655.[6] The Royal Society's Museum of Natural and Artificial Rarities,

Overleaf. 11. Ole Worm's museum, 1655.

MUSEI
WORMIANI
HISTORIA
LUGD· BATAVORUM
EX OFFICINA ELSEVIRIANA
1655·

CONCHILIATA

VARIA

METALIA MINERALIA

CONCHILIA MARIANA

LAPIDES

LAPIDES

LAPIDES

SUCCI FRUCTU

GUMMA

LIGNA

CORTICES

SULPHURA

SALIA

TERRÆ

HERBÆ

RADICES

as described by Nehemiah Grew's 1681 catalogue, included (under 'Humane Rarities') a mummy; 'Coins and other matters relating to Antiquity', some given by John Aubrey; ethnographical specimens catalogued among assorted objects which included Newton's first reflecting telescope, Hooke's cider-press and Wren's bee-hive; and flint arrow-heads classified with crystals and fossils under 'Regular stones'.[7] Gardens were living classified assemblages of plants, inseparably bound up with other collections as the expression of the Royal Society principle of ordered information. John Evelyn was enchanted in 1671 by Sir Thomas Browne's collections in Norwich, 'his whole house and garden being a paradise and cabinet of rarities, and that of the best collection, especially medails, books, plants and natural things'. Robert Burton saw a potential cure for melancholy in such collections. 'What so full of content' he wrote in 1621 'as to read, walk, and see Mapps, Pictures, Statues, Jewels, Marbles ... to peruse old Coyns of several sorts in a fair Gallery; artificial works, perspective glasses, old reliques, *Roman* Antiquities ... Or in some Princes Cabinets ... to see ... *Indian Pictures* made of feathers, *China* works, frames, *Thaumaturgical* motions, exotick toyes *&c.*'[8]

Of the *Musaeum Tradescantium*, the Cabinet, Closet of Rarities or Ark, few items have survived the centuries, but the printed catalogue of 1656 describes this collection formed by the two John Tradescants, father and son, gardeners to Charles I and creators of his Physic Garden in South Lambeth.[9] The museum was arranged by 'materialls', the first group being Natural, and including 'Birds, four footed Beasts and Fishes, Shell-creatures, Insects, Mineralls, Outlandish-fruits and the like'. Here also was the famous 'Dodar, from the Island *Mauritius*' which a century or so later, moth-eaten and despised, was burnt, and only fragments survive. The second group was of 'Artificialls', 'as Vtensils, Householdstuffe, Habits, Instruments of Warre used by several Nations, rare curiosities of Art, &c.', and included Roman pottery and pre-Roman British coins. With this collection we may compare the *Musaeum Thoresbyanum* formed by Ralph Thoresby of Leeds at the end of the seventeenth century and including considerable natural history and ethnographical collections, a good coin cabinet, some British prehistoric antiquities and a much prized Roman Shield: its description and illustration make it, alas, pretty certain that it was a Scottish Highlander's targe of recent date, but a piece of British enthnography unfamiliar to most Englishmen before 1715, when in fact it was published in the printed catalogue.[10]

The Tradescants as royal gardeners must have acquired most of their curiosities by way of their business; Thoresby was an antiquarian wool merchant and begged rarities from his friends as well as buying them. The trade was well established, and Evelyn found in Paris in 1644 'a shop called Noah's Arke, where are sold all curiosities naturall or artificial, Indian or European, for luxury or use, as Cabinets, shells, ivory, porselan, dried fishes, insects, birds, pictures and a thousand exotic extravagances'.[11] Collections could be formed by those of relatively modest means, and certainly went in part with an interest not only mercantile, but also concerned with practical craftsmanship. Tradescant collected 'Mechanick artificiall Works', and the Royal Society had categories of 'Mechanicks' and 'Things related to Mathematicks &c.'. It might be mentioned that of the antiquaries John Aubrey, and William Stukeley who followed him in field archaeology, both recorded how as children they were fascinated by drawing and making things, both keenly watching craftsmen at work, and while Aubrey regretted not living in a town where he could talk to locksmiths and watchmakers, Stukeley as boy first in London avidly frequented the shops of makers of scientific instruments.[12] But the point the collections bring home is that the direct counterpart of these classified museums was the similar assembling of knowledge on paper which produced the county surveys or Natural Histories (including a treatment of antiquities) of Aubrey, Plot, Lhwyd and others.

To a large extent, these surveys had a practical aim, to describe and assess the natural resources of various regions with a view to their exploitation by agriculture, industries and other ventures in trade, and even in medicine and the tourism following the recognition of the appropriate mineral springs. But they ranged far beyond this aspect, and with a county as the unit were often based on questionnaires indicating their scope, such as those issued by Ogilby, Machell, Plot, Aubrey, Lhwyd and Parsons for instance between 1673 and 1697. Antiquities were given a place, sometimes unexpectedly. 'What Horse-Races ? Where ? For what prize ?' asked Machell 'What memorable places where Battles have been fought? Round heaps of Stone, or Earth cast up in Hills, trench'd round about, or otherwise? What fortifications, Camps?'. And Robert Plot, seeking material for his *Natural History of Oxfordshire* (1677), enquired 'Are there any ancient *Sepulchers* hereabout of Men of *Gigantick* stature, *Roman Generals* or *others* of ancient times? has there ever been any apparitions hereabout?', and then went on to ask about fortifications, barrows, coins and other '*British, Roman, Saxon,* or *Danish* antiquities'.[13] Plot was the first Keeper of the Ashmolean Museum, founded as we saw with Trades-cant's collections, and it is characteristic of the age that he became successively Professor of Chemistry, Historiographer to King James II, and Mowbray Herald Extraordinary.[14] Edward Lhwyd served under Plot in the new Museum, and disliked him — 'a man of as bad morals as ever took a doctor's degree'. But in 1691 he succeeded him as Keeper, and embarked on his great Celtic studies, causing notable plans to be made of prehistoric Welsh hill-forts and other monuments as well as pursuing and publishing his famous philological contributions, and producing his internationally admired catalogue of fossils. He did not live to publish more than the first part of the *Archaeologia Britannica,* that dealing with the Celtic languages, but had planned 'An Account of all such Monuments now remaining in *Wales,* as are presum'd to be *British*; and either older, or not much later than the *Roman* conquest: viz. their Camps and Burial Places; the Monuments called *Cromlecheu and Meineugwyr*; their Coyns, Arms, Amulets &c.'.[15]

We must remember that fossils were for long not regarded as the remains of extinct living organisms, not even as relics of the Deluge, but as curious natural 'formed stones' looking decep-tively like fishes, shells or plants. '*Lapides sui generis*' said Lister of fossil shells, 'never any part of an Animal'; Ray and Lhwyd were uncertain; Hooke accepted them as representing organisms and saw the task of the 'Natural Antiquary' as in parallel with that of the student of 'Artificial' antiquities, which were thus closely linked to fossils and minerals.[16] Stone implements pre-sented similar problems in interpretation. The bilateral sym-metry of axe-blades or arrow-heads led to them being placed among the 'regular' formed stones in the Royal Society's museum; they were similarly regarded as 'natural' by Lister; Worm was puzzled by his Danish flint arrow-heads and daggers

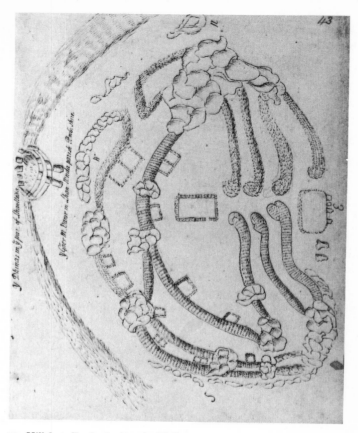

12. *Hill fort, Pembrokeshire, by W. Jones, c. 1700.*

—*de quibus dubito Artisne aut Naturae sint opera*—but one at least he thought *potius Arte quam Natura elaboratum esse*. By 1686, in his *Staffordshire*, Plot accepted flint implements as Ancient British products. The process of fossilisation was not understood, and confused with 'petrifications' from springs such as those at Knaresborough (there were some in the Tradescant collection) and Worm could regard a stone shaft-hole axe as a fossil of an original in iron. In the recognition of ancient stone implements for what they were, the early anti-quaries were facing problems of identification akin to those encountered by the first students of fossils. Both, too, had to face a second conceptual difficulty when moving from identification to interpretation, and seeing fossils or stone tools (and of course field monuments as well) not as an end in themselves, but as potential evidence from which wider inferences, including those of chronology, might be made. The antiquaries had to think, in R. G. Collingwood's terms, of antiquities acquiring an evidential value to those who deliberately sought this quality in them.[17] But this was an intellectual position hardly to be reached before the nineteenth century.

Plot modelled his Oxford book on one by Joshua Childrey of 1660, *Britannia Baconica or the Natural Rarities of England*, which makes the link with Lord Verulam explicit in its title. Antiquities were now coming to be looked at and thought about as phenomena capable of classification, and in his unpublished *Monumenta Britannica* Aubrey attempted for antiquities an archaeology in parallel with John Ray's work in botany and zoology, Martin Lister's in conchology, or Edward Lhwyd's in fossils, and must have been unconsciously forming concepts similar to that explicitly stated by Collingwood, especially in his pioneer attempt to construct a taxonomy of medieval building styles, to which we must return.

This Royal Society approach has an important quality of novelty when compared with the earlier antiquarianism represented by Leland, and at its best by William Camden, whose approach to antiquities was really basically literary and historical, and for whom local history as displayed in the *Britannia* was very much a matter of genealogy and heraldry. Plot was quite clear about the distinction he was making. 'I intend not to meddle with the *pedigrees* or *descents* either of *families* or *lands*' he wrote in 1686 'it being indeed my Designe . . . to omit, as much as may be, both *persons* and *actions*, and chiefly apply my self to *things*; and amongst those too, only of such as are very remote from the present *Age*'.[18] And he was not alone. One of the most significant expressions of the New Antiquarianism was the cooperation of a couple of dozen scholars in a common enterprise which bore fruit in 1695, the editing and enlarging in new terms of Camden's *Britannia* under the direction of Edmund Gibson, later to be Bishop of London and one of the great churchmen of the eighteenth century, but now only just down from Oxford and librarian at Lambeth. It is a striking fact that Gibson could assemble so large and so able a team; he himself was at Queen's College with its 'proluvium of Saxonists' engaged in the study of Old English and of 'Septentrional studies' in general, and with William Nicolson planned things so that not only the south, but the north of Britain was included within his network of correspondents, while Robert Sibbald saw to Scotland and Edward Lhwyd to Wales.[19]

The new field-workers were confronted not only with the obvious ruins of old building in masonry or brick, but with earthworks—banks and ditches, forts and barrows. Recognition and interpretation here was probably easier than for later generations, even if the frame of reference was inevitably military: Civil War earthworks still stood new and raw in the countryside, and a century later Uncle Toby would have looked with understanding and appreciation at the curtains and hornworks of Maiden Castle. The Romans and the Danes were historically attested as builders of forts and camps, but not the Britons, so the two first were the preferred claimants. When Leland had said of the Iron Age fort on Wittenham Clumps that it was 'a castelle in the Britannes tyme' this can hardly have been more than a lucky guess.[20] Barrows were almost universally thought, because of their size, to cover mass burials of those slain in battle rather than a single individual. But non-military earthworks were also still being made: park boundaries and other bank-and-ditch enclosures were everyday occurrences, especially as encoppicement and other new forms of land management increased after the acts of Henry VIII and Elizabeth. To record these antiquities, the antiquaries could employ the practical skills of draughtsman and surveyor which to us today have a professional ring. But in the seventeenth century 'surveying was taught at the Inns of Court, attendance at which formed a normal stage in the education of a gentleman' who would have to manage his own estate in due course. Already in 1621 Robert Burton had written in his *Anatomy of Melancholy* 'What more pleasing studies can there be than the Mathematicks, Theorick or Practick parts? As to survey land, make mapps, models, dials &c., with which I have ever much delighted myself'.[21] Aubrey's plane-table survey of the Avebury stone circles need cause no surprise; Stukeley's background was that of country lawyers, land agents and small gentry, all concerned with land measurement and record.

The discovery of indigenous primitive man in the Americas —uncanonical man, only with the greatest ingenuity to be included among the progeny of Adam or the descendants of Noah—had given European thinkers a profound jolt, and made many think of their own prehistoric forbears. Some, like Arthur Barlowe in 1584, glimpsed the Golden Age among the Virginian Indians: others found Caliban. Most agreed with Thomas Hobbes that primitive peoples 'lived in continual feare, and danger of violent death; And the life of man, solitary, poore, nasty, brutish and shorte'. Aubrey (who knew Hobbes) estimated the Ancient Britons to have been '2 or 3 degrees, I suppose, less savage than the Americans'. But he, with others, used the American Indians as ethnographical parallels. As early as 1612 the poet Samuel Daniel had suggested that the social condition of the early Britons might resemble that of American Indian tribes, and Aubrey seems to have had the same idea when assessing the linear earthworks of Wessex as prehistoric tribal boundaries. He also brilliantly used a New World analogy to explain the formation of a man-made landscape when Edmund Waller asked him whether the then open, turf-covered, downland of Wiltshire had always been clear of woodland. In Jamaica and Virginia, Aubrey replied, the Indians 'did burn down great woods to cultivate the soil', and 'plaines were there made by firing the wood to sowe corne. . . . Who knows but Salisbury plaines, &c., might be made long time ago, after this manner, and for the same reason?' They also talked of the beech-woods on the chalk and Aubrey asked 'In times of yore, when this whole Nation was a Forrest (or Wild) and civilised by the Romanes, why might not the Beeches (being but a Wood and an incumbrance to this ground) be burnt by them, set fire on them on Sarum-plaines, to turn them to Pasturage?'[22] This concept of man's action in clearing original woodland in antiquity was not only new, but hardly appreciated until recent times, when it can be seen how Aubrey anticipated the results of modern palaeo-ecological research.

But we must set this scientific approach against two factors — the appreciation of landscape and 'Nature', and the means of satisfying this by adequate transport. We often forget that many of our emotions concerning the countryside and natural scenery are hardly more than a couple of centuries old, and bound up, from the later eighteenth century at least, with what was then being called 'The Picturesque'.[23] The name gives the quality away: it was countryside that looked, as the Italians had earlier put it, *pittoresco*, in the manner of a painter, and then, of a picture. In painting, landscape had emerged from background to foreground in for instance Patinir or the Breughels, to be developed as a pictorial form by such as Elsheimer and the Brills by around 1600, and then by the giants, Poussin and especially Claude, and in England by topographical artists such as Francis Place (a friend of the antiquary Ralph Thoresby) and Wenceslaus Hollar (the Bohemian emigré who was a friend of Aubrey's and not only illustrated the catalogue of the original Tradescant collection, but the work of Dugdale and other antiquaries). To admire Claude was a demonstration of good taste, and the next step was to look for landscapes that embodied the qualities of his paintings, and so were themselves in good taste, capable of arousing personally and socially desirable and fashionable emotions.

Classical landscapes necessarily included classical ruins, which had to be replaced in Britain by those of the Middle Ages, as we shall see. With ruins went mountains, and in the seventeenth century mountains could arouse passionate dislike, and few found them even tolerable.[24] In 1633 John Donne could ask

> Are these but warts, and pock-holes in the face
> Of th' earth? Thinke so; but yet confesse, in this
> The world's proportion disfigured is.

They were, many thought, an affront to a symmetrically-minded Creator, who, as Thomas Burnett demonstrated later in his widely influential *Sacred Theory of the Earth* (1684), would have called into being a smooth spherical globe. Mountains were emblems of the Fall, ruins and imperfections — 'uncouth, inhospitable, freezing, infruitful, crump-shouldered' wrote Poole in 1657; the Alps, Burnett said 'are plac'd in no Order one with another, that can either respect Use or Beauty . . . there is nothing in Nature more shapeless and ill-figured than an old Rock or Mountain'. And Thomas Hobbes (admittedly describing a natural feature known as The Devil's Arse in the Peak District) had in 1636 reduced mountains to low comedy

> Behind, a ruined mountain does appear
> Swelling into two parts, which turgent are
> As when we bend our bodies to the ground
> The buttocks amply sticking out are found.

Mountains had to wait for new painters and poets, and the later eighteenth century, to make them more respectable than buttocks, more romantic than crump-shouldered, but ruins and antiquities were parts of the picturesque landscape from the first, as they had been in the paintings.

There were of course always those who found an unscientific pleasure in landscape and ruins, and who travelled for the pleasure of looking at ancient monuments rather than, like Celia Fiennes, looking at everything that presented itself. Even if she called the Malvern Hills 'the English Alps', the Lake District for her was no more than 'Desart and barren rocky hills'. John Ray, that great naturalist, liked mountains, and also enjoyed the undramatic downland 'cover'd over with a lovely Carpet of green Grass, and other Herbs, of a Colour not only most grateful and agreeable, but most useful and salutary to the Eye . . . for the Refreshment of our Spirits and our innocent Delight'.[25] This was in 1691, and in the early 1720s the antiquary William Stukeley, whom we shall shortly meet, felt similarly on a Wiltshire hill-top—''Tis a pretty round apex, the turf as soft as velvet. There is the sign of a very old camp cast up on one half of it but unfinished. The air here extremely fragrant . . . the strolling for relaxed minds upon these downs is the most agreeable exercise and amusement in the world . . .' the air 'saluting the nostrils most agreeably and recreating the spirits like taking snuff . . . and all the time upon Nature's tapestry more easy than a plane floor'.[26] William Backhouse of Swallowfield in Berkshire (admittedly an eccentric, believing he knew the secret of the Philosophers' Stone) was a friend of Elias Ashmole and John Aubrey, and the latter recorded in 1696 that 'his custom was, once every Summer, to Travel to see Cathedrals, Abbeys, Castles &c.'.[27] Anthony Wood took a romantic view of such ruins, and at Eynsham in 1657 was 'wonderfully strucken with a veneration of the stately, yet much lamented, ruins of the abbey . . .' and 'spent some time with a melancholy delight in taking a prospect'. The ruins, he said, anticipating as we shall see an emotion of a later century, 'instruct the pensive beholder with an exemplary frailty'.[28] John Aubrey was one of the first to use 'romantic' as an appreciative epithet for landscape: Bagley Wood near Oxford, he wrote to Edmund Halley, 'is a most Romantick place no garden more pleasant and a great variety of plants'.[29] Stukeley as an undergraduate in 1708 'frequently took a walk to sigh over the ruins of Barnwell Abbey . . . lamenting the destruction of so noble monuments of the Piety and Magnificence of our Ancestors'[30] —a sentiment worthy of the heroine of Northanger Abbey.

But in general, to see the countryside as anything more than an unpleasant and uninteresting waste, separating the civilised comforts of one town from another, demanded some degree of improvement in land travel from what were still, before 1650, roads deteriorated from the standards of the Middle Ages, quite inadequate maps, clumsy coaches and unimproved breeds of horses. All the early antiquaries were concerned about the bad quality of the available small-scale county maps, on which roads were only sporadically being marked by the end of the century. Sign-posts were legally required from 1697; the first turnpikes officially date from 1663. But it seems that after the Civil War surplus cavalry horses of an improved type bred in East Anglia now came on the market. These were partly bred from Flemish 'cold-blood' stock which had been imported into England from the Middle Ages onwards, and increasingly as draught animals with the introduction of the first heavy farm wagons from the Low Countries in the sixteenth century, but 'warm-blood' stock was reaching Eastern and Central Europe with the Turkish conquests from the sixteenth century, so that occasional mares of 'oriental' blood came into this country: Cromwell imported six.[31] The development of an improved breed, and its availability in the second half of the seventeenth century, soon raised the standard of the poor breeds, hitherto mostly of pony class, throughout England. A drawing by Aubrey of the 1670s shows him and his friends hawking on the Wiltshire downs with Sir James Long, 'a great falconer and for horseman-ship' (and despite being a Royalist, a friend of Oliver Cromwell, who as we saw was concerned with improving blood-stock). Sir James's mount is a good 'warm-blood' animal contrasting with the three ponies ridden by the others.[32] A gentleman could now ride a horse that engendered a mood for contemplating anti-quities in some comfort and dignity.

William Stukeley, born in 1687, was such an antiquary on horseback, and his life, which we fortunately know in some detail,[33] illustrates to perfection what happened to antiquarian studies as the seventeenth century tradition which I have characterised as that of the Royal Society came to its close, as I suggested, around 1730, to be replaced by something new. Stukeley was educated at Cambridge as a Doctor of Medicine in what was still that tradition; as an undergraduate he collected fossils, botanised with Ray's great Catalogue of Cambridge plants in hand, and knew Isaac Newton. He saw Aubrey's *Monumenta Britannica* MS. around 1718, and was fired by it to visit, and to survey in detail for the first time, the great prehistoric stone circles of Avebury and Stonehenge in Wiltshire and, between 1719 and 1725, to make extensive antiquarian tours on horseback from Portland Bill to Hadrian's Wall. Aubrey had been a good field archaeologist; Stukeley was even better, and no mean topographical draughtsman. But he was better known in his lifetime and for generations to come as the least scientific and most irresponsibly romantic writer on antiquities. What had happened ? There was a turning-point in his life that exactly matched that in the climate of thought at large. He abandoned medicine and was ordained in the Church of England in 1729, and when he published his Avebury and Stonehenge fieldwork in the early 1740s it was strangely interwoven into a very odd religious polemical work.

In 1724 he had in fact published some of his fieldwork (but unfortunately not his best) in objective form, but he reserved Stonehenge and Avebury, reasonably enough, for special treatment, and drafted considerable descriptive passages as early as 1723 which suggest he had in mind a book similar to the *Templa Druidum* chapter of Aubrey's *Monumenta Britannica*, and incorporating comparative material taken from Aubrey's and Lhwyd's MSS. Had he done so we might have had something like Henry Rowlands's *Mona Antiqua Restaurata* of 1723, subtitled 'An Archaeological Discourse of the Antiquities of the Isle of Anglesey'. Rowlands of course could not escape the Druids in an island where they had been specifically placed by Tacitus, and Aubrey had tentatively suggested this prehistoric priesthood as a more likely claimant for the building of stone circles than the other favoured candidates such as Phoenicians, Romans, Saxons or Danes. For Stukeley, Druids moved rapidly from hypothesis to fact, from fact to fantasy. We can chart the changes in his mind in the successive drafts of the projected book just mentioned, starting as the 'History and Temples of the Ancient Celts'; this becomes 'Temples and Religion' and by 1733 'Celts' is ominously replaced by 'Druids'. By 1740–3 his Stonehenge and Avebury books were published as part of a projected seven-volume work on 'Patriarchal Christianity . . . A History of the Origin and Progress of True Religion, and of Idolatry' and were to meet with a warm reception by a new public now looking for just such an approach to prehistoric antiquity.

What had been the New Approach of the Royal Society was by the 1730s failing to satisfy contemporary intellect and emotion. A new 'explanation', in Basil Willey's term, was needed — 'a restatement of something — event, theory, doctrine etc. — in terms of the current interests and assumptions' of the day, satisfying 'because it appeals to that particular set of assumptions, as superseding those of a past age or of a former state of mind'.[34] Now Willey's words were in fact applied to the beginning of the New Science; they apply equally well to what followed its decline. The Royal Society itself was going down hill under the aged Sir Hans Sloane and following him, Martin Folkes. The decline in so many studies at this time has frequently been commented upon: each another 'manifestation of the general lethargy which overtook European science soon after 1700'.[35] The Newtonian mathematics of the universe became an august and sublime realm of knowledge, leaving the mundane enquiries of naturalists, geologists or archaeologists belittled and disregarded. Addison in 1710 felt it to be 'the Mark of a little Genius to be wholly conversant among Insects, Reptiles, Animalcules, and those trifling Rarities that furnish out the Apartment of a Virtuoso'.[36] Parallel with archaeology, the beginnings of palaeontology had developed in the seventeenth century with such as Hooke and Lhwyd, but 'as in other branches of natural science' it has recently been remarked, 'so on the problem of fossils England became an intellectual backwater soon after the beginning of the century'.[37] In geomorphology, 'from 1705 to 1778 there was a period of relapse when the Earth-sciences lay stagnant and forgotten'.[38] The great tradition of Restoration historical studies as is well known, came to an end as the last of its exponents died between 1710 and 1740.[39] On the one hand popularity was now to be accorded to the 'philosophical' and generalising historians and before long to the theorists of social evolution and the 'infancy of society' studied without reference to the evidence of material culture. On the other, the mood was shifting from rational to romantic, from classical calm to barbarian excitement. Though British antiquities were now to become popular, and a part of the country's intellectual and artistic life as never before, they were being seen through very different eyes from those of Aubrey or the young Stukeley.

The architecture of the English Middle Ages had for long been ignored, despised, misunderstood or vituperated. Its internal stylistic sequence from pre-Conquest Romanesque to final Perpendicular was unrecognised, although Aubrey as we saw made a remarkable pioneer effort to arrange architectural details which could be dated by historical documents into a chronological and typological order. Here, in his *Chronologia Architectonica* of the 1670s we see, as Mr Colvin has pointed out, 'the influence of contemporary scientific thought. For its purpose was to classify and compare, and classification and comparison were both features of the new 'experimental philosophy' to which the Royal Society was dedicated'.[40] It was not until 1763 that Warton made the first published historical analysis of English Gothic (in a note to his commentary on Spenser's *Faerie Queene*), and 1817 that Rickman made the definitive classification of styles used in the nineteenth century.

For the late seventeenth and earlier eighteenth century in general, Gothic architecture was a non-classical muddle, and as such unworthy of the Man of Taste. Its unpleasantness could even drive that dull diarist John Evelyn to liveliness when in 1697 he decried the Gothic 'congestions of heavy, dark, melancholy and *Monkish Piles*', with 'slender and misquine *Pillars* . . . ponderous arched Roofs . . . sharp *Angles*, *Jetties*, narrow *Lights*, lame *Statues*, *Lace* and other *Cut-Work* and *Crinkle-Crankle*'.[41] Behind Evelyn lies the Renaissance tradition going back to Vasari's well known outburst against *la maniera Tedesca* in 1550 —'monstrous and barbarous . . . confusion and disorder'; facades on which 'they build a malediction of niches one above another, with no end of pinnacles and points and leaves . . . endless projections and breaks and corbelling and flourishes',[42] and indeed the resemblance is surely not accidental, and Evelyn must have been consciously adapting the earlier diatribe. One could quote similar sentiments from seventeenth and eighteenth century France—Fènelon, Molière and Montesquieu had a low opinion of *le style barbare*. Later, Addison was to take up Evelyn's remarks in a *Spectator* essay, and as late as 1771

Smollett could put into the mouth of Mr Bramble in *Humphrey Clinker* his famous denunciation of York Minster, beginning 'The external appearance of an old cathedral cannot but be displeasing to the eye of every man who has any idea of propriety and proportion' as an expression of an old-fashioned viewpoint.

But by the 1740s Gothic had not only received appreciative attention from many, but had become a fashion. 'A few years ago' wrote a journalist in 1753 'everything was Gothic: our houses, our beds, our book-cases and our couches were all copies from some parts or other of our old cathedrals'.[43] Stukeley was an enthusiastic admirer of Gothic: he seems to have been one of the first in England to make the parallel, again of Renaissance origin, and later to be so popular, between Gothic vaulting and the intersecting branches of a forest glade, and designed some charming ruins as follies, and a notable mock Gothic bridge, in the 1740s. Where ruins did not exist, they could be supplied. At Richmond in 1733 there was a Hermitage 'the Architecture of which is . . . very Gothique, being a Heap of Stones thrown into a very artful Disorder, and curiously embellished with Moss, and Shrubs, to represent *rude Nature*'.[44] And in Lord Bathurst's park at Cirencester, wrote Edward Stephens in 1747:

> A lowly pile with ancient order grac'd
> Stands, half repair'd, and half by Time defac'd,
> Imbrowned with Age, the crusted, mould'ring wall
> Threats the beholder with a sudden fall:
> There fix'd aloft (as whilom us'd) we trace
> Imperfect semblance of the savage race.
> This pile the marks of rolling cen'tries wears
> Sunk to decay—and built scarce twenty years.

It is a famous folly, still extant. Known as Alfred's Hall, it was built between 1721 and 1732, and is reported to have deceived at least one antiquary within a year of its completion.[45] Batty Langley published some very odd Gothic designs from 1742 onwards, Sanderson Miller worked a little later in the same modes, Horace Walpole bought Strawberry Hill in 1747 and had Gothicised it by 1753. To quote Willey again, for an 'explanation' to 'convince us with a sense of its necessary truth, we must be in the condition of needing and desiring that explanation', and the need and desire of the eighteenth century was by now for something that presented the past, and the world in general, not in the objective analytical terms of a scientist, but in more emotive, and if necessary irrational beliefs of Gothick romance and a past full of Noble Savages and mystical Druidry.

Ruins were now very much a part of the landscape, to be seen and appreciated from more than one viewpoint. The idea made popular by Burnett's *Sacred Theory of the Earth* that mountains were the 'ruins of Nature' and emblematic of a broken and imperfect post-Diluvian past was easily transferred to ruined buildings, which could be thought to portray 'the triumph of time over human endeavour'. As Michael Sadleir put it, 'a mouldering building is a parable of the victory of nature over man's handiwork. The grass growing rankly in a once stately courtyard, the ivy creeping over the broken tracery of a once sumptuous window, the glimpse of sky through the fallen roof of a once proud banqueting hall—sights such as these moved to melancholy pleasure minds which dwelt gladly on the impermanence of human life and effort'. Indeed this could be seen in political terms as well, where the ruin becomes a symbol of time's destruction of ancient autocratic power, with the crumbling abbey or decaying castle standing for freedom from the corrupt oppression by monks or barons. 'Creepers and weeds, as year by year they riot over sill and paving-stone, defy a broken despotism; every coping-stone which crashes from a castle battlement into the undergrowth beneath is a small victory for liberty, a snap of the fingers in the face of autocratic power'.[46] Writing of the picturesque qualities of the ruins of abbeys and castles in 1794, Sir Uvedale Price put it charmingly—'The ruins of these once magnificent edifices are the pride and boast of this island; we may well be proud of them, not merely in a picturesque point of view—we may glory that the abodes of tyranny and superstition are in ruin'.[47]

Though Claude and Poussin were not forgotten, the seventeenth century painter Salvator Rosa, with his more exciting romantic vision, came into fashion, and desirable rural scenes comprised

> Whate'er Lorraine light-touched with softening hue
>
> Or savage Rosa dashed, or learned Poussin drew

as Thomson wrote in 1748. New topographical painters appeared in England to influence the public taste in landscape and antiquities, such as Paul and Thomas Sandby, the former as a young man a draughtsman on the Highland Survey directed by General

William Roy in 1747–55; Roy who was to make a most notable study of Roman military antiquities in North Britain.[48] The brothers Buck were touring and publishing their illustrated books of *Antiquities* with romantic (and amateurish) engraved views of ruined abbeys and castles, now such popular objects of the countryside, from the 1720s to the 40s. But the non-romantic approach did not wholly disappear, and Gilbert White's famous *Natural History of Selbourne* of 1789 deserves mention here, because it seems to be, not a product of the new trends which we shall see were emerging at the end of the century, but a legacy of the seventeenth century approach of Aubrey or Plot. As White put it, a parochial history 'ought to consist of natural productions and occurrences as well as antiquities' and accordingly his delightful book begins with topography and fossils, and goes by birds and migrations, salads, leprosy and echoes, to Roman coin hoards and an appendix of medieval documents. White liked landscape and his enthusiasm magnified the distant horizon into 'the vast range of mountains called *The Sussex Downs* . . . which altogether . . . form a noble and extensive outline'. Sir John Sinclair's first *Statistical Account of Scotland* (1791–9) was based on a questionnaire very much in the seventeenth century manner, and of course included antiquities.

Prehistoric antiquities, especially stone circles and ruined chambered tombs, were certainly moving into a favoured position of what has been called 'soft' rather than 'hard' primitivism. The Ancient Britons were seen, as through the later Stukeley's eyes, as Noble Savages, and with Hurons, Hottentots and the like were discovered to have shared the virtues of primaeval innocence—

Nor think in Nature's state they blindly trod,
The State of Nature was the reign of God

wrote Pope in 1733. From this advantageous standpoint they could be seen, together with Stukeley's Druids, as upholders of a British *resistance* against Imperial Rome, as they indeed appear in Thomson's and Collins's *Odes* to Liberty of 1735 and 1747, while Cowper's famous *Boadicea* poem was to come in 1782. 'Britons never will be slaves'—it is worth remembering that *Rule Britannia* first appeared in an antiquarian context, in a masque on King Alfred by Thomson and Mallet in 1740.

And all this was enhanced by what seemed to be the discovery of real Noble Savages, this time the inhabitants of the South Sea Islands, from the 1760s, where a romantic mood was to endure to Gauguin and beyond. Supporting this and supported by it, the home-grown product in British antiquity was found even more convincing, with Gray's *Bard* of 1758, the inventions of Macpherson in the early 1760s, and later the forgeries of Iolo Morganwg, who grafted bogus Druidry on to the genuine if moribund Welsh Eisteddfod in 1819. Side by side with this, Stukleian Druids were blended with the Welsh nonsense of Rowland Jones and William Owen Pughe, and the crazy mythology of Jacob Bryant, by William Blake when writing his Prophetic Books from 1797 to 1804.[49]

Mountains came into favour with ruins and Druids: after all, Druids and their stone monuments were rather a mountainous phenomenon. As early as 1691 John Ray had replied to Burnett's *Sacred Theory*, objecting to the idea that the irregularities of the earth's surface should be thought merely as imperfections: he found landscape 'a beautiful and pleasant object', as we saw, 'affording pleasant and delightful prospects' of mountains and valleys. 'That the Mountains are pleasant Objects to behold, appears that in the very Images of them, their Draughts and Landskips, are so much esteemed'. Stukeley characteristically showed an early appreciation of the Lake District. 'When one stands at the end of these lakes' he wrote in 1725 'the prospect is exceedingly delightful; the mountains on each side rising to a great height, one behind the other the whole length and broke off into short ones, like scenes at a playhouse: nor need a painter go to Italy for variety and gradeur of prospects'. And by the second half of the eighteenth century we have excitingly moved from Mountain Gloom to Mountain Glory, and Thomas Gray, having visited the Scottish Highlands in 1765, writes 'the mountains are ecstatic, and ought to be visited in pilgrimage once a year. None but these monstrous creatures of God know how to join so much beauty with so much horror'.[50]

To descend from the sublime to the practical, we must here think once again of roads and transport. 'All over England' wrote Christopher Hussey of this period, 'the appreciation of scenery, the experiencing of romantic emotions, and the perception of the sublime in nature increased in direct ratio to the number of turnpike acts' for improving the English road system: these had increased by almost five times between 1750 and 1790.

13. *The Queen of Otaheite taking leave of Captain Wallis, 1768.*

And not only roads, but improved and larger scale maps with roads marked on them (and as we shall see, antiquities taken note of), road books and means of transport. As we saw, 'Arab' mares had been sporadically imported for a long time, but the famous stallions, the Darley Arabian, Byerley Turk and Godolphin Barb, came in early in the eighteenth century, up to 1730. Thenceforward half-blood stock was becoming available for hunters and hackneys and for such renowned strains as the Cleveland Bay and the Yorkshire Coach Horse. Although some exceptional performances are recorded in the seventeenth century, such as the 'flying coach' instituted by Dr Fell as Vice-Chancellor of Oxford in 1669, which in summer left All Souls at 6.0 a.m. and arrived in London at 7.0 in the evening, travel was normally very slow, and services very infrequent. At the beginning of the eighteenth century 'the only regular carriage between Oxford and Bath was by a carrier once a fortnight; the same to Birmingham and to Reading: to Shrewsbury once a month; to Exeter once in five weeks; and to Westmorland thrice a year'. By about 1760 the London-Oxford coach ran three times a week, taking two days in winter and one in summer; by the early nineteenth century the journey was done 'with ease and safety' in under seven hours.[51] Coaches and carriages improved with new developments in technology, especially in steel springs, and so did the road surfaces that made lighter and faster vehicles possible, and English coach-builders outstripped the Continent. The Tour in search of the Picturesque, inevitably including antiquities, could now become comfortable, popular and widespread. Tours were made, written up and published. 'Tour writing is the very rage of the times' wrote John Byng, later Viscount Torrington, whose tours in fact remained in manuscript until the 1930s. For his 'Tour to the West' of 1781 Byng provided a title-page in which one looks on to an open landscape through crumbling arches and mouldering vaulting, for all the world like Bentley's fantastic illustration to Gray's *Elegy* of half a century earlier, but on his travels he visits Rollright, Maiden Castle and the Plas Newydd megaliths in Anglesey, for which he makes a strangely modern plea for preservation. The country-house visitor now looked not only for architecture, but for atmosphere. The first Duchess of Northumberland around 1760 carried with her a questionnaire of 150 items, one of which was 'Is the place chearful melancholy romantic wild or dreary?'—and incidentally strikes a very modern note with another query: 'Is there a menagerie?'[52]

With the Tour comes a new development, again with a modern ring, that of antiquarian journalism and the production of handsomely illustrated books of landscapes and ruins—'Tea-table Books' perhaps, with Allan Ramsay's *Tea-Table Miscellany* of the 1720s in mind. These themselves were made possible by the new technologies in book production and illustrating such as aquatinting, first extensively used in this country by Paul Sandby, and later lithography, introduced from Germany by Rudolph Ackermann. He, incidentally, engaged an amusing reprobate, William Coombe, to write verses round a set of drawings by Rowlandson satirising the Tour Industry, where *Dr Syntax In Search of The Picturesque* (1812) says

> I'll read and *write*, and *sketch* and *print*
> And thus create a real *mint*;
> I'll *prose* it here, I'll *verse* it there
> And *picturesque* it everywhere . . .
> With ev'ry other leaf a print
> Of some fine view in *aqua-tint* . . .
> I will allow it is but trash,
> But then it furnishes the cash.

The brothers Buck had led the way, and were now followed by others such as that obese and rather raffish character Francis Grose, the 'Antiquarian Falstaff' and friend of Robert Burns, with his *Antiquities of England and Wales*, and of *Scotland*, between 1773 and 1791; Britton and Brayley published endless *Beauties* and *Antiquities* from 1801 onwards. Not only minor artists undertook antiquarian illustration, as is witnessed by John Sell Cotman's drawings of Norfolk churches, 1811–39, and of Normandy, 1822: Constable's great watercolour of Stonehenge is the culmination of the Romantic iconography of the monument. And side by side with this antiquarian popularisation, and partly stimulated by it, a new reading public was created, encouraging a New Topography, and regional or county histories at a new standard, after the decline of the previous decades. We saw how Gilbert White revived the Royal Society approach in his *Selbourne*, and his correspondent Thomas Pennant was one of the new generation of naturalists and topographers. In such folio volumes as James Douglas's *Nenia Britannica* of 1793, which published the finds from pagan

Saxon cemeteries in Kent in five-shilling numbers to ensure popular sale, or Sir Richard Colt Hoare's *Ancient Wiltshire*, with its proud epigraph 'We speak from facts, not theory' and appearing between 1812 and 1821, we have the first major publications taking the form of a non-romantic, newly objective presentation of the evidence from excavations or field survey. Others took up the task: the brothers Lysons produced pioneer county surveys—the *Magna Britannia*—from 1806 to 1822, and a Romano-British corpus in 1801–17 with outstanding coloured illustrations of mosaic pavements.

In tune with this revived empirical approach to antiquities in the countryside, ruins were being set into the landscape by the map-makers in a manner which would have delighted the topographers of the seventeenth century who had grumbled at the standards of contemporary cartography. Plot had taken great trouble over his Staffordshire and Oxfordshire maps, with a special grid superimposed on the former (of 1686) to assist location of places. Lea's atlas of county maps of 1689 was based on Saxton but had main roads added as an innovation; the 1695 *Britannia* has new maps by Robert Morden, either revised from extant sheets or from original surveys. The exigencies of politics and war had led to a demand for new standards of accuracy at larger scales, and here the Scottish Survey at two inches to the mile, of 1747–55 and under the direction of William Roy, marks a new departure. We saw that Paul Sandby was as a youth employed on this work, and Roy was later to write 'though at that early period, the study of Antiquity was but little the object of the young people employed in that service, yet it was not wholly neglected', and General Melville in 1754 was told by one of the surveyors, à propos of Roman forts, that 'he had been very desirous, according to directions received, to observe and delineate all traces whatever of intrenchments, or other military works'. A special survey of the Antonine Wall was made in the following year.

General Roy moved to his distinguished career as Director General of the Ordnance Survey, whose maps from the beginning of the nineteenth century set new standards. Colt Hoare employed Philip Crocker, a young Ordnance surveyor, as his archaeological draughtsman, part-time from 1805 and wholly in his employment from 1811. Hoare was requested to check the archaeological entries on the Wiltshire one-inch sheets pub-

14. *Stonehenge, watercolour by Constable, after 1830 (detail).*

lished from 1811 onwards, and writing to Daniel Lysons in 1819 he warns him that the plans of ancient earthworks on the Devon and Cornwall Ordnance sheets are not to be trusted—'the government engineers attended very little to antiquities for Col. Mudge was very much obliged to us for our notes on Wilts.' (Mudge was Director General 1798–1820.) Hoare also corrected the archaeology on William Faden's second (1810) edition of Andrews' and Dury's privately produced map of Wiltshire, first published in 1773. It was a good map and attention was paid to archaeological detail from the first: at the hill fort of Ogbury for instance, the original map shows greater relevant detail than does Crocker's plan of the site in *Ancient Wiltshire*.[53]

We have in fact two parallel strands of antiquarianism, the revived empiricism taking up the seventeenth century mood, and the new romanticism which was now flourishing after its tentative start in the 1740s. In such a context, no study, however brief, of early nineteenth century antiquarianism can ignore Scott: no sensible or sensitive man would want to. We may recall first that Scott made his initial impact with his poems, not his novels, and that these began with collection adaptation and imitation of traditional poetry published as *The Border Minstrelsey* in 1802. With all its instantaneous appeal, this came late in an established genre of literary scholarship. Macpherson's Ossianic compositions of 1762–3 had prompted Percy to publish his *Reliques of Ancient English Poetry* in 1765, and he encouraged Evan Evans to print early Welsh poems in the next year; these were amplified by others such as Edward Jones in 1784, while Charlotte Brookes produced her *Reliques of Irish Poetry* in 1789. John Pinkerton collected (and fabricated) Scottish traditional verse, publishing in 1783 and 1786: *The Border Minstrelsey* of a dozen years later falls naturally into place as filling a gap in the collection of regional vernacular poetry in the British Isles.

Scott had chosen between the two streams of antiquarianism and naturally opted for the romantic. The old-fashioned, would-be scholarly antiquarian recording real or imaginary Roman camps was beautifully ridiculed in *The Antiquary* of 1815, the main character being in part based on stories of Sir John Clerk of Penicuik, who was a friend of Stukeley's.[54] But Scott was not uninfluenced by the new school of Scottish academic sociologists who turned to an idealised barbarian past for the first and finest poetry, as to the age of Homer. The 'hunters and shepherds' of 'the deserts and the wild' were the repositories of such poetry, and Scott saw his ballad-collecting in this light: remembering the link between antiquarianism and transport, it is fascinating to note that when he first visited the deserts and wilds of Liddesdale, his coach was the first wheeled vehicle to have been seen there. In his approach to antiquity he directed attention, in the manner of the topographers, to local and visual source material; abbeys, castles and ancient towns as well as ballads and folk tales, the immediate and tangible relics of the past. His influence was wide and diverse, here and abroad, and Trevor-Roper has shown how both Macaulay and Niebuhr, to mention no others, owed a debt to him.[55]

Now, on the eve of Victoria's reign, we leave antiquarianism as it becomes archaeology. The approach to medieval architecture was to be revolutionised by the Tractarians and even more by the Cambridge Camden Society; historical disciplines were being re-shaped into a recognisably modern form. Prehistory was soon to be allied to geology, by now already scientifically respectable and commercially necessary. Intensive study of what had started as amateur natural history 'had turned that genial pursuit into the sciences of geology, biology, palaeontology, zoology'[56] and others: the British Association for the Advancement of Science had been founded in 1831 at the instance of the geologists. Simultaneously came Lyell's 'final breaking of the time-barrier'[57] as a new model of the ancient human past was being envisaged, with the descent of man through remote prehistoric eras. The two worlds of antiquarianism and archaeology were symbolised at a meeting of the Royal Society of Edinburgh in the early 1820s with Sir Walter Scott as President in the chair, when an undergraduate of the University was taken as a guest. The young man remembered the incident in later life when he was himself elected a Fellow: he was Charles Darwin.[58]

NOTES

1 John Aubrey, *Natural History of Wiltshire*, ed. J. Britton, 1847; repr. 1969, opening of Preface. The phrase in brackets is a footnote in the original. Cf. Aubrey's comments on John Wilkins, *Lives*, ed. A. Clark, II, Oxford 1898, 301; No. 1 above.

2 M. Hunter, *Antiq.* LXV, 1971, 113, 187. Cf., too, his *John Aubrey and the realm of learning*, London 1975. For the intellectual background, C. Webster, *The Great Instauration*, London 1975.

3 C. Raven, *John Ray, naturalist*, Cambridge 1942.

4 D. E. L. Haynes, *The Arundel Marbles*, Oxford 1975; M. Allan, *The Tradescants: their plants, gardens and museum*, London 1964; C. H. Josten, *Elias Ashmole* I, Oxford 1966. Despite Josten, it seems difficult to regard Ashmole's action as wholly disingenuous.

5 For early collections, D. Murray, *Museums, their history and their use* I, Glasgow 1904; M. T. Hodgen, *Early Anthropology in the sixteenth and seventeenth centuries*, Philadelphia 1964, Chap. IV.

6 Olaus Wormius, *Musaeum Wormianum seu Historia rerum rariorum . . . quae Hafniae Danorum in aedibus Authoris servantur*, Leyden 1655.

7 Nehemiah Grew, *Musaeum Regalis Societatis or a Catalogue and Description of the Natural and Artificial Rarities Belonging to the Royal Society and preserved at Gresham Colledge*, London 1681.

8 John Evelyn, *Diary*, 17 October 1671; R. Burton, *Anatomy of Melancholy*, London 1621, Pt. 2, Sect. 2, Memb. 4.

9 John Tradescant, *Musaeum Tradescantianum or a collection of rarities preserved at South-Lambeth near London*, London 1656.

10 Ralph Thoresby, *Ducatus Leodiensis*, London 1715, contains a catalogue of the collection.

11 John Evelyn, *Diary*, 3 February 1644.

12 John Aubrey, *Lives*, ed. A. Clark, I, 36; S. Piggott, *William Stukeley: an eighteenth century antiquary*, Oxford 1950, 21.

13 For the parochial questionnaires, S. Piggott, op. cit., 11-13; for Machell, J. E. Ewbank, *Antiquary on horseback*, Kendall 1963.

14 There is a biographical note prefaced to the second edition of Robert Plot, *Natural History of Oxfordshire*, London 1705.

15 R. T. Gunter, *Early Science in Oxford XIV: Life and Letters of Edward Lhwyd*, Oxford 1945; G. Daniel, *Welsh History Review* III, 1967, 345; F. Emery, *Edward Lhuyd FRS, 1660-1709*, Cardiff 1971; Cf. No. VII below.

16 M. J. S. Rudwick, *The Meaning of Fossils*, London 1972.

17 R. G. Collingwood, *The Idea of History*, Oxford 1946, 12.

18 R. Plot, *Natural History of Staffordshire*, Oxford 1686, 392.

19 S. Piggott, *Proc. Brit. Acad.* XXXVII, 1951, 199. F. Emery, *Antiq.* XXXII, 1958, 179; No. III above.

20 *English Place Name Soc. Berkshire* II, Cambridge 1974, 428.

21 H. F. Kearney in C. Webster (ed.), *The Intellectual Revolution of the Seventeenth Century*, London 1974, 230; R. Burton, *Anatomy of Melancholy*, London 1621, Pt. 2, Sect. 2, Memb. 4.

22 John Aubrey, *Natural History of Wiltshire*, ed. J. Britton, London

1847, 10; *Observations*, in *Three Prose Works of John Aubrey*, ed.
J. Buchanan-Brown, Fontwell 1972, 313. Cf. No. 1 above.

23 C. Hussey, *The Picturesque*, London 1927, still holds the ground.

24 M. H. Nicolson, *Mountain Gloom and Mountain Glory*, Cornell
   1959, for comment and quotation.

25 Nicolson, op. cit., 261.

26 S. Piggott, *William Stukeley*, 182.

27 John Aubrey, *Miscellanies*, 1696, in J. Buchanan-Brown, op. cit.,
   80; C. H. Josten, *Elias Ashmole*, 76.

28 A. Wood, 16 September 1657; *Life and Times of Anthony a
   Wood*, ed. Llewelyn Powys, Oxford 1961, 77.

29 J. Buchanan-Brown, op. cit., 361.

30 S. Piggott, *William Stukeley*, 25. Cf. M. Aston, *Journ. Warburg
   & Court. Insts.* XXXVI, 1973, 231.

31 Cf. E. Moir, *The Discovery of Britain: the English Tourists*,
   London 1964; W. Gilbey, *The Great Horse* (2nd ed.), London
   1899; W. Ridgeway, *Origin and Influence of the Thoroughbred
   Horse*, Cambridge 1905; A. A. Dent and D. M. Goodall, *The
   Foals of Epona*, London 1962; J. G. Jenkins, *The English Farm
   Wagon*, Reading 1961; S. Bökönyi, *History of Domestic Mammals
   in Central and Eastern Europe*, Budapest 1974.

32 A. Powell, *John Aubrey and his Friends*, London 1948, 81, 262.

33 S. Piggott, *William Stukeley*, 1950; *The Druids*, London 1968.

34 B. Willey, *The Seventeenth Century Background*, Cambridge
   1934, Chap. I, i.

35 G. L. Davies, *The Earth in Decay: a history of British geomorphology*, London n.d. (*c.* 1969), 95.

36 M. 'Espinasse in C. Webster (ed.), *The Intellectual Revolution* . . .
   London 1974, 347.

37 C. Raven, *John Ray*, 1942, 87.

38 G. L. Davies, op. cit., 95.

39 D. C. Douglas, *English Scholars*, London 1939, is the classic
   study.

40 H. M. Colvin in J. Summerson (ed.), *Concerning Architecture* . . .,
   London 1968, 1; cf. T. H. Cocke, *Journ. Brit. Arch. Ass.* 3rd S.
   XXXII, 1973, 72.

41 J. Evelyn, *Account of Architects and Architecture* 1697, quoted by
   A. O. Lovejoy, *Med. Lang. Notes* XXVII, 1932, 414, reprinted in
   Essays in the History of Ideas, Johns Hopkins 1948, repr. 1960,
   137.

42 G. Vasari, *Lives* . . ., Introduction, I.3.

43 William Whitehead in *The World* no. 12, 1753, quoted by Lovejoy, op. cit., 145.

44 R. A. Aubin, *Studies in Philology* (Univ. N. Carolina) XXXI, 1934,
   408, quoting *Flowers of Parnassus*, 1736, 82; for the hermitage
   and gardens, P. Willis, 'Charles Bridgeman: the Royal gardens', in
   P. Willis (ed.), *Furor Hortensis*, Edinburgh 1974, 41; Pl. 15b.

45 Edward Stephens, 'On Lord Bathurst's Park and Wood', 1747,
   quoted by R. A. Aubin, *Topographical Poetry in Eighteenth Century England*, New York 1936, 134; Barbara Jones, *Follies and*

Grottoes (Second Ed.), 1974, 31; No. VIII below.

46 M. Sadleir, '"All horrid ?": Jane Austen and the Gothic Romance', in *Things Past*, London 1944, 176.

47 Sir Uvedale Price, *An Essay on the Picturesque*: Chapter 'On Architecture and Buildings', Hereford 1794.

48 G. Macdonald, *Arch.* LXVIII, 1917, 161; No. VII below.

49 S. Piggott, *The Druids*, London 1968, Chap. IV.

50 Ray, quoted in M. Nicolson, op. cit., 261; Stukeley, *Itinerarium Curiosum*, London 1776, 48, quoted in S. Piggott, *William Stukeley*, 1950, 79; Gray to Mason, 1765, quoted in Nicolson, op. cit., 357.

51 Anthony Wood, 26 April 1669; Ll. Powys, op. cit., 179; Philip Bliss (writing in 1857), P. Bliss (ed.), *Reliquae Hearnianae*, 2nd ed., London 1869, II, 216.

52 S. Piggott, *Antiq.* XI, 1937, 33; W. Percy and G. Jackson-Stops, *Country Life*, 7 February 1974, 250.

53 L. Hawes, *Constable's Stonehenge* (Victoria & Albert Mus.), 1975; R. Jessup, *Man of many talents . . . James Douglas 1753-1819*, London 1975; G. Macdonald, loc. cit.; C. Close, *Early Years of Ordnance Survey* (ed. J. B. Harley), Newton Abbot 1969, 69; K. Woodbridge, *Landscape and Antiquity*, Oxford 1970; ibid., *Wilts. Arch. & N. H. Soc. Bulletin* X, March 1971, 2; R. H. Cunnington, *From antiquary to archaeologist*, Princes Risborough 1975; O. G. S. Crawford, *Archaeology in the Field*, London 1953, 39; *Andrews' and Dury's Map of Wiltshire 1773* (Intro. E. Crittall), Devizes 1952.

54 I. G. Brown, *Antiq.* XLVIII, 1974, 283; No. VII below.

55 H. Trevor-Roper, *The Romantic Movement and the Study of History* (John Coffin Memorial Lecture), London 1969.

56 C. C. Gillispie, *Genesis and Geology*, Harvard 1951, repr. 1959, 159.

57 S. Toulmin and J. Goodfield, *The Discovery of Time*, 1965; Penguin Books 1967, 209.

58 W. Irvine, *Apes, Angels and Victorians*, New York 1955, repr. 1959, 158.

VII.

THE ANCESTORS OF
JONATHAN
OLDBUCK

'Sir Walter Scott', Andrew Lang once remarked, 'entered literature through the ruined gateway of archaeology'. The influence
of Scott's poetry, and of the Waverley Novels, upon the growing
antiquarian and romantic taste of the early nineteenth century is
a commonplace which needs no enlargement here, but it should
have a particular interest to us as Fellows of the Society of Antiquaries of Scotland, founded for the study of Scottish antiquities
when young Walter was nine years old, and to which he was
elected in 1796. That one of his novels should be called *The Antiquary*, published in 1816, is no mere chance, and in Jonathan
Oldbuck of Monkbarns, who plays the title-role, Scott produced
a character whom he acknowledged as in part a humorous caricature of himself. I should like here to direct your attention to
The Antiquary's, and The Shirra's, archaeological ancestors:
what was the climate of antiquarian thought in which Scott had
been brought up and how it is reflected in his work? I do not
promise anything new in this brief enquiry, but there are points
of interest which may not have been brought together before.

It is, I think, now generally recognised that, great though
Scott's contribution to the romantic and antiquarian movements
in art and literature was, it was less an innovation than a brilliantly successful popularisation of ideas and moods of thought
that had been current for some time. Romantic and antiquarian:
the two are inseparable in Scott, and remained so well into the
later nineteenth century, but when we look further back we find
the partnership not always so firmly established. In fact I hope

133

to show that in Scott's antiquarian background there were two main tendencies of thought, of which one was more susceptible than the other to romantic heightening. One of the spells cast by the Wizard of the North was the closer fusion of romance and antiquarianism into a single emotional experience, at first individual and personal to himself but quickly transmitted by his writing to an ever-widening circle of excited and delighted readers.

Of these two attitudes of mind to the past, the first was shared by Scotland with English antiquarians, had been current since the middle of the seventeenth century and was flourishing at least to the middle of the eighteenth. This we may call the classical tradition, in which the remains of the Romans in Britain were seen as the last tangible links with the civilised world before the severance brought about by the Gothic Middle Ages; with it too was involved the objective scientific study of natural and artificial phenomena which one associates particularly with the founding of the Royal Society. The second mode of thought, originating by the middle and flourishing in the second half of the eighteenth century, seems distinctively Scottish in origin, having its genesis in the philosophical speculations on the origins and development of man, language and society associated with what have been called the Scottish Primitivists, and involving in its speculations the question of the antiquity of vernacular epic poetry. To these one must add of course the less precisely defined but nevertheless powerful interest in monumental field antiquities, were they megaliths or castles or monastic ruins, developing in England in partial response to the improvement of roads under the Turnpike Acts and in Scotland with the new impetus given to travel after the '45 by political settlement and Wade's road system, and all stimulated by that nascent Romanticism that Scott was to foster and encourage.

Before examining these trends of thought, let us look at *The Antiquary* himself for a moment. Scott claimed to have incorporated in Jonathan Oldbuck's quirks and eccentricities certain characteristics of George Constable of Wallace-Craigie, John Ramsay of Ochtertyre and of Sir John Clerk of Penicuik. The last-named, as we shall see, has indeed the best claim of any save Scott himself as a partial prototype, and the best-known incident in the novel, the scene at the alleged Praetorium of the Kaim of Kinprunes, was based almost verbatim on an irreverent family legend of Baron Clerk retailed to Scott by his grandson, John Clerk of Eldin. But Sir Walter enjoyed seeing himself as The Antiquary, and to the unfinished catalogue of the Abbotsford Museum gave the characteristic title of *Reliquiae Trottcosianae, or the Gabions of the late Jonathan Oldbuck Esq.*

As a Scottish representative of the late seventeenth century approach to the past, at once classical and scientific, Robert Sibbald seems to stand alone, but his well documented life and his numerous publications combine to give us a convincing picture of an unusual character. Born in Edinburgh in 1641 and educated at the High School and the University, he was at first destined by his family for divinity, but the contemporary religious dissensions, and the individual protagonists, 'gave me' as he later wrote 'ane disgust of them . . . and I preferred a quiet life, wherein I might not be ingadged in factions of Church or State'. He therefore persuaded his parents to send him to study medicine at Leyden, where in 1660 he was a fellow first-year student with Niels Stensen, the expatriate Dane who was to become Professor of Anatomy at Padua, and under the name of Nicolaus Steno to make distinguished contributions not only to anatomy, but above all to the proper understanding of fossils and geological stratigraphy. Sibbald went on from Leyden to Paris, and after a short stay in London returned to Edinburgh where with Dr Andrew Balfour he created the first Physic Garden (on the site of Waverley Station) in 1667. His career as a doctor flourished; in 1682 he was appointed Physician and Geographer in Scotland to Charles 11, and was knighted, and two years later was made first President of the Royal College of Physicians in Edinburgh, and first Professor of Physic in the University.

From this time on he published extensively on Scottish natural history and antiquities despite an interruption to his career occasioned by a sudden and sentimental conversion to the Roman Church in 1685 which necessitated his removal to London. But his flirtation with the Scarlet Woman lasted no more than a year (during which he was made Fellow of the College of Physicians in London and met scholars such as Robert Boyle, and Walter Charleton who had written a book on Stonehenge in 1663[1]), and he returned to Edinburgh and the Reformed Church. His reputation as the leading Scottish antiquary was recognised by Edmund Gibson's inclusion of him in the team of

15. *Charles Townley with his classical antiques.*

scholars he was organising to prepare the great new edition of Camden's *Britannia* in 1695 — John Aubrey and Robert Plot, Samuel Pepys and Edward Lhwyd, and a couple of dozen more. Lhwyd was to meet Sibbald in 1699 and see his museum, presented to the University and mainly botanical but containing antiquities, coins and Roman inscriptions, and also his library. His publications, increasingly antiquarian rather than on natural history, continued until 1711, and he died eleven years later at the age of 81.[2]

In many ways, Sibbald illustrates the intellectual affiliations of Restoration antiquarianism to perfection. As a medical man using a scientific training to approach antiquities he recalls Sir Thomas Browne, or in a later generation, William Stukeley; in his personal involvement in botanic gardens and the formation of natural history and antiquarian Cabinets of Rarities he comes into the main stream of such activities on the Continent and Britain, from Mercati and Aldrovandi in sixteenth-century Italy to Tradescant and Thoresby in contemporary England. Although never a Fellow of the Royal Society, his qualifications and intellectual temper were appropriately those of the early fellowship, including a distaste for and avoidance of religious and political controversy and dogmatism in a difficult age. But Scotland was a kingdom separated from England and London not only by the constitution but by intolerable difficulties of travel and transport: personal contact and discussion was at the core of the Society's activities, and this demanded residence in or near London. In his attitude to the monuments of the Roman Occupation of Britain, with which he was keenly concerned, Sibbald like Camden before him, and like his younger contemporary in Scottish antiquarian studies, Sir John Clerk of Penicuik (1676–1755), saw them as links with the world of civilised classical antiquity unfortunately severed by the barbarians of later, darker, ages: Goths for Sir John but hardly for Sir Robert, who followed George Buchanan in regarding the Picts as of Gothic descent. In preparing his main book, the *Scotia Illustrata* of 1684, Sibbald distributed a questionnaire in the manner of Plot and the other writers of 'Natural Histories' in England at the time. His sub-title was *Prodromus Historiae Naturalis* . . . and one wonders whether he was making a learned Scottish play on the word *prodromus*, in its two senses of not only an introductory treatise, but also of a wind from the nor'-nor'-east.

Just about half of his thirty published works are in Latin, which would have been old-fashioned in England (and indeed contrary to the Royal Society campaign for plain English) but less so in the traditional world of learning to which Sibbald and Scotland owed allegiance.

So far as prehistoric antiquities were concerned, Sibbald was prepared to accept Scottish hill forts as native constructions before or at the time of the Roman campaigns, but he regarded the prehistoric bronzes he published (including an important and otherwise unrecorded Late Bronze Age hoard from Fife) as Roman, in common with most antiquaries of the day, such as Plot. He also published as Roman four Anglo-Saxon cinerary urns, making the same mistake as did the author of *Hydriotaphia*; Sibbald's illustrations are tantalisingly described as of 'Urnarum *Romanorum* repertarum in *Britannia* boreali' but must represent an unknown pagan Saxon cemetery somewhere in North Britain, and probably in Scotland.[3]

With flint arrowheads he leads us into a curious set of circumstances peculiar to the Scotland of the day. The question they posed to scholars from the sixteenth century was, as is well known, whether they were to be regarded as natural 'formed stones' or human artifacts, and by the end of the seventeenth century the English antiquaries on the whole had accepted them as the latter, largely by recognising ethnographical parallels from North America, as had Dugdale with stone axes in 1656 and Plot with arrow-heads thirty years later. But in Scotland another explanation was widely favoured by, Lhwyd noted when he visited Sir Robert in 1699, 'the most curious, as well the vulgar', that they were made by the fairies, and as 'Elf-bolts' shot by them or by their agents, the witches, to injure men and beasts. The learned and Reverend Robert Kirk of Aberfoyle had in 1691 written what one can only call an anthropological study of the fairy realm regarded as an important system of organisms, supernatural and yet, within the Great Chain of Being, natural, and meriting description like any other corpus of phenomena examined by the Royal Society. He was fully aware of how his parishioners would 'sene or hallow themselves, their corns and cattell from the shots and stealth of these wandring Tribes' of fairies, 'to save them from these arrowes that fly in the dark', and, as he wrote to Robert Boyle, 'I have had Barbed arrow-heads of yellow flint, that could not be cut so

smal and neat, of so brittle a substance, by all the art of Man'.[4]
Sibbald (who must have been one of the 'most curious' who
believed this) was torn between European science and Scottish
superstition. He catalogued an arrow-head in his own Cabinet
of Rarities under 'Regular Stones' and referred to 'Elf-arrows'
in the entry; in 1684 and again in 1710 he repeats in Latin the
legends of their fairy origins, calling them *sagittae lamiarum*,
with its sinister undertones of the use of *lamia* not only for elves
but witches.[5] Sir Robert had been 21 when the trial for witch-
craft of Isobel Gowdie of Auldearne took place, when she confessed not only to 'spanging' elf-bolts at a gentleman (and fortunately missing him) but to having seen them being made by
the Devil in the fairy-land she visited under the Downie Hills.[6]
Surprisingly Sibbald's arrow-heads and stone axes seem to have
been the first Lhwyd encountered—he had never seen them in
Wales, he wrote to Richard Richardson, and did they occur in
England? He instantly identified them for what they were,
quoting Amerindian parallels, but there is no mention of Plot's
statement of a dozen years before. Lhwyd, we may remember,
very much disliked his chief in the Ashmolean. As for fairy bolts
dropping out of the air, 'for my part I must crave leave to sus-
pend my faith, untill I see one of them descend'. And presumably he had to be tactful in Scotland about Druidic Snake-
Beads: 'not onely ye vulgar but even gentlemen of good education are full persuaded ye snakes make these stones . . . though
they are as plain glass as any in a bottle'. At all events he
appreciated Sir Robert's hospitality and conversation. 'He is'
he wrote to Martin Lister 'a gentleman no less obliging and
communicative than learned and curious; has a tolerable collection of natural curiosities and a library of 8,000 volumes'.

But one of the most significant and endearing personalities
among the early eighteenth century antiquaries in Scotland is
Sir John Clerk of Penicuik, Baron of the Exchequer.[7] Sir John,
born in 1676, started his education at Glasgow University and
continued it in what he, like Sibbald, found a more congenial
atmosphere in the University of Leyden, where he studied
jurisprudence and attended lectures on classical antiquities by
Voorbrock and Gronovius, took drawing lessons, became a com-
petent musician and formed a friendship with Boerhaave, the
distinguished physician. Sir John indeed seems to have introduced him to porridge: perhaps tactfully he described it as

nutrimentum divinum. From Holland in 1697 he set out on a tour of Italy: in Rome, he says, 'my two great diversions were Musick and Antiquities', and he looked back on his visit there with pleasure for the rest of his life. He practised as an advocate, took a considerable part in the negotiation of the Act of Union of 1707, and was appointed a Baron of the Exchequer in the following year. From the 1720s onwards his classical tastes were developing in two directions—an interest in the Roman antiquities of North Britain, and the practical application of his archaeological learning by designing buildings in what was in Scotland still an unfamiliar and somewhat daring mode, the classical styles which one associates with Palladio and his followers, notably Lord Burlington. These two activities must be seen as two parts of a whole, as closely linked as the writing of the Waverley Novels to the building of Abbotsford.

The taste for classical antiquities inculcated in Rome by the virtuosi such as Chaprigni was expressed on Sir John's return to Scotland in more than one way. He soon entered into correspondence with the English antiquaries of the day, becoming a member of the circle which included William Stukeley, Roger and Samuel Gale, Ralph Thoresby and the other members of the Society of Antiquaries of London, to which he was elected in 1724. His local interests were reinforced by his purchase of the Cammo estate near the important Roman fort at Cramond, where he lived from 1710 to 1722, and he maintained his concern with Roman Scotland throughout his life, eventually consenting to publish five years before his death a much revised Latin dissertation on the subject. That he wrote in Latin is significant, and one remembers Sibbald; his only other published work, the *Dissertatio de stylis Veterum* . . . was again in Latin, but it also appeared in an English abridgement made by Roger Gale for the Royal Society, and the substance of the other dissertation was in fact incorporated in English by Alexander Gordon, in the 'Additions and Corrections' to his *Itinerarium Septentrionale*, published separately in 1732, the original *Itinerarium* appearing in 1726, as we shall see. He wrote little and revised much, conscious of and quoting the advice of Horace, and as an impassioned lover of the classical tradition would have felt it a betrayal of standards and a deplorable display of bad taste to make a learned communication in the vernacular.

His second classical outlet was the formation of a notable

collection of inscriptions, sculptures and coins at Penicuik House, the bulk of which, including 16 inscriptions and altars from North Britain, was given to the museum of the Society of Antiquaries of Scotland by Sir George Clerk in 1857: it included the bronze Roman stylus in its case which occasioned his second dissertation. But the collection was strictly a gentleman's cabinet of classical art, in the manner of the Arundel Marbles or of Charles Townley, and not a scientific collection based on a nucleus of natural history such as those of Sibbald or Thoresby; it represents the aristocratic approach to the ancient world. Sir John saw this as a duty, facilitated by Britain's mercantile position and wealth which enabled the advantageous purchase of classical antiquities to be made abroad. As he wrote in his unpublished poem *The Country Seat* (1727)

> All must submit, the highest Walls and Towrs
> Cannot resist Britannia's golden Showers.

He also pursued his interests in the field, encouraging and acting as patron to Alexander Gordon, who accompanied him on tours in 1723 and 1724, the second to Hadrian's Wall. The tours were satisfactorily mixed with business (such as visiting the Baron's coal mines) or sport ('We found some heath game amongst the shrubs which grow in these ditches, and killed two' he reported from Sewingshields) and it was these that largely lay behind Gordon's *Itinerarium Septentrionale* of 1726, a copy of which Scott portrays his Antiquary, Mr Jonathan Oldbuck, carrying off in triumph on the Queensferry coach at the opening of the novel. We must turn to Gordon shortly, but another aspect of Sir John Clerk's classicist approach must be touched on. As Iain Brown has shown, his feelings with regard to the Roman conquest of Britain are interestingly ambivalent. Hadrian's Wall represented not only Roman military and architectural achievement, but in its very greatness paid a compliment to the foe beyond its frontier — 'our Forefathers were a very numerous and terrible people to the Romans that they were at such immense pains, labour and expense to fortify themselves against us'. The Caledonians would join the other Ancient Britons who stood for the sturdy native virtues opposed to the insidious charms of the foreign conqueror and the indignities of subjugation:

> Such, such of old the first born natives were
> Who breathed the virtues of Britannia's air

Their realm when mighty Caesar vainly sought
For mightier freedom against Caesar fought

as Henry Brooke (father of Charlotte, who published the first collection of ancient Irish poetry) wrote in his verse tragedy *Gustavus Vasa* of 1739, and the sentiment was common at the time. But to Sir John, a civilised Scot who not only devotedly admired the art and letters of ancient Rome, but whose day-to-day activities were profoundly concerned with bringing into effect the Act of Union of 1707, while the Wall could be seen as 'the Great Boundary of the British Liberty and Servitude', nevertheless the Romans 'Wall'd out humanity from us'; 'it is a reproach to a nation to have resisted the humanity which Rome laboured to introduce'. Such cultural isolation could only lead to what Gordon called '*Gothicism*, Ignorance and a bad Taste', in antiquity or today, and indeed Sir John once reproved Gordon for accepting the speech of Galgacus as a genuine utterance of national feeling and not a well-worn literary artifice.

It is in this light that Sir John's architectural and landscape gardening activities should be seen. In his long poem *The Country Seat* he set out his views on these subjects, and already in 1723 he had designed himself a house in the classical mode at Mavisbank 'under the correction of one Mr. Adams, a skilful Architect', and it is typical enough of William Adam. But on his London visit of 1727 he was entertained by Lord Burlington, looked keenly at London buildings by Inigo Jones, Gibbs and Vanbrugh, met Lord Pembroke and visited Wilton House. He returned entranced and intended to rebuild the old house at Penicuik as an architectural tribute to the new version of the Roman cultural tradition, but it was left to his son Sir James to design and build, with the architect-mason John Baxter, the new house in 1763, in the Burlingtonian Palladianism which had so impressed his father 40 years before and was now out of fashion. And in the splendid stable block he further commemorated the Romans in Scotland by adorning it with a dovecot which is a full-sized replica of a unique circular Roman building once standing in southern Scotland, which as we shall see was destroyed in 1743 to the disgust of the Baron and all other antiquaries of the time.

Alexander Gordon was born about 1692 in Aberdeen and educated in the University there.[8] His varied career began as a music master (he seems to have studied in Italy), and certainly in later life he painted portraits. He became a friend of Sir John Clerk and through him of Roger Gale and others of the English archaeological circle which included William Stukeley and gave distinction to the early days of the Society of Antiquaries of London, founded in 1717. Gordon moved to London and succeeded Stukeley as Secretary to the Antiquaries in 1736, holding his office until 1741, when he emigrated to America as secretary to James Glen, Governor of South Carolina, where he died in 1754. In 1726 he published his *Itinerarium Septentrionale*, 'containing an Account of all the MONUMENTS of *ROMAN* ANTIQUITY found and collected in that Journey', with a second part 'Of the several Invasions of the Danes'. The 65 plates, some engraved by Gerard van der Gught, friend of Stukeley and engraver of some of his Avebury plates, comprise plans of sites, inscriptions, coins, antiquities (mostly prehistoric bronzes thought to be Roman), Pictish stones, and other monuments including the brochs of Dun Troddan and Dun Telve in Glen Elg. Gordon records that he was 'particularly encourag'd to proceed in this Work' by reading Stukeley's account of the famous circular Roman building known as Arthur's O'on (or Oven) near Falkirk, published in 1720, 'the destruction of which in 1743 has come to be regarded as the greatest antiquarian scandal of the eighteenth century'. Stukeley never visited the site, but used drawings made for him at his request by Andrews Jelfe, architect to the Board of Ordnance charged in 1718–19 'to repair and make some Forts in Scotland', and these (with Sir James Clerk's replica already mentioned) constitute our basic record of the monument, almost certainly a temple.[9]

The subscription list for the *Itinerarium* includes half a dozen antiquaries, the architects William Adam and James Gibbs, nine bishops and over 60 members of the Peerage, a tribute perhaps rather to Gordon's powers of sales promotion than to a passion for Roman antiquities in high places. The Clerk family were to remember him as 'a grave man, of formal habits, tall, lean and usually taciturn', but a less kindly acquaintance said he had 'some learning, some ingenuity, much pride, much deceit and very little honesty', and a modern estimate is that 'his carrer suggests that he was a shifty and not over-scrupulous adventurer'. His book has a value for the first-hand observations rather than his plans, which are unreliable, but his two plates of

16. *Arthur's O'on, by Roy, after Stukeley, after Jelfe, c. 1773.*

bronzes (L, LI) are very good for the time, and superior to what were to follow in for instance the early volumes of *Archaeologia Scotica*. But only six years after the publication of the *Itinerarium* what 'was undoubtedly the most judicious treatise that had up to that date been compiled on Roman Britain' appeared in the form of John Horsley's magisterial *Britannia Romana* of 1732. Horsley was an Edinburgh graduate, and a presbyterian minister and schoolmaster in Morpeth in Northumberland, dying in the year of the publication of his great life-work.[10] Mr Oldbuck was perhaps deliberately portrayed as out-of-date and uncritical in his preference of Gordon over Horsley: Scott must have known the *Itinerarium* well, for as George Macdonald pointed out, he not only made a point of introducing it by name in his novel, but put quotations from it into the mouth of the Antiquary.

In the continued investigation of Roman Scotland the Clerk family once again make their contribution, when in 1751 Captain (later Lieutenant-General) Robert Melville visited Penicuik with an introduction from his brother officer Matthew Clerk, the Baron's youngest son. Fired with enthusiasm by Sir John and his collection of Roman antiquities and inscriptions, Melville turned to active field-work on Roman Scotland, making an extensive tour on foot with John Clerk of Eldin and his young brother in 1754 which led to the discovery of unsuspected forts and marching-camps. Already William Roy, later Major-General and first Director-General of the Ordnance Survey, was working in Scotland on the 'Duke of Cumberland's Map' of the Highlands and interesting himself in Roman antiquities: 'upon my return to Edin^r', Melville wrote later, 'my first proselyte was the present Gen Roy', and by 1773 Roy's great *Military Antiquities of the Romans in North Britain* was completed, though not published until 20 years later, after his death, by the Society of Antiquaries of London. The book, Sir George Macdonald wrote, 'remains one of our archaeological classics . . . the permanent value . . . is due mainly to its careful plans . . . as a storehouse of trustworthy topographical information regarding Roman sites, it can never be entirely superseded'.[11] It is the visual record, the surveys, that count rather than the text, a period piece too often vitiated by acceptance of the forged itinerary of Richard of Cirencester. We must remember how standards of draughtsmanship and accurate delineation vary not so much in response to the technical ability of the artist, but in the demands or expectations of his patron or public. Sir Ernst Gombrich illuminated the whole question when he pointed out that a pictorial representation 'is not a faithful record of a visual experience, but the faithful construction of a relational model . . . such a model can be constructed to any required degree of accuracy. What is decisive here is clearly the world "required". The form of a representation cannot be divorced from its purpose and the requirements of the society in which the given visual language gains currency'.[12] The visual requirements of the late seventeenth and early eighteenth century antiquaries in the scientific tradition were not only more exacting than those of Leland's or Camden's day but also of those who followed in the late eighteenth century when tastes had again changed.

Scotland shared with England the general decline in standards which affected so many studies including history, many of the earth and life sciences, and antiquarianism itself, after about 1730. The founding of the Society of Antiquaries of Scotland in 1780 came at an unpropitious time, and like its senior counterpart in London it did little to improve the situation in archaeological investigation and publication. The Society was brought into being by a group of noblemen and gentlemen of great respectability under the aegis of the eleventh Earl of Buchan; James Boswell's name appears on the original list of 38 interested persons, but he was not one of the fourteen who went by invitation to Lord Buchan's house to 'consider the propriety of forming a Society upon the plan suggested' by him. Lord Bute was elected President, Buchan the senior of five Vice-Presidents and James Burnett, Lord Monboddo (whom we shall shortly meet again), the second. Three years later the Society obtained a Royal Charter in the teeth of the combined opposition of the University of Edinburgh, the Advocates' Library, and the Philosophical Society (or Society for Improving Arts and Sciences) which became the Royal Society of Edinburgh in 1783. Ten years later the membership totalled some 425, with a Council of 33; an Ordinary Membership of 107 based on Edinburgh and the neighbourhood; 181 Correspondent Members widely scattered in Scotland and England; 81 Honorary Members including Horace Walpole (who must have been surprised), Bishop Percy, Sir William Chambers, Robert Adam and Thomas Pennant; Buffon, Diderot and Grim Thorkelin (who in 1815 was to publish the first edition of *Beowulf*); and many other foreign scholars and institutions including the Vatican and Douay. A final group of 23 'Artists Associated' are differentiated from the nobility and gentry, and include the historical painters Alexander Runciman and Gavin Hamilton; under 'Architects' John Baxter, the builder and mason with whom Sir James Clerk designed and built Penicuik House in 1763, and a final tail of engravers, surveyors and booksellers. In all, it is a fascinating microcosm of contemporary Scottish society.[13]

The great and permanent memorial to the Society's early activities was the founding and maintaining of the archaeological collections which were to form the nucleus of the National Museum of Antiquities of Scotland today. Accessions began from the start: a Late Bronze Age hoard from Duddingston Loch found in 1778 was split between the landowner, Sir Alexander Dick (whose share later went to Sir Walter Scott), George III (now lost) and to the Society's Museum, where it was registered in 1781 and was later re-united with Sir Walter's pieces. In 1792 it was reckoned that over the decade there had been 1,130 donors of 16,000 objects: Scott of course collected antiquities himself at Abbotsford, the most famous of them, the Early Iron Age bronze horse-cap and horned mountings from Torrs in Kirkcudbrightshire, given to him in 1829, was eventually bought by the National Museum in 1921.[14]

The Society's first publication, *Archaeologia Scotica* Volume I, with a format, type-face and layout closely resembling the London Society's *Archaeologia*, by then in its sixth volume, appeared in 1792, but Volume II was not published until 1822. London and Edinburgh both show archaeology in decline. Contemporary critics said of *Archaeologia* at this time that anyone looking for 'profound researches' would find it to 'contain only amusing fugitive papers'; others complained of 'vile drawings of paltry pitchers, and rude masses of Druidical rocks'; Horace Walpole was of course pettish and carping.[15] The Scottish volume mainly contained non-archaeological papers — two long parochial surveys; historical documents; original poems by a Corresponding Member in Lowland Scots and printed in his own phonetic notation of 42 characters. There were some prehistoric finds, like the Inshoch bronze hoard, very unsatisfactory drawings of Dun Carloway and Dun Cromore brochs in Lewis, and of the medieval cross at Eccles in Berwickshire. The 1822 volume was much the same, with rather more illustrations of dubious quality of Pictish stones, the Barmekin of Echt fort and now-destroyed stone circles, the find of a Roman bathhouse at Inveresk and of a medieval heart-burial, as well as the inevitable essay on 'The Language of the Pehts'.

The popularisation of antiquities in England was leading to a new literature closely connected with improved roads and transport, and summed up in The Tour, so often in search of the Picturesque, in which by now ruins and ancient monuments were essential ingredients. Scotland was soon to be included; Gray had experienced ecstatic emotions among the natural scenery of the Highlands as early as 1765, and the Road to the Isles, already signposted by Martin Martin in his *Description of the Western Islands*, was opened to a public eager for such novel experiences by Thomas Pennant, who made and published Tours not only of his native Wales, but of Scotland in 1769 and again, with a *Voyage to the Hebrides*, in 1774. This was an immediate success not only at home, but abroad, where for instance German romanticism led to Ebeling's translation published only five years later.[16] Pennant is interesting in that he continued the earlier tradition of the naturalist-antiquary, for his *British Zoology* (1766) and *History of Quadrupeds* (1781) were well esteemed works of the day, and he, and Daines Barrington, were the correspondents to whom Gilbert White addressed his famous *Natural History of Selbourne* (1789), a work very much in the tradition of the early Fellows of the Royal Society such as Plot. Pennant took note not only of topography and natural history, but antiquities and contemporary ethnography such as black houses and shielings, querns and cloth-waulking and other features of the traditional life of the West Highlands.

Archaeological journalism and popularisation too was represented by the picaresque figure of Captain Grose, who lumbers across the Scottish scene as a friend of Robert Burns, the 'chiel amang ye takin' notes' to write up as his *Antiquities of Scotland* in 1789–91. Sir John Sinclair was of course primarily an improving landlord who set Scottish agriculture on a new footing at the end of the eighteenth century, but in his original *Statistical Account* of 1791–9 he was not only using the system of parochial enquiries in the manner of the earlier English topographers and of Sibbald, but included information of local antiquities provided by ministers whose scholarly interests were turning to such matters in response to the new antiquarian climate of thought. One such, the Reverend Dr John Ogilvie of Midmar in Aberdeenshire, not only wrote on the lyric poetry of the ancients, but published anonymously a romantic poem, *The Fane of the Druids*, prompted by a recumbent stone circle in the neighbourhood in 1787: the 'favourable reception' it received encouraged the author to publish a second part 'Comprehending an account of the origin, progress, and establishment of society in North Britain' in 1789. And a remarkable little monograph of 1777 by John Williams, a 'Mineral Engineer', descriptive of Craig Phadrig and other vitrified forts, shows a new scientific and practical approach linked to commercial geology

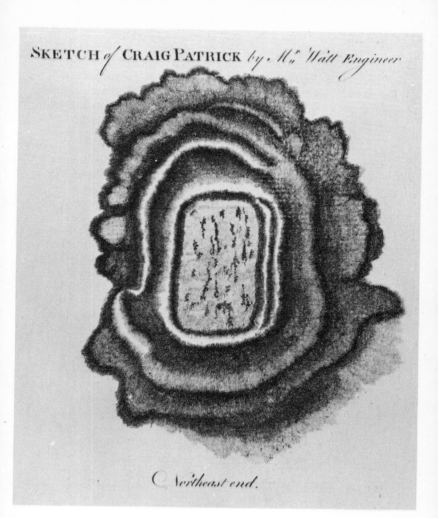

SKETCH *of* CRAIG PATRICK *by* M͞r Watt *Engineer*

Northeast end.

17. *Craig Patrick, by James Watt, 1777.*

and the beginnings of the Industrial Revolution, addressed to George Clerk-Maxwell (son of the Baron and one of the founders of the Society of Antiquaries of Scotland), and with a technical appendix and surveys of the fort by James Watt.

It was from this background then that Scott drew certain elements in Mr Oldbuck—his passionate interest in Roman castrametation, the ludicrous episode on the 'Praetorium', and his proud acquisition of Sandy Gordon's folio. The general growth of popular interest in antiquities would make such a character acceptable and topical. The introduction of a Roman camp into a novel, with attendant antiquary, was a motif employed by at least three other writers between the 1770s and 1831, the last being Thomas Love Peacock in *Crochet Castle*.[17] Mr Chainmail, too, in the same novel, has many features which recall Sir Walter, though his prototype is usually considered to be Sir Edward Strachey. Scott certainly appears in another Peacock novel as we shall see. But to return to Scott and *The Antiquary*. Whatever use he may have made of the Scottish tradition of Romano-British archaeology as it existed in the second half of the eighteenth century, Scott could not have found this field of study congenial to his own temperament. He was a poor classic anyway, and the romantic in him would hardly choose the Roman Occupation of Britain as a period of the past to be idealised. Rather, like Gordon, he would accept Galgacus' speech at its face value; the Baron would have shaken his head at this 'Gothic taste'. Sir Walter, as Iain Brown points out, 'returns to the medieval, romantic past in which to find an identity for Scotland. Clerk, keeping within the classical tradition, goes back to the Caledonia of the Roman Period'.

It is not my purpose here to develop the well-worn theme of antiquarianism and the Romantic movement, which had already begun to join forces by the time Scott wrote his poems or started his collection of Border ballads. All this is familiar enough, but there is another, peculiarly Scottish, development of thought about antiquity in the middle and latter eighteenth century which deserves attention. Perhaps it can best be introduced by Peacock, that acute and witty observer of the foibles of his age, who in *Crotchet Castle* (already mentioned) has a splendid episode when at the end of a most convivial dinner, Mr McQuedy, the Modern Athenian, tries repeatedly to read the company a paper which opens 'In the infancy of society . . .'. He was fortunately never allowed to get very much further, but Peacock's joke at the expense of the Edinburgh political economists brings out the point I wish to make — the interest of Scottish thinkers of the time in the ultimate origins of man, the nature of primitive society and the beginnings of language and literature.

The development of historiography in the later eighteenth century which led to the 'philosophical' approaches of the Enlightenment, associated especially with France and the Encyclopaedists, has frequently been the subject of comment in recent years. With what would now be thought of as sociological rather than historical aims, *les philosophes* looked for broad general 'laws' analogous to those being established in the sciences, governing the development and behaviour of human societies; in modern jargon, nomothetic models of the past. In such enquiries hypotheses can acquire greater intellectual prestige than the elucidation of the raw material of prehistory and history by archaeologists, archivists and palaeographers, and such a dichotomy indeed developed in eighteenth century France. In Britain the situation was interestingly diversified when, from before the middle of the century there arose in Scotland but not in England a highly influential school of theoretical sociology which, with great inner conviction, set out the nomothetic schemes Mr McQuedy was longing to expound: Peacock points out that his name is an acronym of *Quod Erat Demonstrandum*. This thinking not only has a most interesting but perhaps rather neglected place in the history of archaeology but its eventual repercussions down the centuries end with Marx. Based in part on the current ideas which were introducing a temporal element into the hitherto eternal and immutable Great Chain of Being and its correlative doctrine of the plenitude of the Creation, it must be remembered that it was avowedly theoretical and although concerning itself with prehistory, it did not and could not use the archaeological evidence because that evidence had not yet been recognised for what it was.[18]

It grew up in the intellectual centres of the Universities of Edinburgh and Aberdeen and its exponents were the still bright stars of the Scottish Enlightenment. One of the earliest thinkers of these lines was Thomas Blackwell, Professor of Greek at Marischal College from 1723 to 1757 and including among his pupils James Burnett, later Lord Monboddo;[19] to the Aberdeen circle also belonged James Macpherson of Ossianic fame and John Ogilvie of the Druidic poems. In Edinburgh (and of course there was much coming and going between the cities) there were Lord Kames, David Hume, Adam Smith and Adam Ferguson, William Robertson and the rest. Their speculations on the development of human societies, institutions and language had started before the mid-century and therefore antedate Rousseau's *Discours sur l'inégalité* of 1755, but the Scottish taste for claret no less than philosophical discussion formed a link with another French thinker, for Lords Morton and Elibank ordered their wine through the Baron de la Brède et de Montesquieu, who was a close friend of Mr Black the Bordeaux wine merchant, father of Joseph Black who brought about the Adam Ferguson connection. The *Esprit des lois* was published in 1748 and David Hume assisted the author in bringing out the Edinburgh edition two years later.

Dugald Stewart in his retrospective survey of the movement in his biographical essay on Adam Smith of 1794 describes Smith's concern with what 'I shall take the liberty of giving the title of *Theoretic or Conjectural History*'. On such problems as the earliest stages in social development, Stewart goes on, 'on most of these subjects very little information is to be expected from history' because such phases lie beyond its range; 'many of the most important steps' must have been taken in what we would now call prehistoric times. 'A few insulated facts' can be obtained from the narratives of travellers 'who have viewed the arrangements of rude nations' but 'in this want of direct evidence, we are under the necessity of supplying the place of fact by conjecture'. Lord Monboddo wrote explaining his method: as his enquiry was 'not the subject of what is commonly called *History*, I have been at great pains to collect Facts . . . from Travellers both dead and living, and to compare these with the Facts related by the ancient Authors'. Do we here perhaps hear the rustle of the wind in the Golden Bough growing on an ancient Scottish oak, as James Burnett and James Frazer share a methodology and with it, its inherent traps and pitfalls as well as its rewards ? At all events, it is with what we should now call anthropological parallels that the eighteenth century enquirers were concerned, except that the parallels sought were with hypothetical social situations in the past, and not those inferred from archaeological evidence.

The developmental schemes proposed were of varying degrees of elaboration but all shared one basic concept, that of classifying societies in terms of their subsistence-economics and the provision of food supplies, together with their developing technologies. The fundamental distinction made, going back to Montesquieu in 1748, is between the stages of savagery and barbarism; 'there is this difference between savage and barbarous nations: the former are dispersed clans, which for some particular reason, cannot be joined into a body: and the latter are commonly small nations, capable of being united.˙The savages are generally hunters; the barbarians are herdsmen and shepherds'. The 'gradual progress of man from the savage state' said Adam Smith in 1774, always seemed to follow the same pattern, 'beginning with hunting and fishing, advancing to flocks and herds, and then to agriculture and commerce'. Hugh Blair in 1763 and James Beattie in 1790, with many others, see the complete sequence as four stages: hunting and fishing, pasturage, agriculture, and commerce; but some, notably Rousseau, Condercet, and Monboddo, went further. The first in his often misunderstood (and admittedly frequently self-contradictory) scheme, started with man as a solitary animal, nasty and brutish and indeed going back to Hobbes, and without language. There followed a long period of technological development, including the invention and adoption of tools, weapons and speech, in which the first human societies were formed and there was limited possession of property, culminating in a third stage of patriarchal hunter-fisher societies enjoying the amenities of song and dance. This man-achieved state was Rousseau's Golden Age, not the first brutish state of pure Nature, but in a fourth stage deterioration set in with agriculture, metallurgy, private property and capital. For Monboddo, the most interesting, original and scholarly of all the theorists, man 'was at first a quadruped', and solitary; 'the next step of man's progress is to the herding life' (living himself in herds or social units) 'yet he has no art of fishing and hunting'. Owing to population pressure 'then and not till then, they took to hunting and fishing' and so to agriculture and the invention of language, and finally the 'state of civility and arts' represented by the ancient civilisations known from history.

For Monboddo, his second stage was represented by the anthropoid apes as known to him from travellers' tales, his third by the similar reports on Hottentots, American Indians and the Pacific where 'the golden age may be said yet to exist in some of the countries that have been discovered in the South Sea, where the inhabitants live, without toil or labour, upon the bounty of nature, in those fine climates'. I have discussed elsewhere the pervasive Golden Ages of the eighteenth and earlier centuries;[20] Martin Martin in 1698 had found one near home (and in a less than fine climate) in the inhabitants of St Kilda—'what the condition of the people in the golden age is feigned by the poets to be, that theirs really is'. We must shortly return to the idealisation of the Highlands, but in the meantime Adam Ferguson used his North American Indian parallels to sound effect, as had John Aubrey long before, when considering the narratives of Tacitus and Caesar—'What should distinguish a German or a Briton, in his habits of mind or his body, in his manners or apprehensions, from an American, who, like him, with his bow and his dart, is left to traverse the forest?' Nor were the Scottish social theoreticians alone, for others such as Thomas Pownall were aware of the problem: he had first-hand experience of Indians as successively Lieut-Governor of New Jersey and Governor of Massachusetts between 1755 and 1760, and produced in 1773 a very interesting variant scheme with a dual division between 'Woodland-men living on the fruits, fish and game of the forest', and the 'Land-workers' or agriculturalists.[21]

Commenting on a later elaborated but basically similar scheme, Glyn Daniel wrote 'It was based primarily not on archaeological evidence but on the comparative study of modern primitive peoples, the arrangement of these existing economies and societies into an evolutionary sequence, and the projection of this hypothetical sequence into the prehistoric past'. This was the scheme set out by the American anthropologist Lewis Morgan in his *Ancient Society* of 1877, of whom Engels was to write in 1884 'Morgan is the first man who with expert knowledge has attempted to introduce a definite order into human prehistory'.[22] It seems a pity that Lord Monboddo, Adam Smith and their friends have not been given their due as contributors to Marxist historical doctrine, for Morgan's scheme is theirs. It has proved a good model of the past, much of it receiving support from modern studies in prehistoric subsistence-patterns.

Before we turn to the circumstances in which Sir Walter

Scott becomes involved in such thinking in Scotland (and he has not been forgotten in pursuit of an irrelevance) there are two points to make. The first is, that though in Scotland the evolutionary scheme for human societies was put up by the most respected members of the Establishment, it completely avoids conflict with the Biblical account of the origins of mankind by the simple expedient of making no reference whatever to Adam and Eve, the Garden of Eden, the Fall or the Flood. The Old Testament is used as an anthropological document and indeed provided the evidence for a pastoral state — 'Pasturage' wrote James Beattie 'we learn, from the history of the patriarchs, to have been one of their earliest vocations'.[23] Rousseau we know was well aware of the issue and skilfully avoided it, but in Scotland the dilemma to be posed in the nineteenth century between the antiquity of man and revealed religion seems not to have disturbed those who like Lord Monboddo, happily accepted earliest man as an inarticulate and ungregarious quadruped, and took the ourang-outan in his evolutionary stride. The scheme did, in the second place, although a theoretical construct, at least make possible the concept of a time-scale extending back beyond written history in two or three developmental stages of prehistory. In Scotland the social theorists and the antiquaries seem to have had no point of contact or common ground, but with the low level of antiquarian studies at the time it is not surprising that the former should not seek alliance with ineffective amateurs pottering about among Pictish Towers or the site of Mons Graupius. Had John Frere known of it in 1797 he might have found a place in it for his palaeolithic hand-axes which he was tempted 'to refer to a very remote period indeed; even beyond that of the present world'; Rousseau, with Lucretius in his mind, put the use of metals not earlier than his fourth stage, and throughout there seems an implicit assumption that sticks and stones were not replaced by metals until relatively late. It had to wait for the formulation of a technological three-ages system founded empirically on prehistoric artefacts by Danish archaeologists between 1813 and 1836 to begin the process of archaeologically testing the eighteenth century Scottish theories of social evolution which continues today.[24]

From the speculations on the origin of language and literature among members of the Monboddo circle in Aberdeen and Edinburgh there arose the view that 'poetry is as old as mankind, coeval with the human race'. It was not a wholly new idea, and indeed in the late sixteenth century Richard Puttenham had thought that rhymed verse was the earliest form, and an agent in civilising primitive peoples who had previously 'remained in the woods and mountains, vagarant and dispersed like wild beasts, lawlesse and naked, or verie ill-clad'.[25] 'In order to explore the rise of Poetry', wrote Blair in 1783, 'we must have recourse to the deserts and the wilds; we must go back to the age of hunters and of shepherds; to the highest antiquity'. It was thought of as a product of the earliest stages of social evolution once language was achieved. If you were a classic you could turn to Homer, for by a development of the basic idea of poetry and song as man's first coherent utterance it was thought that epic poetry was the earliest form: 'nature and common sense had supplied to these old simple bards the want of critical art, and taught them some of the most essential rules of Epic Poetry'. But Homer, alas, was not a Scot, and there was nothing nearer than the Scandinavian *Edda* when one looked for a home-grown product. To the rescue came James Macpherson, who in 1750 produced the first of his alleged fragments of ancient Gaelic epic poetry, and within a few years *Ossian* had made its mark in Macpherson's nicely calculated Romantic invention. Here was what one writer called a 'noble confirmation' of the theory of primitive poetry; *Ossian* was seriously and elaborately compared with the *Iliad*, on at least one occasion to the disadvantage of the latter. The Golden Age in St Kilda was not far away.

You may think I have strayed far away from my avowed theme, the antiquarian antecedents of Sir Walter Scott. But can one ignore in any consideration of his poems and novels this episode in Scottish thought, these conjectures on 'the infancy of mankind', making possible on the one hand the romantic idealisation of the past and on the other finding in the ancient barbarian world the origins of poetry, whether in Homeric Greece or with Fingal and Ossian? Percy, whose *Reliques* are an acknowledged influence on Scott the collector (and inventor) of Border ballads, was fully involved in the ideas on the origins of epic poetry we have been reviewing, and Scott himself may well have regarded his championing of the ballads as the most ancient recoverable Scots poetry as the Lowlander's answer to Macpherson. Indeed, something of this may be implicit in the Antiquary's ridicule of Ossian in his conversations with the

Highlander Hector McIntyre. In his Introduction to the *Minstrelsey* Scott expresses the view that 'the more rude and wild the state of society, the more general and violent is the impulse received from poetry and music. The muse ... records in the lays of inspiration, the history, the lays, the very religion of savages'. And so in the romantic medievalism of the poems and the no less romantic approach to the past in the Waverley Novels, Scott was writing for a public already favourably inclined to such sentiments as the result of ideas that had been in the air for half a century or so and which had themselves contributed in no little measure to Scott's own temper of thought.

To sum up then we see in Sir Walter Scott, and in his creation of Jonathan Oldbuck, the meeting-place of two traditions of antiquarian thougnt. Of these the senior was that directly deriving from the Renaissance, coming through from Sibbald to Sir John Clerk and General Roy; empirical, questioning, practical; heir to the lucidity and formality of classical thought and language. To Scott the man of romantic sensibility, poet and story-writer, such a tradition could never but be alien; even, as on the Kaim of Kinprunes, a target for his particular ridicule. But the novel speculations on ancient man, even though they had originated in the uncongenial setting of professors, lawyers and political economists, allowed of a more liberal and poetic interpretation. The general decline in British historical studies in the second half of the eighteenth century made an idealised version of the Middle Ages easier to accept than in the more critical atmosphere of the high scholastic traditions of the Restoration, and in England this romantic approach, especially to medieval architecture, had been in full swing since the 1740s: Strawberry Hill was finished by 1753. With the ideas of the origins of epic poetry evolved by the Scottish primitivists in the air, the ballads, real and invented, would be sure of a sympathetic reception, and Scott as Mr Derrydown in Peacock's *Melincourt* (1817), asserting the superiority of *Chevy Chase* and *Auld Robin Gray* over *Paradise Lost*, reminds us not a little of the champions of Ossian as against Homer. *Melincourt* too, in Sir Oran Haut-ton, has a character supplied by Monboddo, and documented by extensive footnote references from his works. Just as Sir John Clerk had built Mavisbank as a tangible memorial to his faith in the classical tradition, Abbotsford finally emerged as the architectural embodiment of the fictitious Middle Ages which Scott had created as the inspired spokesman of the romantic antiquarianism which he had so eagerly encouraged to take its place.

NOTES

1   For Charleton, 'very much the intellectual barometer of his age', cf. C. Webster, *The Great Instauration*, London 1975, 278.
2   Sibbald deserves full-length treatment. He wrote an autobiographical sketch up to 1692: *Autobiography of Sir Robert Sibbald . . .*, Edinburgh 1833; *The Memoirs of Sir Robert Sibbald* (ed. F. Paget Hett), London 1932. His collections were given to the University of Edinburgh and catalogued in *Auctarium musaei Balfouriani e museo Sibbaldiano . . .*, Edinburgh 1697; his library was sold on his death, with sale catalogue *Bibliotheca Sibbaldiana . . .*, Edinburgh 1722. His MSS. are in the National Library of Scotland. For Steno M. J. S. Rudwick, *The Meaning of Fossils*, London 1972; Lhwyd, R. T. Gunther, *Life and Letters of Edward Lhwyd*, Oxford 1945, 418; J. L. Campbell and D. Thomson, *Edward Lhuyd in the Scottish Highlands* Oxford 1963. Cf. No. VI above.
3   *Miscellanea quaedam eruditae antiquitatis . . .*, Edinburgh 1710, Tab. 1-3.
4   R. Kirk, *Secret Commonwealth of Elves and Fairies* (1691), ed. S. Sanderson, Folklore Soc. 1976, 51, 107. Cf. No. VI above.
5   R. Sibbald, *Auctarium . . .*, 55, 58; *Miscellanea . . .*, 35.
6   G. F. Black, *Proc. Soc. Ant. Scot.* XXVII, 1892-3, 433. Isobel Gowdie's phrase about the 'Elf-boyes, who whyttis and dightis them with a sharp thing lyk a paking neidle' sounds uncannily like a description of the pressure-flaking technique used in such flint working by recent stone-using peoples.
7   For Sir John Clerk, J. M. Gray (ed.), *Memoirs of the life of Sir John Clerk of Penicuik . . .* (Scot. Hist. Soc. Pubs. XIII), Edinburgh 1892; A. Rowan, *Country Life* CXLIV (August 1968), 383, 488; W. Spink, 'Sir John Clerk of Penicuik: Landowner as designer', in P. Willis (ed.), *Furor Hortensis*, Edinburgh 1974 31; S. Piggott, *William Stukeley . . .*, Oxford 1950; 'Sir John Clerk and the "Country Seat"' in H. M. Colvin and J. Harris (eds.), *The Country Seat: Studies . . . presented to Sir John Summerson*, London 1970, 110; I. G. Brown, *Antiq.* XLVIII, 1974, 283; ibid., *Antiquarian Sir John . . .*, unpub. MA dissertation, University of Edinburgh, 1972. I am grateful to Mr Brown for allowing me to use and quote from this, which anticipates a full-length study.
8   For Alexander Gordon, D. Wilson and D. Laing, *Proc. Soc. Ant. Scot.*, X, 1872-4 363; D. Wilson *Arch. and Prehist. Annals of Scotland*, Edinburgh 1851, 371; G. Macdonald, *Roman Wall in Scotland* (2nd edn.), Oxford 1934, 75.
9   K. A. Steer, *Arch. Journ.* CXV, 1960, 99; I. G. Brown, *Antiq.* XLVIII, 1974, 283.

10 G. Macdonald, *Arch. Aeliana* 4th S, x, 1933, 1.
11 Ibid., *Arch.* LXVIII, 1917, 161. Cf. No. VI above.
12 E. Gombrich, *Art and Illusion*, New York 1960, 90; S. Piggott, *Antiq.* XXXIX, 1965, 165.
13 *Arch. Scotica*, I, 1792, iii.
14 J. M. Coles, *Proc. Soc. Ant. Scot.* XCIII, 1959-60, 122; R. J. C. Atkinson and S. Piggott, *Arch.* XCVI, 1955, 197.
15 J. Evans, *History of the Society of Antiquaries*, Oxford 1956, 187.
16 J. B. Ebeling, (trans.) T. Pennant, *Reise durch Schottland und die Hebridischen Inseln*, 2 vols., Leipzig, 1779-80.
17 S. Piggott, *Review Eng. Lit.* VII, no. 3, 1966, 21; No. VIII below.
18 A. O. Lovejoy, *Mod. Philology* XXI, 1923, 165; ibid. XXX, 1933, 275 (reprinted in *Essays in the History of Ideas*, Johns Hopkins 1948, Nos. II and III); Lois Whitney, *Mod. Philology* XXI, 1924, 337; *Primitivism and the idea of progress in English popular literature . . .*, Baltimore 1934; 1965.
19 E. L. Cloyd, *James Burnett, Lord Monboddo*, Oxford 1972.
20 S. Piggott, *The Druids*, London 1968.
21 For Pownall, B. Orme, *Antiq.* XLVIII, 1974, 116. Ethnographers had been making comparisons between ancient and recent peoples since the beginning of the eighteenth century: J. Lafiteau, *Moeurs des sauvages Ameriquains . . .*, Paris 1724, is important here (M. T. Hodgen, *Early anthropology in the sixteenth and seventeenth centuries*, Philadelphia 1964, 346). Later, A-Y. Goguet, *De l'origine des lois, des arts et des sciences*, Paris 1758, is interesting, and significantly enough was published in an English edition in Edinburgh in 1761 (R. F. Heizer, *Man's discovery of his past*, Englewood Cliffs 1962, 11). Jens Kraft published similar observations in Denmark in 1760 (K. Birket-Smith, *Folk*, II, 1960, 5).
22 G. Daniel, *A hundred and fifty years of archaeology*, London 1975, 186. He also notes that Coleridge used the basic scheme, and one may observe its persistence through Tylor to Gordon Childe (*Social Evolution*, London 1951) and Grahame Clark (*From savagery to civilisation*, London 1946).
23 J. Beattie, *Elements of moral science*, Edinburgh 1790-93, quoted by J. S. Slotkin, *Readings in early anthropology*, London 1965, 458.
24 G. Daniel, op. cit.
25 R. Puttenham, *The arte of English poesie . . .*, London 1589, quoted by M. T. Hodgen, op. cit., 341.

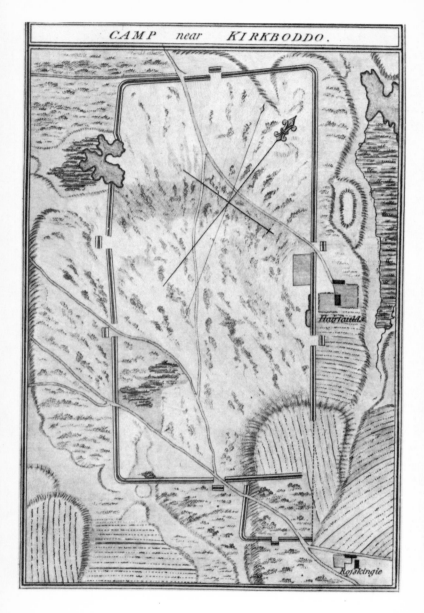

CAMP near KIRKBODDO.

Haerfaulds

Rofskingie

18. *Roman Camp, Kirkboddo, by Roy, 1773.*

VIII.

THE ROMAN CAMP AND
FOUR AUTHORS

One of the best known of the humorous passages in Scott's novels is the scene in Chapter IV of *The Antiquary* of 1816 on the site of the alleged Roman camp at the Kaim of Kinprunes.[1] The Antiquary, Mr Jonathan Oldbuck of Monkbarns, has taken young Mr Lovel

> . . . through one or two pasture meadows to an open heath or common, and so to the top of a gentle eminence.
>
> 'Here' he said, 'Mr Lovel, is a truly remarkable spot'.
>
> 'It commands a fine view' said his companion, looking around him.
>
> 'True, but it is not for the prospect I brought you hither; so you see nothing else remarkable ?—nothing on the surface of the ground ?'
>
> 'Why, yes; I do see something like a ditch, indistinctly marked'.
>
> 'Indistinctly!—pardon me, sir, but the indistinctness must be in your powers of vision—nothing can be more plainly traced—a proper *agger* or *vallum*, with its corresponding ditch or *fossa*. Indistinctly! why Heaven help you. . . .'

And so Mr Oldbuck goes on, referring to Roman forts at Ardoch and at Birrenswark, telling of the discovery of an inscribed stone on the site, quoting from other antiquaries and his own Essay upon Castrametation, and finally appealing to the unbelieving young man:

> 'I appeal to people's eyesight—is not here the Decuman

gate? and there, but for the ravage of the horrid plough, as a learned friend calls it, would be the Praetorian gate. On the left hand you may see some slight vestiges of the *porta sinistra*, and on the right, one side of the *porta dextra* well-nigh entire . . . From this very Praetorium. . . .'

It is at this point that Edie Ochiltree, the licensed beggar, enters to declare that the Praetorium is no more than the grass-grown ruins of a building that he remembers being made ('I mind the bigging o't') and explains the inscribed stone in irreverent terms.

Scott himself said that the character of The Antiquary incorporated characteristics taken from various persons, such as George Constable of Wallace-Craigie, John Ramsay of Ochtertyre and Sir John Clerk of Penicuik. Lockhart records a tradition in the Clerk family, passed on to Scott by John Clerk of Eldin, according to which the antiquarian Sir John was thought to have discovered a Roman camp at Drumcrieff, only to be told by a local inhabitant that he had himself 'made it wi' a flachter spade', and this has usually and reasonably been regarded as the source of the final episode at the Kaim of Kinprunes.[2]

The ludicrous possibilities of an antiquary mistaking a modern construction for an ancient monument had however been explored by a novelist over forty years earlier. In his curious picaresque production ridiculing the Methodists, *The Spiritual Quixote* of 1772, Richard Graves brings his hero Mr Wildgoose, and his faithful Sancho Panza Jerry Tugwell, to Lord Bathurst's park at Cirencester, where they meet with a keeper who shows them the renowned works of landscape gardening, planting and folly-building which had been begun early in the century. Among these was the mock-Gothic structure known as Alfred's Hall, built between 1721 and 1732 with the cooperation of Alexander Pope, and as they stood

> before the Gothic house, there arrived a tall elderly gentlemen with his servant, whose curiosity had brought him to see the place . . . alighting from his horse, and surveying the structure, which represents the ruin of a castle overgrown with ivy; 'Ay', says he, 'a very ancient place! Probably one of the *castra aestiva*, or summer camps, of the Romans; some appendage to Cirencester, I suppose, which was one of the *castra hiberna*, or winter stations, of the Roman legions. The castle itself was probably built during the

barons' wars, in the reign of Henry the Third, or King John'. — 'Aha! look ye there now' says the keeper, smiling, 'so several gentlemen have thought; but, sir, I assure you, it was built by my present lord, but a few years ago: and his lordship used to say, he could have built it as old again if he had had a mind'.[3]

Mr Wildgoose was not amused: 'I don't at all approve of these deceptions, which must necessarily mislead future antiquaries, and introduce great confusion into the English history'. By 1772 the story was of long standing, for only a year after the folly was finished Mary Granville, then Mrs Pendarves and later the well-known Mrs Delany, wrote to Swift telling him how Lord Bathurst had 'greatly improved the wood house which you may remember but a cottage, not a bit better than an Irish cabin. It is now a venerable castle and has been taken by an antiquarian as one of King Arthur's, "with thicket overgrown and wild"'.[4] The same building was commemorated as 'Sunk to decay—and built scarce twenty years' in Edward Stephen's verses *On Lord Bathurst's Park and Wood* of 1747.[5] Graves is thought to have ridiculed his antiquarian father, and the *castra aestiva* and *hiberna* do have something of the ring of the *porta sinistra* and *dextra* of Monkbarns, but the joke really lies in the pseudo-medieval folly of King Alfred or King Arthur, and not in any visible remains attributed to the Romans. Moreover, the antiquary is not demonstrating his views to a sceptical young man. Connection with Scott is therefore tenuous, though possible.

But twenty years before 1816, when *The Antiquary* appeared, a minor English writer had introduced into a novel an episode which in mood and construction is closely akin to the passage we are discussing. Robert Bage (1728–1810) published in 1796 his last novel, *Hermsprong, or Man as he is not*, following *Man as he is* of 1792. Chapter VI of *Hermsprong* opens with a scene in which the local rector, Dr Blick, meets the young hero, Charles Hermsprong, at this point still incognito to the reader, at an ancient encampment:

> The Reverend Doctor Blick seldom walked, but he rode sometimes out in his chariot; and as he was a profound antiquarian, would sometimes stop to view the remains of the castle, the convent, or a remarkable place which had much the appearance of an encampment. It was at the latter place,

the day after the affair of the preceding chapter, he observed a gentleman viewing it attentively. The Doctor alighted, and giving the stranger the good-morrow, said, 'This place, Sir, seems to take your attention, and is indeed worthy of it. I presume you know this was once a Roman camp'.

'No, Sir,' the stranger replied, 'I do not know it'.

'Nothing can be plainer, Sir. You see it was a square. Here must have stood the praetorium, here the augurale; that, Sir, must have been the decuman gate'.

'I see, indeed, ground on which these things might have been,—nothing to indicate with certainty that they were'.

'I have studied the place so long, Sir, and with so much attention, that I can demonstrate it. I can tell you exactly where were the stations of the *volites*, the *hastati*, the *triarii*; their centurions and tribunes'.

'They cannot arise to contradict you, Sir; nor shall I'.

'I wish to convince you'.

'Do not take the trouble, Sir. I have seen many places of encampment like this, some where the Romans never were. But they shall be all Roman to oblige you'.

The temper of Bage's novel is sharp and satirical: Dr Blick is presented as a pompous old fool and, while to the modern reader Hermsprong is an infuriatingly ill-mannered prig, he is intended to represent all the virtues of the unprejudiced and emancipated mind. But, however different in characterisation from Monkbarns and Mr Lovel, the two are brought together in circumstances curiously similar, and lacking only the dénouement which we have seen was likely to have been taken by Scott direct from a comic story current in a friend's family.

Is it then possible that the Roman Camp episode in *The Antiquary* owes something, consciously or unconsciously, to Robert Bage and *Hermsprong*? The novel was popular and widely read: it was not only in Scott's library at Abbotsford,[6] but he wrote an introductory memoir on Bage for a selection of his novels (not including *Hermsprong*), published in Ballantyne's Novelist's Library in 1824.[7] It was the humour in Bage that appealed to Scott, rather than the radical philosophy—'a light, gay, pleasing air carries us agreeably through Bage's novels', he wrote; however much we may disagree with his philosophy, he goes on, 'we are reconciled to the author by the ease and good humour of his style'. Whether the recollection was conscious or unconscious, it does look as though Scott, perhaps starting with the story of Sir John Clerk's discomfiture on a bogus Roman site, contrived an episode in *The Antiquary* which echoed the meeting of Dr Blick and Hermsprong in the work of an earlier novelist he found entertaining.

The fortification in Bage's scene was evidently a genuine antiquity, and Dr Blick, it is implied, is being a dogmatic and die-hard classic in forcing on it a Roman interpretation supported by little or no evidence on the ground. This is itself interesting, and we must return to it later, but for the moment there is a fourth author to consider, who sets a scene of old and young in an ancient earthwork. This is Thomas Love Peacock, and the episode is in *Crotchet Castle*, published in 1831 and likely, from its topical allusions, to have been written within the previous couple of years.[8]

Here Chapter III, entitled 'The Roman Camp', opens with the vicar of the parish in which Mr Crotchet's villa or castle lies, The Reverend Dr Folliott, walking home from a notable breakfast-party with his friend, past an ancient earthwork from which in fact Mr Crotchet has named his country seat. Here he sees a young man 'sitting on a camp stool with a portfolio on his knee, taking a sketch of the Roman Camp', who begs apologies for trespassing. He is assured however by the 'portly divine' that 'all the arts and sciences are welcome' on Mr Crotchet's domain, enumerating some of these, from music and painting to transcendentalism and fish for breakfast. There then follows the dialogue:

> *The Stranger.* A pleasant association, sir, and a liberal and discriminating hospitality. This an old British camp, I believe, sir?
>
> *The Rev. Dr Folliott.* Roman, sir; Roman: undeniably Roman. The vallum is past controversy. It was not a camp, sir, a *castrum*, but a *castellum*, a little camp, or watch-station. . . .

In some ways we are here perhaps even nearer to Bage than in *The Antiquary*. The mood is of course mellow rather than satirical: Dr Folliott is an engaging scholar and gastronome, unlike the odious Dr Blick, and The Stranger, soon to be revealed as Captain Fitzchrome, is very different from the ineffable Charles Hermsprong. But the local antiquarian-minded clergyman meets an unknown young man on an ancient earthwork, which the latter thinks to be prehistoric rather than Roman, and in contriving such a scene (which has no particular bearing on the rest of the story) one can only wonder again whether in this instance Peacock may have been influenced by the similar episode in *Hermsprong*. I know of no direct evidence for Peacock's interest in Bage, but he was an omnivorous reader from early youth, and *Hermsprong*, published a year after his birth, would have been by no means an obsolete novel when he was a young man. From the beginning of his friendship with Shelley in 1812 he would have had every opportunity of encountering this novel of radical, revolutionary and Jacobin ideas, and for one who turned to Lord Monboddo's works for comic inspiration in *Melincourt*, Bage would hardly count as an obscure source. *Melincourt* with its splendid scenes of comedy based on the primitivist ideas of Monboddo and his Scottish circle, was being written while Shelley was staying with him at Marlow in 1817, and he could well then or at other times have been intrigued by the primitivism and Noble Savage ideas used by Bage in the portrayal of his hero.[9]

There remains an additional point of interest in the *Hermsprong* passage, already touched on, and present again in Peacock. In the climate of antiquarian thought of the late eighteenth (and indeed the early nineteenth) century the ascription of the earthworks and encampments to a prehistoric rather than to a Roman past is sufficiently unusual to call for comment. It is perhaps significant that it is the young man in each instance who voices this opinion: the older men, representatives of the classical and clerical tradition, are for the Romans. They had indeed tradition, and the opinions of most contemporary antiquaries, to support them, and even so acute a fieldworker as William Stukeley on the whole held this view. In Scotland, Mr Oldbuck could (and did) quote not only Stukeley, but Sir Robert Sibbald, Alexander Gordon and General Roy as authorities on Roman forts, and indeed he might well have added his part-prototype, Sir John Clerk.[10] But curiously enough it is from Scotland that what must be one of the earliest eighteenth-century references to a British hill-fort comes. Significantly for us, it is not in antiquarian literature at all, but in a popular poem, James Thomson's *The Seasons*.

Thomson was a minister's son from Roxburghshire in southern Scotland, and 'Spring', the third of *The Seasons* to be published, came out in 1728. A shepherd is depicted, a conventional figure in a conventional scene, but the hills are unlikely to be other than those among which the poet had been born and spent the first twenty-five years of his life. With the shepherd is his flock:

> . . . his sportive lambs
> This way and that convolved, in friskful glee,
> Their frolics play. And now the sprightly race
> Invites them forth; when swift, the signal given,
> They start away, and sweep the massy mound
> That runs around the hill; the rampart once
> Of iron war, in ancient barbarous times,
> When disunited Briton ever bled
> Lost in eternal broil . . .

Here we clearly have a typical Roxburghshire hill-fort of the Early Iron Age, perhaps indeed that on Southdean Law, above the school where Thomson was taught.

A minute search of the minor topographical poets would no doubt produce more examples comparable to this. Caesar or Tacitus provided literary sources for the urban or stay-at-home poet. It was in Caesar that George Richards found a British fort to adorn his Oxford Prize Poem of 1791, on *The Aboriginal Britons*:

> But plain and simple, in the shadowy wood,
> The shapeless rude-constructed hamlets stood:
> O'er the deep trench an earthy mound arose,
> To guard the sylvan town from beasts and foes.

Others ventured into alternative non-Roman origins for hill-forts, as for instance William Hay, in *Mount Caburn* (1730), which opens in The Caburn, an Early Iron Age hill-fort near Lewes in Sussex:

> This Mount to Mind domestick Discord brings;
> For in a SAXON CAMP my muse now sings.

By the early nineteenth century the Ancient Briton was becoming a Noble Savage—indeed, George Richards had made him that in the 1790s, comparing him with the South Sea Islanders, those paragons of savage nobility of the day, who dwell, in the words of John Ogilvie's *Fane of the Druids* of 1788 (where their life is compared to that of the ancient Britons), 'in the depth of Tahaitean groves' and 'lead the dance on Monootopa's strand'.

Francis Skurray, describing the two adjacent Wiltshire hill-forts of Scratchbury and Battlesbury in *Bidcombe Hill* (1824) obviously approved of the stern virtues of their builders:

> Nor ye vicinal hills, where shepherds lead
> O'er earth constructed battlements their flocks,
> Must ye remain unsung. From your high tops
> Dress'd in the rude habiliments of war
> The sturdy Briton view'd the gleaming mail
> Of foes. . . .

But by this time we are in a world of antiquarian thought where the idea of pre-Roman hill-forts was being generally accepted. Sir Richard Colt Hoare was 'of opinion that the greater part of them may claim a British origin' and indeed noted features that 'bespeak a British origin', specifically at Scratchbury. His *Ancient Wiltshire* of 1812, in which these opinions are recorded, made a deservedly great impression both on antiquaries and on the educated public at large.

A final question arises: were actual ancient earthworks likely to have been envisaged by any of our authors? It seems fairly certain that Scott had no actual prototype on the east coast of Scotland for the Kaim of Kinprunes, for the whole mood of the episode depends on the non-existence of any real antiquity. The Cirencester folly is genuine, and indeed exists today, but the 'Roman camp' is imaginary. But we must pause a moment with Bage, where the scene might allow of an actual site being in the author's mind. *Hermsprong* is set on the Devon-Cornwall border of Dartmoor, but there is nothing to show that the Derbyshire paper-maker knew that part of England on the ground: Godwin in fact commented on his very limited range of travel.[11] The place-names have a wholly unconvincing and fictitious ring: Dr Blick is Rector of Grondale and Sithin, and the main action of the novel takes place in the former village. Place-names ending in -dale are characteristic enough of Derbyshire and North England,[12] but not of the south-west, and the two places seem named with the same craggy oddity as the persons in the novel, an oddity it seems deliberate in Bage, for Hermsprong's name provokes the comment 'a very ugly name—it sounds monstrous Germanish' from Miss Fluart (herself strangely named, unless she is a printer's error for 'Stuart'), and Mr Chestrum confesses his own 'is but an odd sort of name'. A real location therefore seems very unlikely, and anyway the few hill-forts on the eastern edge of Dartmoor are none of them well-known or conspicuous.

Peacock does in fact give what may be a spurious air of topographical precision to the location of Crotchet Castle. It was in the chalk country of the Thames Valley, on downland 'which rose from a steep, but not precipitous, ascent, from the river to the summit of the hill'; there 'were the manifest traces, on the brow of the hill, of a Roman station, or *castellum*, which was still called the castle by the country people'. There were 'primitive mounds and trenches, merely overgrown by greensward, with a few patches of juniper and box on the vallum'. 'The castellated villa at Streatley or Goring—or is it Henley-on-Thames ?' Mr David Garnett has asked the question but has left the answer open.[13] A Roman camp in this Thames Valley context is in fact archaeologically impossible, but prehistoric claimants might be found in the forts of Danesfield or States House above Marlow and Medmenham, or Bozedown above Goring,[14] if one feels that actual topography was ever intended by Peacock. At all events, it looks as though Dr Folliott was wrong, and Captain Fitzchrome right.

NOTES

1   My grateful thanks are due to Dr J. C. Corson of the University of Edinburgh for advice and help on Scott and his possible sources.

2   Cf. S. Piggott, *Antiq.* XXIX, 1955, 150; No. VII below.

3   *The Spiritual Quixote*, 1772, Vol. I, Bk. IV, Ch. v. I am very grateful to Dr Clarence Tracy of the University of British Columbia for drawing my attention to this passage after the original publication of the essay.

4   Mrs Pendarves to Dr Swift, 24 Oct. 1733: *Autobiography and Correspondence of Mary Granville, Mrs Delany*, ed. Lady Llanover, London 1861, I, 421. Cf. Barbara Jones, *Follies and Grottoes* (Second ed., London 1974), 31; David Verey, *Gloucestershire I—The Cotswolds* (Buildings of England, Penguin Books, 1970), 185-6.

5   Quoted in R. A. Aubin, *Topographical Poetry in XVIII Century England*, New York 1936, 134-5. Cf. No. VI above.

6   *Catalogue of the Library at Abbotsford*, Edinburgh 1838, 333.

7   Sir Walter Scott, *Miscellaneous Prose Works*, Edinburgh 1847, I, 338.

8   I have used throughout the introductions and notes to *The Novels of Thomas Love Peacock*, ed. D. Garnett, London 1948.

9   This is a well-trodden path: cf. H. N. Fairchild, *The Noble Savage: A Study in Romantic Naturalism*, New York 1928, repr.

1961; L. Whitney, *Primitivism and the Idea of Progress in English Popular Literature of the Eighteenth Century*, Baltimore 1934.

10 For the antiquarian background, cf. my *William Stukeley: An Eighteenth Century Antiquary*, Oxford 1950; and No. VII above.

11 In a letter to Mary Woolstonecraft, June 1797, quoted by L. Whitney, op. cit., 270.

12 A. H. Smith, *English Place-name Elements* (Eng. Place-name Soc. xxv), Cambridge 1956, 126-7.

13 D. Garnett, op. cit., 645.

14 The evidence is conveniently presented in the Ordnance Survey's *Map of Roman Britain*, 3rd ed., 1956, and *Map of Southern Britain in the Iron Age*, 1962.

IX.

THE ORIGINS OF
THE ENGLISH COUNTY
ARCHAEOLOGICAL
SOCIETIES

The origins of the archaeological societies, on a county or a regional basis, and as a part of Victorian social life, seem hardly to have been considered either by historians of that period, or by archaeologists themselves. One great scholar did however comment on the subject some 45 years ago, and that was Francis Haverfield, in the course of his lectures on Roman Britain at Oxford. 'The study of Roman Britain in the earlier part of the nineteenth century', he wrote, 'was of a different order' from the researches of Mommsen and the German school he had been describing. 'There was new life enough in the country' he went on. 'The reforms of the franchise and the poor law, the development of churchmanship, of elementary education and the public schools are obvious examples of it. In archaeological matters the new growth was perhaps most closely connected with the new religious movement. The antiquarian and the tractarian have much in common. The ascertainment of primitive practice must, or at least ought, to be dear to both, and the two movements, though not in origin the same, probably helped one another.' The new development of interest then 'moves along lines characteristic of the early Victorian age through the formation of societies. This social tendency towards groups is, indeed, one of the most striking features in the educated life of England during the last seventy or eighty years'.[1]

What Haverfield said is of the greatest significance, and it is interesting to compare his views with those of a distinguished nineteenth-century archaeologist, Romilly Allen, published forty years before Haverfield's posthumous volume, in 1884. Allen, discussing the past, present, and future of British archaeology as he saw it, perceived that 'two great causes have operated to raise archaeology in the present century from the level of a learned pastime to that of an exact science', and these he believed to be the Oxford Movement in the church of the 1840s, and the development of geological studies, especially those associated with the names of William Buckland and Boucher de Perthes.[2]

Now Romilly Allen was not specifically concerned with archaeological societies, as Haverfield in part was, but archaeology as a whole. But it is surely significant that both mention the religious movements of the early nineteenth century, and for Allen these represented events of only forty years earlier, embodying ideas and emotions still well remembered and active when he wrote. In fact, if we are to look at the social structure of early Victorian England, of which our older local societies were beginning to form a part, we cannot ignore the religious life of the period. Religion, throughout the last century, played a part in every department of British life and thought in a way that a younger generation at least today may find it difficult, or even repugnant, to credit. But whether we find ourselves sympathetic or not, we ignore this aspect of the age at our peril: in parenthesis, it is sometimes alarmingly ignored by those who should perhaps know better, as when Professor Asa Briggs's popular book, *Victorian People*, omits entirely the churchmen and ministers who moulded so much of nineteenth-century life and thought.

But before we turn to take up this aspect, the importance of which was apparent to Romilly Allen and to Haverfield, we should briefly consider the former's second factor in British archaeological development, geology. Here, while no one would doubt the validity of attaching high importance to the new concepts of the antiquity of man in Victorian archaeology as a whole, can we regard them as factors in the founding of local archaeological societies early in the century, which is our concern? Geological studies had developed in advance of archaeology, with the accompanying formation of specialist societies; the Geological Society itself dates from 1807; among local societies we may notice the Royal Geological Society of Cornwall in 1814; William Smith's famous geological map appeared in 1815, and the Geological Survey was founded in 1835. The subject had become popular in a way irresistibly similar to archaeology today. Professor Buckland's lectures at Oxford were famous from 1820 onwards:

> His eloquence rolled like the Deluge retiring
>> Where mastodon carcases floated;
> To a subject obscure he gave charms so inspiring
>> Young and old on geology doated.

That unpleasant man, Gideon Mantell, was another popular lecturer in geology of the time in Sussex, driving his wife out of his house before the incoming tide of his collection of fossils, while drawing huge audiences to his public addresses; Buckland's *Reliquiae Diluvianae* of 1824, a contemporary wrote, was instrumental in bringing geology 'in favour with the church, and even securing the countenance of the drawing-room'. But it was not only the Church and polite society that were captivated; more important, commerce was involved from the start.

The Cornish society reminds us of the mining interests, and the Industrial Revolution needed geologists on every front — railways, canals, iron-founding, potteries. A bewildered German, Herr Schönbein, attended a meeting of the British Association at Birmingham in 1839, and reported that Buckland in an impressive lecture demonstrated that the Divine Will alone could have brought beds of iron-ore, coal, and limestone into such convenient commercial juxtaposition around Birmingham, and that this fact 'expressed the most clear design of Providence to make the inhabitants of the British Isles, by means of this gift, the most powerful and the richest nation on the earth'. The same sentiment was put more starkly (as befits a Scot) by Hugh Miller in 1841. 'Geology', he wrote, 'in a peculiar manner supplies to the intellect an exercise . . . of ennobling character. But it has also its cash value'.[3]

But an interest in geology associated with Birmingham goes back further than 1839. Josiah Wedgwood in particular, and the other members of the famous Lunar Society in the late eighteenth century in general, were concerned with geology from a purely practical and commercial point of view. They were indeed businessmen who were little concerned with the non-utilitarian aspects of research. John Whitehead, writing to Wedgwood in connection with the impending visit of a pupil of Linnaeus's, puts it bluntly: 'I don't See the Utility of bottony and therefore cant say a word about that pursuit'.[4]

It is not surprising therefore that the manifold interests of the Lunar Society did not include the study of antiquities, except for Wedgwood's practical concern in making copies and versions of the Greek vases which at that time were thought to be Etruscan. One interesting and early example of the application of technological methods to prehistory does however link the Lunar Society to antiquarian studies. When John Williams, himself a 'Mineral Engineer', published his pioneer essay on Scottish vitrified forts in 1777, he included in it not only a plan and section of the Craig Phadrig fort near Inverness by James Watt, then in partnership with Matthew Boulton at the Soho Works, but a technical appendix by Watt in the form of a letter dated from Birmingham and addressed to George Clerk-Maxwell, to whom Williams also dedicated his little book. He was a son of the antiquarian Sir John Clerk of Penicuik, a member of Stukeley's circle, and ancestor of the famous scientist James Clerk-Maxwell, first professor of experimental physics at Cambridge in 1871: the whole episode shows a fascinating interweaving of antiquarian and scientific interests over a century.

Geology, I feel, had already by the 1840s, the period of the first county archaeological societies, become at once too separate and too professional a discipline to play any part in their formation, though of course amateur geology and other natural sciences were often included within their ambit from the start. It was already too late. 'By the 1820s', it has been said, 'geology was acquiring the internal coherence and complexity of a developed natural science'.[5]

And not everyone was swept along in those enthusiastic diluvial lectures of Buckland. An undergraduate attending them in 1821 recorded his impressions of geology:

To tell the truth, the science is so in its infancy that no regular system is formed. Hence the lectures are rather an enumeration of facts from which probabilities are deduced, than a consistent and luminous theory of certainties, illustrated by occasional examples. It is however most entertaining, and opens an amazing field to imagination and to poetry.

The undergraduate was John Henry Newman, whose search for a luminous theory of certainties was to lead him over twenty years later, in 1845, to be accepted into the Roman communion.

In the intervening couple of decades he and others at Oxford, and like-minded young men at Cambridge, brought about a revolution in the Church of England which had repercussions extending far beyond questions of doctrine or belief, among them, as Romilly Allen and Haverfield successively saw, important effects on the development of British archaeology.[6] It is not for nothing that Keble's Assize Sermon on National Apostasy was delivered in 1833 and the Oxford *Tracts for the Times* ran from that year to 1845, while the British Archaeological Association and the county societies of Northamptonshire and Lincolnshire were founded in 1844, the Norfolk Society in 1846 and the Cambrian Archaeological Association in 1847, the Sussex, Bedfordshire, and Buckinghamshire Archaeological Societies in the same year, followed by Lancashire and Cheshire in 1848, Somerset in 1849, Wiltshire in 1853, Surrey in 1854, and Leicestershire in 1855, to mention only some of the first decade.

This is not the time or place, nor have I the competence, to discuss the strictly religious aspect of what became conveniently called the Oxford Movement in the English Church. As G. M. Young put it, at the beginning of the nineteenth century, 'in dogma, there was little to choose between a worthy clergyman of evangelical cast and a worthy dissenting minister'. Before the 1840s there had been 'a somewhat formless individualism' in the Dissenting bodies — Unitarians, Independents, Baptists, and many others — which were to be welded together by the example of Wesleyan Methodism as developed by such leaders as Jabez Bunting, and were to become a very important element in lower-class and lower-middle-class circles, particularly in mercantile and mining regions, and powerfully affecting the constitution of political parties and the Trade Unions. On the other hand, the Anglican church was shaken out of what had at worst been an effete aristocratic inertia and at best a smug evangelical pietism, by the demand by the younger members of Oxford and Cambridge, 'enchanted by Scott and bemused by Coleridge', for a new 'Anglican self-consciousness, parallel to the self-consciousness of the Protestant denominations, based on the assurance of apostolic descent, and inevitably, tending to sympathy, at least, with the one Church whose apostolic origin could not be denied'. The Tractarians and their followers were directing the thoughts of the Anglican clergy to the past of their faith and of their Church, and from the Church to their respective parish churches was not only an easy but, in the circumstances of a revised liturgy, an inevitable transition. 'Liturgical science became a passion with the younger clergy, and the wave of restoration and church building brought with it a keen, sometimes a ludicrous, preoccupation with symbolism'.[7] But not only this. In turning the attention of the parson, the squire, and the churchwardens to the structure and fabric of their church, the movement injected a stiff dose of medieval archaeology and architectural history into the clerical and lay population of parish after parish.

It is perhaps difficult now to realise the appearance of English churches, particularly in country parishes, 150 years ago. Archdeacon Francis Wrangham, reporting on his Visitation of Cleveland in 1820, wrote:

> In many places during my late Visitation I could not help contrasting the unventilated and gloomy Parish Church — its tattered Books, ruinous Seats, green Walls, rugged Pavement, dilapidated Turrets and broken Fences — with the clean and airy Conventicle.[8]

Wakeman, writing later in the century, evoked 'the whitewashed walls, the damp stone floors, the ceiled roof, the high stiff pews with mouldy green baize cushions and faded red curtains . . . the mean table with a moth-eaten red cloth upon it in the chancel . . . the dirt . . . the indescribable dank smell of decay'. We see such interiors, even if transmuted by a great artist, in many of John Sell Cotman's water-colours; churches where you well might find the fonts 'filled with candles and brushes', if not wholly removed for 'horse-troughs, or as ornaments to a publick teagarden'.[9] Monuments, as Charles Stothard found on these antiquarian tours he described so gaily and charmingly in his letters, would almost inevitably be covered thickly by 'a barbarous coat of whitewash or other plastering (called by country churchwardens *beautifying*)', brasses mutilated or vanished since their last record, sold by the churchwardens or in use by workmen in the churchyard as a frying-pan.[10] The Dean of Exeter, addressing the Diocesan Architectural Society in 1842, reminded his audience that 'we may now see in most of our rural churches a rabble of boors and boys seated on the very rails and steps of the altar, and the altar itself used to place their hats on'.[11] Nor was decorum much better observed by the gentry. 'The tedium of a long service, or the

19. *W. Dereham Church, by Cotman, c. 1810.*

THE TOWER OF W... DEREHAM CH'RCH

To Thomas Harvey Esq.
this Print is Respectfully Dedicated by his Obt Hum'le Ser.

J S Cotman

appetite engendered by it, was relieved by the entry of a servant with sherry and light refreshment' in many an eighteenth-century church and, as late as 1842, the same year as Dean Lowe's address, J. M. Neale, whom we shall shortly encounter again, wrote of Tong in Shropshire: 'The Squire has built a pew in the Chancel; when the Commandments are begun, a servant regularly enters at the Chancel door with the luncheon tray!'.[12]

There were indeed sightseers of a kind already visiting cathedrals at least. Neale in 1843 has no patience with the 'holyday-making artizans and shopkeepers of provincial towns' who were 'entertained during a visit to a cathedral' by vergers who should have known better — 'who can reprobate the apathy and remissness in too strong terms, who not only allow, but even encourage, the grossest acts of irreverence ?', retailing 'some low joke or scurrilous jest to the low minded party that they were conducting, who rewarded it with a laugh'. At St Albans, the vergers organised a blindfold race from the west door to the choir, so that you might 'see three or four persons at once playing at this profane species of blind man's buff, staggering about the nave and aisles, and affording the highest amusement to the spectators'.[13]

But by the turn of the century we are in a different world: such conditions would hardly have been tolerated in Trollope's cathedral or diocese of Barchester, and even his Archdeacon Grantly (by no manner of means a ritualist, one imagines) would, one feels, in G. M. Young's words, 'hardly suspect the hand of the Pope at work when the Communion Table ceased to be a depository for hats, the font a receptacle for umbrellas'. The world is that of the English parish church of today, but it is infrequently realised by those anxious, and rightly anxious, to preserve its appearance against change, that they are campaigning to perpetuate (and I quote the Reverend B. F. L. Clarke) 'the expression of the ideals of a small pietistic society founded by undergraduates at Cambridge at the beginning of the reign of Queen Victoria. So powerful [he goes on] is the influence of faith, even if it be mistaken, and so irresistible is the force of obstinacy'.[14]

The Cambridge society in question is little known to most people today, though its effects are visible in almost every Anglican church in Britain. Independently, but virtually simultaneously in 1839, there were founded two societies, one The

Oxford Society for Promoting the Study of Gothic Architecture
and the other, The Cambridge Camden Society, so named after
the sixteenth-century antiquary.[15] The Oxford society was later
to alter its name to The Oxford Architectural and Historical
Society, under which it still flourishes and produces its distinguished archaeological journal *Oxoniensia*; the Cambridge
group eventually formed the nucleus of the London-based
Ecclesiological Society in 1846, which came to an end in 1862.
Both were directly related to the new movements in the Church,
and the Camdenians, who had been founded by two undergraduates, J. M. Neale and Benjamin Webb, set out their aims
as 'the study of Ecclesiastical Architecture and the restoration
of mutilated architectural remains'. The High Church Angli-
cans asserting their claim to represent a church with a continuous past going back before the Reformation, needed the
right kind of buildings in which to perform the English rite—
'long chancels, choir stalls, returned stalls for the clergy, fonts
and altars raised on steps, frontals, altar crosses. . . . This was
the new ideal; and as a result of it there arose also a new society
and a new word'.[16] The Society was the Cambridge Camdenians,
the word ecclesiology, and ecclesiologist. Very much a vogue-
word in the 1840s, it too is almost forgotten today unless we
remember our Betjeman:

> Broad of church and broad of mind
> Broad before and broad behind
> A keen ecclesiologist
> A rather dirty Wykehamist.

The two societies, as one views them across a century, had
contrasted characters from the first. The Cambridge group, as
we saw, was an undergraduate idea from the start, and in the
persons of Neale and Webb had two vehement, tactless, and
arrogant young men, full of architectural rectitude and a hideous
consciousness of their liturgical superiority: the Society issued
pamphlet after didactic pamphlet—*A Few Words to Churchwardens*, *A Few Words to Church Builders*, *Twenty-three Reasons
for Getting Rid of Church Pues* and so on. They were instantan-
eously successful. *A Few Words to Churchwardens* sold 5,000
copies in the first six weeks of publication; 13,000 had been
circulated by 1843, and, as has been said, 'probably a copy
reached almost every parish in England'. They sharply and
publicly criticised ecclesiastical architects and offered their

expert help in terms nearer to a demand for the submission of their working drawings in advance, and this indeed was not infrequently done. Oxford was less vociferous and less fierce. The Society, although from the beginning including junior members of the University, also contained an impressive series of Establishment figures in the form of senior dons, heads of houses, and distinguished architects. It wielded power in the architectural world in the manner of Camdenians, but more tactfully and less shrilly. It moved quietly with the times, by the 1860s if not before, by dropping its original exclusive interest in church architecture, liturgy, and symbolism, and becoming a local archaeological society of the normal later Victorian type.

The importance of the architectural as well as the liturgical changes was of course noticed at the time. Tom Mozley, in his *Reminiscences* of the Oxford Movement, wrote of 'the great ecclesiological and ritual revival which has changed not only the inside of our churches but the face of the land'.[17] Newman, however, remained unaffected by the changing of setting and ceremony, and continued while still a member of the Anglican church to perform his religious services in the traditional manner of the previous century.

The original Cambridge Camdenians were by no means consistent in their ideas about the nature of ecclesiology and its origins. Archdeacon Thorpe, President of the Society in 1844, looked to the romantic poets: Wordsworth, he said, 'might be considered one of the founders of the Society. He had sown the seed' which had led 'to the recall of whatever was pure and imaginative',[18] and I shall dwell on this topic for a moment later on. J.S. Howson, however, writing in the first number of *The Ecclesiologist* three years earlier, took up what we might today think of as a more distinctively Cambridge archaeological viewpoint when he declared that 'Ecclesiology, like Astronomy and Geology, is an Inductive Science'.[19] The phrase is newly-minted Cambridge coinage itself, invented by William Whewell, Master of Trinity, whose *History of the Inductive Sciences* had come out in 1837, his *Philosophy* of them in 1840. And this is not all. Whewell was a very remarkable man, to whom, incidentally, we owe as deliberate inventions not only the words *scientist* and *physicist*, but many others, such as *anode* and *cathode* in electricity and *miocene* and *pliocene* in geology.[20] But his far-reaching interests did not stop with theology, philosophy, mathematics, mineralogy, and international law, but included ecclesiology, and he published the first edition of his *Architectural Notes on German Churches* in 1830, thus showing not only the wide range of his own studies, but the irresistible contemporary appeal of the subject. He later, in 1838 and 1840, wrote some very poor light verse on the digging of a group of Roman barrows known as the Bartlow Hills, at which he seems to have been present.[21]

However much we criticise the early church restorers, and with reason, and however hard we may find it to appreciate many of the new churches built at that time, we cannot escape from the recognition that it was the proselytising vigour of the Camdenians that brought an appreciation of ancient buildings —and by an easy extension, ancient monuments in general— into the lives of the English upper and middle classes in the 1840s as never before. For restoration or for new designs both societies built up archives of notes and drawings of medieval churches on as wide a front as possible. The Camdenians issued an elaborate questionnaire which was used by both societies, listing every possible feature of a church and its fittings in systematic order and under elaborate classified headings, the precursor of the record cards which were used by the staff of the English Ancient Monuments Commission.

It was all very earnest, rather priggish, and dangerously doctrinaire, but its results were extraordinary. People started looking at their churches in a new way, and the question of restoration or rebuilding might easily be contentious and always a topic of discussion: churches could no longer be ignored. Many ecstatic phrases were used of the new work by contemporaries, but furious disapprobation was equally expressed. The Bishop of Manchester ran amok in the newly restored church of St John's, Higher Broughton, and 'gave an exhibition of maniacal fury. He cast down cushions and altar cloths; he screwed off carved ornaments and dashed them on the pavement', while shouting that he hoped the local boys would soon break the new windows.[22] Churches were lively subjects for discussion, and so automatically was medieval architecture, and the whole question of the preservation and conservation of ancient buildings. 'Do not let us talk of restoration' wrote Ruskin in 1849 .'The thing is a lie from beginning to end', and in 1854 he proposed to the Society of Antiquaries the formation of a committee for the preservation of ancient monuments. William Morris was equally alarmed and even more outspoken: there is a story of his stamping down the aisle of an over-restored church shouting 'Beasts! Pigs! Damn their souls!'.[23] In 1877 he founded the Society for the Preservation of Ancient Buildings, anticipating the wholly permissive first Ancient Monuments Act by five years, and this by definition did not concern itself with functioning churches. Local societies now began to come into existence to bring together the increasing number of persons, especially in rural districts, who wanted to meet and talk about such things.

Reading the literature of the period one notes straight away the involvement of archaeology with religion, even when in no sense concerned with the dangerous topics of ancient man and geology. In the early days of the Royal Archaeological Institute a member threatened resignation because someone had been elected to the Council who was a Socinian: he denied the divinity of Christ, and was therefore a heretic. I suppose, though, this is only as if someone today objected to a Maoist or a supporter of apartheid as an officer of the Institute: our prejudices are transferred to other forms of faith. In the early days of the Lincoln-shire Society for the Encouragement of Ecclesiastical Anti-quities (founded in 1844) there was overt expression of religi-ous intolerance. 'One of the most distinguished architects in the county, Edward James Willson, was a Roman Catholic. Al-though he could do work for the dean and chapter — who were not thought sound on the new architectural gospel — and col-laborated with Welby Pugin, he never became a member. Nor was there any place for dissenters. When in 1857 the Revd. G. B. Mellor, a Wesleyan minister at Grimsby, was proposed for election as *Mr* Mellor, it was declared that the proposal was dis-pleasing to a portion of the committee, and his name was with-drawn'.[24]

It is perhaps surprising to find E. A. Freeman, later to become Regius Professor of modern History at Oxford, objecting to the Archaeological Institute's attitude to medieval archaeology. He felt indeed that 'the grand objection to the Institute seems to me to be what its name expresses, that it is merely archaeological on points where mere archaeology is worse than useless'. One might think Freeman went on to deplore an insufficient use of docu-mentary sources, but no: 'the Institute is wrong in applying to higher matters the merely antiquarian tone which belongs to inferior ones', and making an archaeological approach to 'painting, sculpture, architecture . . . without recognising either their aesthetical or their religious character. . . . Their manner of treating heathen remains would be absurd, unphilosophical, unartistick; when applied to sacred things, it is all this, and irreverent into the bargain'.[25] Freeman, at least as a young man, was deeply committed to the Tractarian cause, and could write purple passages about church ornaments almost indistinguishable from those of Pugin. And I can quote what seems to me a curiously parallel passage from an archaeological address of only a few years ago. 'The methods of prehistory', said Dr Joan Evans in her Anniversary speech to the Society of Antiquaries, 'have, in the younger generation, begun to take over historic and well-documented periods in which more subtle, more aesthetic, and more civilised methods of approach should primarily be employed'.[26] I trust I am not being irreverent into the bargain.

I hope you will not think I have dwelt too long on the influence which I believe the Tractarian Movement had, indirectly, on the development of British local archaeology between about 1840 and 1860. It was not of course the only factor leading to the foundation of the societies with which we are concerned today, and I shall suggest others shortly. In the meantime we must remember that though many of our older county societies were formed around the middle of the century, there are certain senior bodies. The Gentlemen's Society of Spalding, founded in 1710, has always had antiquarian interests, but was not primarily formed with this object. But from the founding of the Society of Antiquaries of London in 1717 sprang two junior archaeological bodies, the Society of Antiquaries of Scotland in 1780, and that of Newcastle upon Tyne in 1813. Both represent the great development of cultural activities in the North once the affairs of 1745 had been settled, and in Edinburgh the Antiquaries soon had, as their scientific counterpart, the Royal Society of Edinburgh, founded in 1783. The philosophical questions of early human society were the subject of much discussion among Scottish men of learning at this time, and Lord Monboddo was even asking awkward questions about men and apes, and in such a climate of thought a new interest in the monuments of Scotland's past arose.

Here we should turn for a moment to consider the profound

influence of Sir Walter Scott and other romantics of his time on British antiquarian interests at large. The field has been well covered and much discussed, but a few points may be made which have direct bearing on our enquiry into the first local archaeological societies. To recall dates and indicate the force of popular interest, the Waverley novels (I would remind you that the name derived not from any romantic Scottish stronghold, but from a comfortable country house in Surrey) began publication in 1814, and over the next 25 years there were 266 paintings based on them exhibited in public galleries; *Ivanhoe* was published in 1819 and thereafter two pictures each year illustrated scenes from this novel alone, and in 1820 dramatised versions were running concurrently in six London theatres. The Tower Armouries, opening in 1828, were immensely popular as a public exhibition, drawing up to 40,000 visitors a year, and medievalism was given its most famous and ludicrous advertisement in the ill-starred Eglinton Tournament of 1839, when Lord Londonderry, as King of the Tournament, survived the cloudburst that descended on the spectacle by riding in procession in medieval armour under a large green umbrella.[27] It was in this heady atmosphere of Scott's poems and novels, and, as Archdeacon Thorpe saw, the influence of other romantic poets such as Wordsworth, that the seeds of the first local antiquarian societies were sown.

But there is another, less superficial aspect, recently surveyed with erudition and elegance by Professor Trevor-Roper, the very nature of the romantic approach to history.[28] Historiography in the eighteenth century, the approach of Montesquieu or of Hume, was on the whole a philosophical exploration, in terms of the contemporary rationalism of the Encyclopaedists, of a generalised human past, seeking for a demonstration of universal processes of sociological development. The attitude was Olympian and detached, and in France those who held it were *les philosophes*, sharply to be distinguished from those inferior beings *les érudits*, who were antiquarians, epigraphists, and paleographers. Gibbon, whose greatness lay in his appreciation of both approaches, was shocked by encountering this dichotomy when visiting France in 1763, and contrasted 'the intolerant zeal of the philosophers' with the 'good sense and learning' of those who concerned themselves with the hard facts of antiquarian studies.[29] The romantics such as Scott found the subject-matter of their study of the past not in philosophical abstractions but in the local and particular, in ballads and traditions, in abbeys and castles, in the antiquities and land-scape of a region known deeply and personally. The new poets, with Wordsworth supreme, again expressed their deep attach-ment to the *genius loci*, whether among the Lakes or elsewhere.

In such a changing view of history—and Trevor-Roper shows how not only writers in this country, but historians in Germany were moving towards this new model of the past at this time—local antiquarian studies bulked large: a climate of thought and feeling was created in which the foundation of regional archaeological societies was almost inevitable, and by the late 1830s the new ecclesiastical movements in Oxford and Cambridge acted as the decisive catalyst. It is curiously interest-ing to the historian of ideas to see among archaeologists today something of a restatement of the eighteenth-century position, with the appearance of *les philosophes* among those who seek an intellectual alliance with the generalising disciplines of theo-retical sociology, as against *les érudits* of an older tradition of empirical studies.

The ludicrous can often illuminate an aspect of an age as well as the serious, and we should remember for instance that Bill Stumps made his mark on epigraphical studies (through that notable local society the Pickwick Club) in 1827. Still more to the point is the enormous popularity enjoyed by the comic mock-medievalism of the Reverend Richard Harris Barham's prose and verse *Ingoldsby Legends*, which appeared between 1837 and 1843; the first a prose tale, including a house-party picnic in a ruined abbey complete with Mr Simpkinson of Bath, the FSA, probably intended as a caricature of John Britton. Here, too, is a memorably funny interchange between Miss Simpkinson, who writes romantic poetry about ruins, and the engaging Cockney vulgarian Mr Peters:

'Did you ever see an old abbey before, Mr Peters?'

'Yes, miss, A French one; we have got one at Ramsgate; he teaches the Miss Joneses to parley-voo, and is turned of sixty.'

Barham is linked to Scott by a common intimate friendship with Mrs Hughes, wife of a Canon of St Paul's, and a great repository of local Berkshire stories, most genuine, but some likely to have been invented: from her Scott got the legend of

Wayland's Smithy and Barham that of the Pyes of Faringdon. Her grandson was Thomas Hughes of *Tom Brown's Schooldays* and *The Scouring of the White Horse* of 1859, which contains an antiquary based on J. Y. Akerman. *The Ingoldsby Legends* were in their way a reaction to the Tractarians, ridiculing the *Lives of the Saints* edited by Mark Pattison and J. A. Froude: Canon Hughes roundly stated that the object of Barham's verses was 'to quiz that spirit of flirtation with the scarlet lady of Babylon which has of late assumed a pretty marked aspect'.[30]

Scotland had become accessible to travellers after the '45 by the improved road system, and this is something which is I think closely related to the emergence of the English county archaeological societies in the 1840s and 1850s. The improvement of the public highways had begun at the end of the eighteenth century as a result of the new legislation embodied in the Turnpike Acts, and improvement was long overdue. Roads were in a medieval, a Dark Ages state of disrepair and neglect. 'But, my dear Sir, what am I to say of the roads in this country! The turnpikes! as they have the assurance to call them, and the hardiness to make one pay for . . . mere rocky lanes, full of hugeous stones as big as one's horse, and abominable holes'. So Arthur Young, writing from Chepstow on his *Southern Tour* of 1768. In Suffolk he found 'ponds of liquid dirt, and a scattering of loose flints, just sufficient to lame every horse that moves near them', and vehicular traffic over long distances might be impeded by a failure of the wheels to fit the local ruts. Commenting on Gloucestershire ruts, Young 'found by them they build their wagons with their wheels full three inches nearer to each other than in the eastern counties . . . a *Norfolk* or *Suffolk* wagon would not stir even in this *turnpike road*'.[31] This is an interesting observation, and is confirmed by the measurements of the wheel tracks of recent farm wagons in east and west England.[32] Good roads were beginning to be built, however, and Young is enthusiastic about the Salisbury-Romsey highway: the number of turnpikes increased by almost five times between 1750 and 1790. With better roads came increasing mobility, and as Christopher Hussey put it 'All over England the appreciation of scenery, the experiencing of romantic emotions, and the perception of the sublime in nature increased in direct ratio to the number of turnpike acts'.[33] The Romantic Tour, the Search for the Picturesque, were now beginning, and with this came ancient monuments, so many of them picturesque before the restorers tidied them into neat gravel-pathed rockeries in the safest suburban taste. The keen ecclesiologist is about—'the church visitor, with his knapsack on his back, his sketch-book, and note-book, and foot-rule, and measuring-tape in his pocket, his good oak stick in his hand, with fair weather, and a fine tract of churches before him', sharply distinguished by Neale from his predecessors, the 'amateur church sketchers and Gothick archi-tecture connoisseurs . . . Oh! preserve me from such people! I cannot bear their slang about grotesque ornaments, Gothick side-aisles, Saxon doorways and all the rest'.[34] But there was not only the individual church visitor, there was the Archaeo-logical Excursion.

An underrated factor in all this was I am sure the sheer in-tolerable boredom of the winter in country house or rectory, parsonage or gentleman's place. The spirit that drove Chaucer's Canterbury pilgrims gratefully to travel in the spring must have pricked the corages of many more down the centuries whose delights were not in the hunt or the shoot, and the tour or the excursion allowed one to escape, alone or in congenial company, from rooms grown all too familiar and relatives far too well known. It also not only allowed men to escape, but intelligent women, in a society where they were normally expected to find all the amusement they needed in being a pious mother, like Christina Pontifex, or a dutiful daughter of the house, engaged in that 'faddling twaddling and the endless tweedling of nose-gays in jugs' that so annoyed the young Florence Nightingale in 1839.[35] The early archaeological societies all contained women members, associates or hangers-on, and so just slightly loosened the constricting bonds of contemporary convention. Tennyson's *Princess* of 1847 is concerned with this attitude. Set in Sir Walter Vivian's park and house, it gives us a glimpse of a private museum, where:

> on the pavement lay
> Carved stones of the Abbey-ruin in the park
> Huge Ammonites, and the first bones of Time;
> And on the tables every clime and age
> Jumbled together; celts and calumets,
> Claymore and snowshoe.

And while the Mechanics' Institute are conducting philoso-phical experiments in the park, Aunt Elizabeth appears, and

> then the maiden aunt
> Took this fair day for text, and from it preach'd
> An universal culture for the crowd.

The archaeological societies were also to contribute in their way
to popular education, by bringing together people of common
interests, at winter lectures or in summer excursions. Here we
can turn to the Cambrian Archaeological Association.

This had been founded in 1847 by two Welsh clergymen,
Longueville Jones and John Williams, the former a very keen
ecclesiologist and archaeologist, the latter a patriot deluded by
the nonsense of Iolo Morganwg and Owen Pughe. They had
been brought together by a church controversy in 1836 about
the merging of the dioceses of St Asaph and Bangor, and as Sir
John Lloyd put it, 'ecclesiastical policy led to archaeology'.[36] In
the first year of their existence (just when Aunt Elizabeth was
preaching) they visited Strata Florida, and the local newspaper
report, now a well-known collector's piece, bears repetition:

> The scene at the Abbey was at one time a most interesting
> one, several ladies having joined the party. Architects and
> draughtsmen were measuring and sketching portions of old
> buildings and one dignitary of the church was transferring
> the resemblance of the gateway to his sketch-book. . . . All
> seemed to vie with each other who should do most towards
> the advancement of the object of the excursion; and whilst
> intelligent commoners were measuring the building, an
> enthusiastic nobleman might be seen busily washing the
> tiles and ornaments for removal and preservation.[37]

This has everything: the ladies, the architects, church digni-
taries, commoners and noblemen, thoroughly enjoying the
excursion, and although the snobbish tone is enchantingly comic
today, the power of such meetings in breaking, however parti-
ally, through the strict divisions of the rigidly stratified social
structure of the day can have done nothing but good.

An anonymous writer in 1856 reassures his readers that
archaeologists are not all musty old gentlemen, 'and especially
the most interesting part of that section [of the public] the
"young lady" portion' is reminded 'that there are *young* archaeologists as well as *old*; and that even "military young gentlemen"
are not infrequently brought within the magic circle of archaeology, and that "papers" at "Institutes" have been positively
lisped from beneath as faultless and magnificent a pair of

moustachios as ever graced a parade, or did their resistless execution in the ball-room'.[38] And later, in lecturing to the Oxford Architectural and Historical Society in 1870, J.H. Parker stands firm on women in archaeology.

> When archaeology is made part of the system of Education in Oxford, as I trust it will be ... any educated man will feel it a disgrace to be ignorant of it ... the ladies are already taking the lead in this matter ... I have frequently observed in society that to find out whether a young lady knows anything of Archaeology or not, is a test whether she has been highly educated or not. The daughters of our higher nobility ... are almost always well acquainted with Archaeology. Some of my favourite pupils have been young ladies of this class, our future Duchesses or Countesses.[39]

In *The Princess*, some of you may remember, Tennyson had dreamed of women's colleges

> With prudes for proctors, dowagers for deans,
> And sweet girl-graduates in their golden hair—

and if Parker had his way, they would all no doubt be reading archaeology.

But, more seriously, I think we have touched on some significant points. The impact of the architectural expression of the High Church movement in the 1840s; the new romantic approach to history, the improvement of transport with new roads and, of course, for long-distance travel between towns, the railways (the London and Birmingham from 1828); the receptive temper of the times—earnest, anxious for self-improvement, socially ambitious; the development of geology and prehistory: all these combined to make the emergence of local archaeological societies inevitable around the middle of the last century. Social ambition and self-improvement should not be ignored: we must remember the Mechanics' Institutes which figure (as we saw) in *The Princess*, and the Working Men's College, founded by F.D.Maurice in 1854, of which Neddy Baily, in Thomas Hughes's *Scouring of the White Horse* (1859), was an enthusiastic eighteen-year-old member five years later: Hughes was Principal of the College from 1872 to 1883.

Opinions could be divided on the question of railway travel. Neale thought that 'the traveller on the railway has many new and beautiful scenes opened out to him; and much the advantage, if he be gifted with any power of abstraction, over the traveller by the old method, in point of picturesqueness'. But on the other hand, he would 'agree with every one as to the immense moral mischief that railroads have caused and will cause to England, making it one huge manufacturing town' by promoting population mobility.[40]

On a personal level too the societies could provide escape from a constricting home background; an opportunity for mixing among different classes of men, and a chance for women to think and talk about antiquarian problems in common with members of the opposite sex. One of the Camdenian publications is in the form of a conversation in a Wiltshire church between Mr Herbert, the incumbent, his wife and daughter, and an ill-informed Miss Newmarsh who is indoctrinated by the others in ecclesiology: no doubt such discussions did take place, privately or at local societies' meetings.

I mentioned a few founding dates earlier on: a dozen or more local architectural and archaeological societies in the decade 1845–55 came into being in response to a new social need over much of England. There are of course others, but these are representative enough. What does emerge, if we admit the great part played by the Tractarians, is that the earliest societies are practically all in those parts of England dominated by the Anglican church and with an agricultural and squirearchical background, and not in the industrial Midlands and North where Nonconformity of some kind was prevalent, and naturally without any interest in the fabrics of the ancient churches which represented all the misguided traditions from which the various sects had dissented and seceded. North of the Border this situation was intensified and exacerbated, with the sour smell of the success of Calvinism, and the sad neglect or destruction of church fabrics. 'But above all, what misery is it to make a church-tour in Scotland! I think nothing can surpass the desecration there', wrote Neale in 1843.[41] The industrial areas were of course not without their learned societies, but these were concerned with interests other than antiquarian, and were broadly 'philosophical' in the eighteenth-century sense. The Lunar Society at the end of that century is one of the more renowned of these, parallel with the more formally constituted Literary and Philosophical Society of Manchester, founded in 1781, or the Philosophical Society of Derby, of 1783. In Birmingham, a Philosophical Institution dating from 1800 had scarcely 50 years of life, but by 1854 the Birmingham and Midland Institute was founded, from which the Archaeological Society emerged in 1870.

We have come to a point which I touched on some years ago in my Presidential Address to the Prehistoric Society—the concept of British social geography. Commenting on the precocious development of prehistoric studies, particularly in the field, in the 1920s and 1930s, I said 'The distribution in the countryside and in the smaller provincial towns of persons of taste and education, leisure and intellectual ability, was and is very unequal in Britain. . . . It was this country-dwelling middle class, in those areas where it was to be found, that initiated and fostered archaeological development . . . and an index to its intensity or scarcity would be the flourishing, or dimly functioning, or the non-existence of a local archaeological society'.[42] Now I think that behind the 1930s we can see the 1830s. Well before the middle of the nineteenth century the Industrial Revolution had disrupted the traditional pattern of rural life in much of England, from Birmingham to Bradford and beyond. In the traditional pattern, 'whatever differences existed in the lives and outlook of a gentleman, a yeoman, and a cottager were mitigated by their common subjection to the ebb and flow of the world, the seasons and the hours . . . the traditional morality and culture of England were based on the patriarchal village family in all degrees . . . on Sunday they went together, great and small, to worship in the village church'. This was the southern, rural, order of things. 'Lying outside the orbit of the old ruling class, neglected by their natural leaders, the industrial territories were growing up as best they might, undrained, unpoliced, ungoverned, and unschooled'.[43] The Two Nations had come into existence: Disraeli's *Sybil*, with this phrase as a sub-title, was published in 1845.

Over thirty years ago I wrote a juvenile essay relating British archaeology to the Romantic Movement in literature and the visual arts, a movement arising in the educated middle and upper classes and intimately linked with the non-industrial countryside, even if blast-furnaces or mines could on occasion be accepted as lurid and horrid aspects of the Picturesque.[44] In many of its aspects, the Tractarian Movement in the Anglican church had its origins in much the same sentiments, and to go

21. *Queen Mary's Chapel, E. Lothian, c.1842.*

back to Haverfield's phrase, 'the antiquarian and the tractarian have much in common' in the middle of the last century. To provide for shared common interests in archaeology and antiquities, the county societies came into being in Anglican, rural England. The societies were an answer to an intellectual and emotional need; they were desirable and approved social artifacts, and remained this while the temper of middle-class English society had not itself unduly changed from that at the time of their inception.

I have put before you a necessarily brief but I hope not too superficial outline of what seem to me to have been the social and intellectual forces which brought into being the local archaeological bodies in England from the 1840s onwards. From that time until today they have formed the framework of our insular archaeological activity: whether this framework is still the right one to accommodate the changes in our society and our archaeology which have taken place since the nineteenth century is not for us to decide today.

[Queen Mary's Chapel at Seton, in East Lothian, already noticed in page 167, affords a beautiful specimen of the religious Gothic; and the state of ruin in which it now exists is just such as to render it a pleasing subject for the artist, without depriving the antiquary of the means of fully enjoying it.—E.]

NOTES

1 *The Roman Occupation of Britain*, Oxford 1924, 81.

2 J. R. Allen, *Arch. Camb.* 1884, 232 ff. I am grateful to Dr D. V. Clarke for drawing my attention to this source.

3 The foregoing brief sketch of the geology of the period is taken from C. C. Gillispie, *Genesis and Geology*, New York 1951, with the quotations from Buckland, Schönbein and Miller.

4 R. E. Schofield, *The Lunar Society of Birmingham*, Oxford 1963, 95, 101; Watt and Williams, 175.

5 S. Toulmin and J. Goodfield, *The Discovery of Time* (Penguin Books, 1967), 199.

6 The quotation from Newman is in G. Faber, *Oxford Apostles* (Penguin Books 1954), 71.

7 Quotations from G. M. Young, *Victorian England: Portrait of an Age*, London 1944. My indebtedness to the late author extends beyond the study cited here, in the form of conversations over many years on the topics here discussed.

8 M. Sadleir, 'Archdeacon Francis Wrangham 1769-1842' in *Things Past*, London 1944, 223; Wakeman quoted by Faber, op. cit., 93.

9 Cambridge Camden Society, *A Few Words to Church-wardens II*, 5th edn., Cambridge 1842, 8.

10 Mrs Charles Stothard, *Memoirs . . . of the late Charles Alfred Stothard*, London 1823, 88; Anon., *Essex Naturalist* III, 1889, 199 (brasses).

11 J. F. White, *The Cambridge Movement*, Cambridge 1962, 4.

12 J. R. Abbey and J. H. Overton, *English Church in the Eighteenth Century*, ii, London, 423, quoted in M. S. Briggs, *Goths and Vandals*, London 1952, 132.

13 J. M. Neale, *Hierologus: or the Church Tourists*, London 1843; these dialogues 'recording, for the most part, the incidents and impressions of church tours' made with Benjamin Webb, were published when Neale was 25 and Webb a year younger. I am very grateful to Professor Giles Robertson for bringing this fascinating source to my knowledge.

14 B. F. L. Clarke, *Church Builders of the Nineteenth Century*, London 1938, 106.

15 For the Cambridge Camden Society, White and Clarke, opp. cit.; Oxford, W. A. Pantin, *Oxoniensia* iv (1939), 174; S. L. Ollard, ibid., v (1940), 146.

16 Clarke, op. cit., 75.

17 White, *The Cambridge Movement*, 21.

18 Ibid., 28.

19 Ibid., 49.

20 P. B. Medawar, *Induction and Intuition in Scientific Thought*, London 1969, 10, with refs.

21 C. G. B. Daubeney (ed.), *Fugitive Poems connected with Natural History and Physical Science*, London 1869, 216-23. I am indebted to Prof. J. V. S. Megaw for this reference.

22 J. F. White, op. cit., 101.

23 M. S. Briggs, *Goths and Vandals*, 203, 211; Joan Evans, *A History of the Society of Antiquaries*, Oxford 1956, 309.

24 Sir Francis Hill, *Lincs. Hist. & Archaeology* I, 1966, 59.

25 Quoted by Pantin, loc. cit.

26 Anniversary Address to the Society of Antiquaries of London, 1961; *Antiq. Journ.* XLI, 1961, 149.

27 I. Anstruther, *The Knight and the Umbrella*, London 1963, *passim*.

28 H. R. Trevor-Roper, *The Romantic Movement and the Study of History* (John Coffin Memorial Lecture), London 1969.

29 J. Seznec, *Essais sur Diderot et l'Antiquité*, Oxford 1957, especially chap. V; A. Momigliano, 'Gibbon's contribution to historical method', *Studies in Historiography*, London 1966, 40. Cf. No. VII above.

30 J. B. Atlay, Introduction to *The Ingoldsby Legends*, London 1903. The Wayland's Smithy legend appears to have been first recorded by Francis Wise, *A letter to Dr Mead concerning some antiquities in Berkshire*, Oxford 1738, 37. The absence of finds of ancient or recent small change in the extensive excavations of 1962-3 is curious.

31 A. Young, *A Six Week's Tour of the Southern Counties of England and Wales*, London 1769, 153, 143.

32 Cf. the measurements in J. G. Jenkins, *The English Farm Wagon*, Reading 1961, App. I.

33 C. Hussey, *The Picturesque*, London 1927, 100. Cf. No. VI above.

34 Neale, *Hierologus*, 92.

35 C. Woodham-Smith, *Florence Nightingale* (Penguin Books, 1955), 34.

36 J. E. Lloyd, 'Introduction' to *A Hundred Years of Welsh Archaeology* (Cambrian Arch. Ass. n.d.), 11.

37 *The Welshman*, September 17, 1847, quoted by Evelyn Lewes in *Out with Cambrians*, London 1934, 30; *Antiq.* XI, 1937, 37.

38 Anon., *Stories by an Archaeologist and his Friends*, London 1856, i.p. 2.

39 Lecture given in the Ashmolean Museum, November 2, 1870; quoted by G. Daniel, *Origins and Growth of Archaeology*, Penguin Books 1967, 141.

40 Neale, *Hierologus*, 92.

41 Neale, *Hierologus*, 117.

42 S. Piggott, *Proc. Prehist. Soc.* XXIX, 1963, 2.

43 G. M. Young, op. cit.

44 S. Piggott, *Antiq.* XI, 1937, 31.

ACKNOWLEDGEMENTS

I owe much to the help of others, and individual acknowledgements are made in the text. My thanks are due to the Universities and other learned bodies whose invitations to lecture in this field of study were the occasion of writing most of the essays published here. In general, and over many years, I have had the continuous help, encouragement and a generous share in their knowledge of the by-ways of early antiquarianism from Mr Howard Colvin, Professor Glyn Daniel and Sir Thomas Kentrick. I have had unfailing help and courtesy from the staff of many libraries, notably the Edinburgh University Library and the Bodleian Library, but in particular I owe a personal debt of gratitude to Mr John Hopkins, Librarian to the Society of Antiquaries of London and to Mr A. R. Turnbull, my publisher.

The originals of these essays were published as listed below, and the author and the publisher gratefully acknowledge permission to reprint them here: 1. Antiquarian Thought in the 16th and 17th Centuries, from *English Historical Scholarship in the 16th and 17th Centuries*, ed. Fox, Oxford Univ. Press, 1965. 2. Brazilian Indians on an Elizabethan Monument, *Antiquity*, XXXVIII, 1964. 3. William Camden and the Britannia, Reckitt Archaeological Lecture, *Proc. Brit. Acad.* XXXVII, 1957. 4. Celts, Saxons and the Early Antiquaries, O'Donnell Lecture, Edinburgh Univ. Press, 1966. 5. First publication. 6. Ruins in a Landscape, Ford Special Historical Lecture, Oxford 1975. 7. The Ancestors of Jonathan Oldbuck, lecture, Society of Antiquaries of Scotland, *Antiquity*, XXIX, 1955. 8. The Roman

Camp, *Rev.Eng.Lit.* VII, 1966. 9. The Origins of the English County Archaeological Societies, Centenary Lecture 1970, *Trans.Birm.and Warw.Arch.Soc.* LXXXVI, 1974.

The publisher gratefully acknowledges the source of the following illustrations: The British Library, Pl. 1, from MS Egerton 3029, f. 30; The Bodleian Library, Pl. 6, from MS Eng. Misc. 665, and Pl. 8, from MS Top. gen. c. 25, f. 107; Edinburgh Univ. Library, Pls. 5, 18, 19, 20; Nat. Gall. Scot., frontispiece; Nat. Library Scot., Pl. 7; Radio Times Hulton Picture Library, Pl. 13; Nat. Mus. Dublin, Pl. 2; Mr Patrick Wise, Burford, Pls. 3, 4; Burnley Bor. Coun., Towneley Hall Art Gall. & Mus., Pl. 15.

Pl. 10 is from 'Designs by Mr R. Bentley for six poems by Mr T. Gray', London, Dodsley, 1753. Pl. 11 is from Olaus Wormius, 'Musaeum Wormianum seu Historia rerum rariorum . . .' Leyden 1655. Pl. 17, from 'An Account of Some Remarkable Ancient Ruins . . . by John Williams, Mineral Engineer'. Edinburgh, Creech, 1777. Pl. 21, 'Sir Uvedale Price on the Picturesque . . .' Edinburgh, Caldwell, Lloyd & Co., 1842.

INDEX

emergence, 101
empirical, 15-21, 101-11, 121,
127, 134, 135, 137, 157
in 16th and 17th Cs, 1-21
in 18th C., 21, 49-50, 117-8,
146
influence of Baconian science,
15, 101-2
intellectual background of
Elizabethan, 33
journalism and books on, 125,
127, 148, 150
medieval, 5-6
new empiricism, 127, 128
new 'explanation', 117-8
observation and experiment,
101-2
popularisation, 125-7, 133-4,
147-8
public interest, 14-15, 44, 127
romanticism and, 117-8, 121-4,
128-9
Royal Society and, 101-11, 134
Scott and, 128-29, 133-4, 150,
157-8
Scottish, 135-50, 157
Scottish Primitivism and, 134,
150-8
transport and, 129, 134, 147,
187-8
visual representation, changing
forms of, 145
antiquarian, antiquary
Celts, Saxons and the early,
55-75
emergence of, 3
Scott's view of, 50, 129, 133,
134-5, 162
topographer-, 6, 34-5, 42-3, 52
Antonine
Itinerary, 48, 50
Wall, 49, 127
aquatints, 125
Archaeological societies
Cambridge Camdenians, 179-
181, 185
church restoration, 176, 178,
181-2
condition of 18th C. churches,
176, 178

dates of founding, 175
excursions, 188-90
geological studies and, 172-4
influence of Scott and the
romantics, 184
interest in medieval history,
176, 181
lectures, 189
local antiquarian studies, 185
location, 191-3
origin of the English county,
171-93
Oxford Movement, 172, 174-83
Oxford Society, 178-9, 180, 185
romantic approach to history,
184-5, 190
social geography and, 192-3
social life and, 171, 172, 188-
190, 191
tractarianism and, 171, 175-83,
190, 191, 192-3
transport and, 187-8, 190
women in, 188, 189-90, 191
Archaeology
as a separate discipline, 21
Aubrey's contribution, 16-17,
107
beginnings, 2, 3
beginnings of field, 101-2, 107
classificatory techniques, 110
critical approach, 33-4
decline, 49-50
empirical enquiry, 14-21
geology and, 129, 148, 150, 172-
174
interest in field, 17-20
medieval field, 5-6
remains as natural wonders, 4-5
relation between history and, 3
revival of scientific approach, 21
Stukeley's contribution, 6, 21,
48, 66, 71, 107, 116, 137
supplementary documentary
evidence, 2-3
techniques of enquiry, 2-3
testing of social evolution
theories, 155
Architecture
Aubrey's interest in medieval,
17, 20, 110, 118